Disasters and Social Resilience

T0361207

The interconnectedness of communities, organisations, governing bodies, policy and individuals in the field of disaster studies has never been accurately examined or comprehensively modelled. This kind of study is vital for planning policy and emergency responses and assessing individual and community vulnerability, resilience and sustainability as well as mitigation and adaptation to climate change impacts; it therefore deserves attention.

Disasters and Social Resilience fills this gap by introducing to the field of disaster studies a fresh methodology and a model for examining and measuring impacts and responses to disasters. Urie Bronfenbrenner's bioecological systems theory, which looks at communities holistically, is outlined and illustrated through a series of chapters, guiding the reader from the theory's underpinnings through research illustrations and applications focused on each level of Bronfenbrenner's ecosystems, culminating in an integration chapter. The final chapter provides policy recommendations for local and national government bodies and emergency providers to help individuals and communities prepare and withstand the effects of a range of disasters.

This book will be of great interest to scholars and students of disaster and emergency management, disaster readiness and risk reduction (DRR), as well as more general climate change and sustainability studies.

Helen J. Boon is a Senior Lecturer at the College of Arts, Society and Education, Division of Tropical Environments and Societies at James Cook University, Australia.

Alison Cottrell is an Associate Professor with the Centre for Disaster Studies and Associate Dean Research Education within the College of Marine and Environmental Sciences at James Cook University, Australia.

David King is an Associate Professor in the College of Marine and Environmental Sciences at James Cook University, Australia, and is Director of the Centre for Disaster Studies, and the Centre for Tropical Urban and Regional Planning.

Routledge Explorations in Environmental Studies

Disasters and Social Resilience
A bioecological approach

Helen J. Boon, Alison Cottrell and David King

Routledge
Taylor & Francis Group

LONDON AND NEW YORK

First published 2016
by Routledge

2 Park Square, Milton Park, Abingdon, Oxfordshire OX14 4RN
711 Third Avenue, New York, NY 10017

Routledge is an imprint of the Taylor & Francis Group, an informa business

First issued in paperback 2017

British Library Cataloguing-in-Publication Data
A catalogue record for this book is available from the British Library

Library of Congress Cataloging-in-Publication Data
Names: Boon, Helen J., author.
Title: Disasters and social resilience : a bioecological approach /
Helen J. Boon, Alison Cottrell and David King.
Description: Abingdon, Oxon ; New York, NY : Routledge, [2016] |
Series: Routledge explorations in environmental studies
Identifiers: LCCN 2015048454 | ISBN 9781138933125 (hb) |
ISBN 9781315678726 (ebook)
Subjects: LCSH: Natural disasters–Social aspects. | Human ecology. |
Hazardous geographic environments. | Emergency planning–
Environmental aspects.
Classification: LCC GB5014 .B66 2016 | DDC 363.34–dc23
LC record available at http://lccn.loc.gov/2015048454

ISBN: 978-1-138-93312-5 (hbk)
ISBN: 978-0-8153-6436-8 (pbk)

Typeset in Goudy
by Wearset Ltd, Boldon, Tyne and Wear

Contents

Figures

Tables

1 Introduction

Helen J. Boon

Bronfenbrenner's bioecological systems theory and climate change

This book is intended to outline and describe a method for estimating social resilience to disasters based on Uri Bronfenbrenner's bioecological systems theory. The need to estimate and measure resilience to disasters is a consequence of global climate change effects which have led to an increase in natural hazards. Governments worldwide have recognised that an effective way to avoid natural hazards becoming disasters is to strengthen and empower communities and individuals to manage the impacts of floods, severe storms, droughts and the like. This is particularly important for developing countries, which are more vulnerable to the vagaries of the weather and other natural hazards such as tsunamis, landslides, pandemics and so on, because they often have less developed infrastructure and monetary resources to protect residents and rebuild damaged property. Climate change adaptation and its corollary, disaster risk reduction, are considered to be building blocks for lessening risk and resilience enhancement. There is, therefore, a great need to understand the processes that operate at local and individual level within particular contexts in order for governments and relevant bodies such as emergency management organisations to be able to strengthen those that build resilience in the face of an impending hazard.

This introduction is organised into six sections. It begins from a discussion of the context – climate change – and flows on to conceptualisations of responses deemed to deal more effectively with the problems arising, specifically the increase in natural hazards. It concludes with the approach we believe is salient to understanding resilience to disasters. The approach uses Bronfenbrenner's bioecological theory as a conceptual framework, to model relevant influences upon a person or community entity so that interventions can be targeted to strengthen their resilience.

The context: climate change

Around the world most scientists, and the majority of governments, acknowledge that we are living in an age of climate change. Whether the cause of this climate change is human activity – that is, whether it is anthropogenic, or part of a natural cycle – the fact remains that it is giving rise to an increased number of natural hazards. Floods, tornados, droughts, wildfires and hurricanes/typhoons/cyclones are experienced with more frequency globally. Some even contend that earthquakes and volcanic eruptions can be linked to climate change. This is because, they argue, an examination of the earth's past history, when the ice-age climate warmed naturally, shows evidence that earthquakes, tremors and even volcanic activity along pre-existing fault lines were triggered as a result of the climate change. The explanation is centred on the idea that the large ice sheets covering much of the planet were so heavy that the release of pressure when they melted caused the earth's crust to 'bounce back' (McGuire 2012). Many of these natural hazards are severe in intensity, such as the devastating category-5 Hurricane Katrina of 2005, category-4 Cyclone Yasi of 2011 and category-4 Typhoon Usagi of 2013. The number of Category-4 and 5 hurricanes worldwide nearly doubled between the early 1970s and the early 2000s. Moreover, both the duration of tropical cyclones and their strongest wind speeds have increased by about 50 per cent over the past 50 years. Of course there are also natural hazards that are not unanimously thought to be directly linked to climate change; for example, the magnitude-6.0 earthquake in the Emilia Romagna region of Italy, which resulted in more than €150 million in economic losses, and the 2011 6.3-magnitude Christchurch earthquake, which killed 185 people and cost New Zealand NZ$40 billion. According to UNISDR (United Nations Office for Disaster Risk Reduction), in the years 2000–2011, 1.1 million people were killed by natural hazards and 2.7 billion directly affected, with economic damage to the value of US$1.3 trillion reported globally. The year 2011 was recorded as the costliest year, with estimated disaster losses of US$380 billion. Using a new risk model UNISDR estimates that annual losses just from earthquakes and cyclonic winds will be in the range of US$180 billion annually this century (UNISDR 2013).

The human lives lost to such events, not to mention the economic costs from the hazards' impacts upon households, infrastructure and essential services, reflect the vulnerability of individuals and their communities to specific hazards. For example, vulnerability of individuals and communities in coastal zones depends on an ability to cope with the consequences of natural and socioeconomic impacts of storms, rises in sea level or other phenomena induced by climate change. Socio-economic factors, such as disparities in income and asset distributions in a community, are critical in determining vulnerability and intimately linked with the risk exposure that individuals might experience as a result of a natural hazard.

To illustrate, a city located on the coast, such as Sydney, New Orleans or Manila, is more vulnerable to risks associated with sea-level rise than cities located further inland on higher ground. As a rule of thumb, a 0.1 m rise in sea level increases the frequency of flooding by a factor of about three. This effect is multiplicative, which means that an increase in mean sea level of 0.5 m will increase the frequency of flooding by a factor of roughly 300. Therefore an event which presently only occurs on average once every 100 years (the '100-year return event') will happen several times a year after sea level has risen by 0.5 m (ACECRC 2012). It is clear that for communities such as Manila that are vulnerable to flooding, sea-level rise and the like, the level of vulnerability of a household will depend on a number of factors. The location of a dwelling, its construction, the household's resources and the individual and collective coping of those living in it will impact upon a household's vulnerability. It is also clear that the lens used to assess vulnerability will affect what is observed. For instance, different results will be gathered depending on whether one examines individual psychological vulnerability, ecological vulnerability (of a particular ecosystem, such as the Great Barrier Reef) or economic vulnerability as it impacts the livelihood of groups of residents or the very fabric of a whole town and its continued existence as a demographic and geographic entity, that is, whole-community vulnerability.

Even though there are clear differences between ecological and socio-economic vulnerability, it should be obvious from the foregoing that these are intrinsically connected. Individuals reside within specific ecological systems, which are in turn governed and managed by social organisations and institutions. The physical and ecological characteristics defining a community, whether it is situated up a mountainside in Austria or deep in the rainforest of Papua New Guinea, affect the social institutions, governance, culture and customs, both in terms of what is needed and what is available. Conversely the social and socio-economic milieu of the community invariably has an impact, direct or indirect, upon the ecological system in which it is embedded. Of course the complexity of a community invariably increases with the size of its population. Therefore to examine one without due consideration of the other will lead to an incomplete and possibly inaccurate assessment of vulnerability. Some examples will help to illustrate the point.

Natural hazards, extreme weather events or human activity, including over-fishing or coastal and industrial development, can result in changes in water quality, which in turn affect coastal habitats, leading to different composition of fish species. Such an ecological change can have social and economic ramifications, including conflicts over resources. For instance, climate change or a severe cyclone making landfall in particular Australian coastal areas may affect fish abundance and distribution. This can lead to conflicts between traditional Indigenous, recreational and commercial fishers over quotas, access and harvest of marine resources. Organisations and decision-makers negotiate and manage the emerging issues by seeking to agree upon fishing routines for all stakeholders to increase or at least avoid depleting the quality of life of stakeholders and to ensure the continued economic viability of the broader community, since fishing might be the main occupation of its members. This constitutes an important adaptive strategy for the future viability of the impacted ecological and socio-economic communities. Thus a disaster, namely the erosion of a whole vulnerable community, can be averted.

Clearly local contingencies are crucial considerations when examining vulnerabilities of people and places. Let's look at the case of Charleston, South Carolina. Like many coastal cities, its physical environment is critical in moulding the social fabric of the city. It has a flat topography with downtown Charleston comprising an eight-square-mile peninsula, although the city as a whole has grown to a total of 110 square miles. The population has also expanded in pace with the extension of city limits, and the many new settlers in the region are employed in the main industry of the city, tourism. The vast majority of these new residents have not experienced Charleston's natural hazards: hurricanes, floods, earthquakes and ice storms. Given that tourism is the city's main industry, what can be done to prevent a natural hazard from rendering the city a disaster zone? The large population and extent of the built environment present complex systems requiring multi-dimensional policies and negotiations between institutions and government bodies, as well as between local residents. Time and resources will be required to assess the potential vulnerability of groups of residents, their livelihoods, the built environment and essential infrastructure and services, in order to set up processes that will secure the safety and sustainability of the city.

Some lessons have been learnt from more extreme, devastating scenarios, which have been observed with regularity in developing and developed countries alike. One recalls the Indian Ocean tsunami of 2004, which led to over a quarter of a million deaths around the Indian Ocean. An example of a lesser tragedy, at least in terms of human lives lost, occurred in Australia in 2011: on 10 January 2011, the town of Grantham, Queensland, was inundated with a flash flood in which 12 of the town's 370 residents drowned. Grantham was one of more than 70 communities and 200,000 people in Queensland that were affected by flooding between December 2010 and January 2011. During this time the overall damage bill for Queensland was AU$2.38 billion (US$2.4 billion), with 35 deaths and more than three-quarters of the state declared a flood disaster zone. For Grantham, the flash flooding resulted in the unusual decision to relocate parts of the community of Grantham physically in March 2011. The Lockyer Valley Regional Council acquired a 377-hectare (932-acre) site to enable affected, vulnerable residents of Grantham to swap their properties voluntarily with equivalent-sized lots in a higher location less prone to flooding. To facilitate the unusual resettling process, planning regulations were set aside to streamline the relocation of a portion of the town. Grantham's response to the disaster, following the community's severe loss, ensures that damage will be less likely to reoccur with the same severity.

To avert or lessen the likelihood of a disaster following a natural hazard it is important to estimate and model how particular natural hazards might affect a community. Such thinking leads to assessments of vulnerability. A focus on the vulnerability of particular entities, whether at the level of individuals or on a much bigger city-wide scale, is designed to determine how much exposure and sensitivity to risk can be endured and how far disaster can be averted. Much effort has been devoted to disaster risk reduction.

Disaster risk reduction

Disaster Risk Reduction (DRR) aims to reduce the damage caused by natural hazards like earthquakes, floods, droughts and cyclones, through systematic and timely preparedness and prevention strategies. Disasters can follow natural hazards. A disaster's severity depends on the severity of a hazard's impact on communities and the environment. The scale of the impact in turn depends on the choices we, or previous stakeholders, have made for the way we live and conduct business and for our environment. These choices relate to how we conduct agricultural practices, produce our food, where and with what materials we build our homes, the sorts of infrastructure we give privilege to, the kind of government we elect, how our taxes are applied and even what we teach future generations, our children, in schools. Each decision and action has the potential to make us more vulnerable to natural hazards and prone to disasters – or more able to cope and withstand them.

Disaster risk reduction involves the reduction of disaster risks through systematic efforts to analyse and reduce the causes of disasters: reducing communities' and households' exposure to hazards; lessening the vulnerability of people and property; employing appropriate management of land and the environment; and improving preparedness and early warning systems for natural hazards. To this end, the United Nations Office for Disaster Risk Reduction (UNISDR) emphasises that there is no such thing as a 'natural' disaster, only natural hazards. It is now more than 10 years since the World Disaster Reduction Conference, held in Kobe, Hyogo, Japan in January 2005, led to the development of the Hyogo Framework for Action (HFA) 10-year plan to make the world safer from natural hazards. The HFA vision aimed to influence countries to develop policy, legislative and institutional frameworks for disaster risk reduction. These will enable countries to develop and track progress towards more disaster-safe communities through specific and measurable indicators. Indicators will be used to manage risks and to achieve widespread consensus for engagement in, and compliance with, disaster risk reduction measures across all sectors of society, in both developing and developed countries. A consequence of this drive to reduce disaster risk has been a focus on building resilience to disasters.

Resilience

Emergency management policy focuses on building resilience into global communities as an essential preamble to coping with climate change and concomitant disasters. Resilience, in particular community resilience, is becoming the most frequently used framework for enhancing community-level disaster preparedness, response and recovery, and for adaptation to climate change. The enhancement of disaster resilience has been the topic of recent high-level reports in the United States (National Academies 2012), the United Kingdom (UK Foresight 2012) and the United Nations (UNISDR 2012). This focus on resilience has emerged from observations that show some communities have been able to respond and recover from disasters more quickly and effectively than others. These communities have been characterised as resilient. Key attributes of resilient communities include the ability to assess and manage risk, a preparedness to face threats and capacity to absorb shocks. Communities that exhibit strong social cohesion, where individuals are highly socially connected and have a strong sense of place, and communities containing networks that foster social connectivity with external agencies are more likely to be resilient (Boon 2014).

But what exactly is resilience? There have been reams of papers variously describing resilience over the past 60 or more years, with definitions that depend on the academic background of the theorist. Moreover, resilience has been understood in a different way depending on the level of analysis, for example, individual, community or ecological system. For instance, from an engineering perspective, a vitally important perspective when looking at strengthening neighbourhoods to withstand the impact of natural hazards, Uda and Kennedy (2015) consider three types of resilience:

- Engineering resilience, which looks at an entity's resilience as if it were a machine that can break in a crisis and would need to be fixed back to its original state.
- Ecological resilience, as applied to a biophysical ecosystem, is understood as the ability to reorganise and move into one of several possible states after a disturbance.
- Evolutionary resilience, which contends that there is no set ideal state or set of states for an entity to return or transition to, so an entity's resilience is its inherent capability to adapt and transform.

Others have described socio-ecological resilience, the capacity of ecosystems to sustain societal development and progress with essential ecosystem services (Berkes et al. 2003). More essentially, resilience describes the capacity of a person, community or ecosystem to persist in the face of shocks and disturbances without changing fundamental structures and functions. It is often associated with 'resistance', 'return to a previous state' or 'transformation', as well as combinations of these three terms (Dale et al. 2011). 'Resistance' refers to the capacity of the entity to resist shocks; 'return to a previous state' means that entity will return to its previous state after a disturbance; while 'transformation' refers to the capacity of individuals, organisations or the whole community to deal with challenges and persist, perhaps in an altered or novel state, despite adversity.

A debate about the range of definitions is still raging at this time and will likely continue. Most definitions however, tend to incorporate a stressor, the notion of adaptation and a return to pre-stressor levels of functioning, whether at individual or community level. We would stress that a return to pre-stressor functioning or a shift to a new state of adaptive functioning is the minimum expectation that is required for an individual or community to be considered resilient.

Given the interconnectedness and interdependence of human and socio-ecological systems, resilience-building strategies should address risks upon individuals, their livelihoods, food security and the natural environment as integral aspects. Consideration should be given to integrating disaster and climate risk management into enhanced social protection schemes and programmes that are resilient to shocks, while simultaneously improving standards for safety, health, capital assets and well-being. Similarly poverty-reduction initiatives such as employment-guarantee schemes, conditional cash transfers, micro-finance and insurance are key features of protection against disasters due to severe impacts from natural hazards. As a minimum, access to essential services and (unemployment) income, including protection from the risks of disasters, is now recognised as a universal human right that must be guaranteed to every individual (ILO 2011).

Implicit in disaster risk reduction is building resilience into critical infrastructure, such as transport conduits, schools and hospitals, not only to ensure continued basic social services but also to prevent long-term social and economic impacts that can result when, for example, education is disrupted by a disaster. With a focus to future generations, safe schools must include safe learning facilities, disaster preparedness and integration of disaster risk reduction into the curriculum. Comprehensive planning approaches that focus upon children and youth have also been known to mobilise communities. Children and youth have been instrumental in bringing together parents, local government and other institutions, and contributing to building whole-community resilience in many different countries (Back *et al.* 2009).

Of course, disaster risk reduction and resilience building are immense undertakings. Referring to efforts made in the United States, the National Research Council (NRC 2015) stresses the need for a multi-sectoral approach by national and local programmes to replace the prevailing ad-hoc and project-centred approach that is currently observed. The challenges of preparing resilient communities and increasing national resilience were documented in the United States report *Disaster Resilience: A National Imperative* (National Academies 2012). This report, sponsored by eight federal agencies and a community resilience organisation, extended to stakeholders beyond the Washington, DC governmental community. Its message was to emphasise the need for accurate information so that an understanding of national resilience could be embedded in communities across the United States. Among the findings issued by the committee was one underpinning the thrust of the rationale in this book, namely the need for a quantitative, numerical means of assessing resilience. This is so that the priority needs of communities are identified for interventions, to monitor incremental changes to resilience and to compare the cost benefits required for this undertaking. The overall aim of disaster risk reduction policy is to avert or minimise disasters, as illustrated in Figure 1.1.

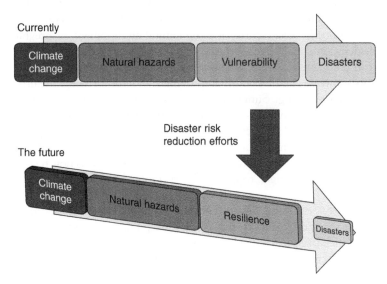

Figure 1.1 The aim of disaster risk reduction policy.

Challenges

Given that measuring, as well as defining, resilience is a challenge, measures and indicators to evaluate progress and incremental increases in resilience are deemed essential in tackling disaster risk reduction efforts. Moreover the data necessary to establish those measures are critical: communities need to define what resilience means for them and to develop and prioritise resilience investments. In the National Academies (2012) report, the committee reviewed the strengths and challenges of different frameworks for measuring resilience, and in so doing identified four essential facets of a reliable system to measure resilience. They noted that this system must include indicators or measures that assess:

- Vulnerable individuals, assessed via factors that capture special needs of individuals and groups, through minority and health status, mobility and socio-economic status indicators.
- Infrastructure, giving a snapshot of the ability of, for example, water and sewerage, transportation, power and communications to recover from hazardous events.
- Societal factors that enhance or limit a community's ability to recover, including variables underpinning social capital: education facilities, armed forces, governance, financial structures, cultural facilities and workforce.
- The built environment, indicating the ability of buildings to withstand the impact of natural hazards, assessing entities such as hospitals, local government offices, emergency response facilities, schools, businesses, bridges and roads.

The NRC described the United States as not having a consistent basis for measuring resilience that includes all of the above-mentioned dimensions, making it difficult for communities to monitor improvements or changes in their resilience. One of the recommendations from the 2012 report was that government entities (at federal, state and local levels) and professional organisations should partner to help develop a framework for communities to adapt to their circumstances and begin to track their progress towards increasing resilience.

It is beyond the scope of this book to document the efforts of individual countries to incorporate risk reduction approaches into their local and national policies. However, for those interested in investigating the progress made by a particular country the UNISDR website holds an extensive database with a large number of HFA (Hyogo Framework for Action) National Progress Reports, which are freely available. By way of a quick summary, 82 countries have begun the process of organising their disaster risk management by putting together disaster loss databases: 15 in Africa, 27 in the Americas, 26 in Asia-Pacific, 10 in Arab States and 4 in Europe (UNISDR 2015). National disaster loss databases systematically account, measure and analyse disaster losses associated with both hydro-meteorological and geological hazards. This is a crucial first step to generate the information necessary for risk estimation and to inform public investment in disaster risk reduction and climate change adaptation.

One of the key messages emerging from the foregoing discussion is the importance of finding and using a framework that is capable of organising and measuring facets of importance to socio-economic resilience: a resilience framework that could be used to help identify barriers to resilience, prioritise actions and measure progress aligned with disaster risk reduction goals and their associated monitoring processes. Such a framework, one moreover which has been tested and can be applied to diverse settings and conditions, is the one that was originally designed as a way to study and understand the range of influences that act upon the development of children: Uri Bronfenbrenner's bioecological systems theory.

Bronfenbrenner's bioecological systems theory

Uri Bronfenbrenner was a Russian-born American developmental psychologist who developed the ecological systems theory of child development. His work, which was instrumental in the establishment of the Head Start Program in 1965 in the USA, was highly influential in changing the perspective of developmental psychology because it acknowledged the importance of environmental and societal influences on child development. Bronfenbrenner's ecological systems theory has been widely used by psychologists interested in understanding individuals in context. A search in Google Scholar reveals that *The Ecology of Human Development* (Bronfenbrenner 1979) has been cited over 15,000 times. Bronfenbrenner is credited with focusing the attention of developmental scientists to the contextual variation that is observed in human development. He was instrumental in helping to move developmental psychology from what he derisively referred to as 'the science of the strange behaviour of children in strange situations with strange adults for the briefest possible periods of time' (Bronfenbrenner 1977: 513) to more 'ecologically valid' studies of developing individuals in their natural environment. The theory has been used to understand how particular contexts or settings influence the emergence of a range of attributes. Research based on his theory have been successfully used to explain a range of phenomena, including adolescent motivation and academic outcomes (e.g. Boon 2006), developmental risk and protective factors for substance use (e.g. Szapocznik and Coatsworth 1999), youth activity engagement (e.g. Rose-Krasnor 2009), family influence on gender development (e.g. McHale et al. 2003) and more recently the development of disaster resilience (Boon et al. 2012).

Bronfenbrenner theorised that developing children are subject to a range of effects arising from the processes and events that occur in the consecutive layers comprising their social and environmental milieu, which he visualised as a set of nested Russian dolls (Bronfenbrenner 1979: 3). Figure 1.2 shows the most usual conceptualisation of the theory as originally posited by Bronfenbrenner. He viewed the developmental context as being the sum of effects that take place in five sequentially nested spaces. Development refers to stability and change in the characteristics of human beings over the life course and across generations. The inner circle – the microsystem – describes the settings in which the developing individual has direct, face-to-face interactions with significant people, such as family, friends, co-workers and teachers. This is where a person's time is spent, where daily life takes place and where development and learning occur. There are cross-relationships among these small settings – parents talk to peers, or teachers, for example – and these interconnections form a network called the mesosystem (Bronfenbrenner 1979: 25). Beyond this is an outer circle of people and organisations that indirectly influence a person's development, such as the parents' employers, health care workers and the media; this is called the exosystem (Bronfenbrenner 1979: 25). Bronfenbrenner also described a macrosystem (the prevailing cultural and economic conditions of a society) and a chronosystem (the element of time, which impacts upon changes and shifts upon each system; see Figure 1.2). Table 1.1 outlines the various systems and their descriptions extracted from Bronfenbrenner's original conceptualisation.

A range of studies have used this theory to identify contextual predictors or processes that emanate from sources outside of the individual and impact upon his or her development. In other words, research has sought to determine the environmental, social and physical factors that moderate and modulate a person's development, learning and behaviours. For example, Evans, Chen, Miller and Seeman (Evans et al. 2012) from Cornell University have shown through longitudinal studies in the USA that children who have been exposed to chronic stress and poverty display significant differences from typical children in their emotional regulation; these persist into adulthood and are found to be hard wired in their brain anatomy as adults. Countless other longitudinal studies by the same group of researchers have shown that social determinants translate

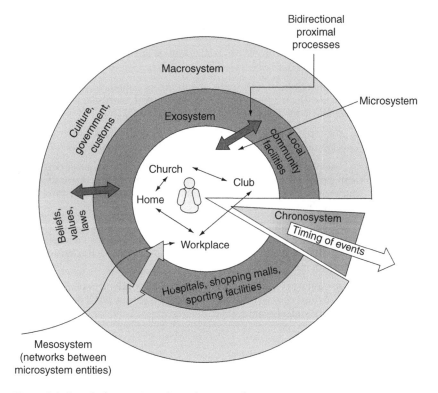

Figure 1.2 Bronfenbrenner's ecological systems theory.

into outcomes such as lower academic achievement and material success as well as higher predisposition to illness and obesity.

Bronfenbrenner believed behaviour and learning to be the product of the individual's way of perceiving certain contextual factors and responding to them. The basis of this theory is succinctly captured in the following extract:

> Throughout the life course, human development takes place through processes of progressively more complex reciprocal interaction between an active, evolving biopsychological human organism and the persons, objects, and symbols in its immediate external environment. To be effective, the interaction must occur on a fairly regular basis over extended periods of time. Such enduring forms of interaction on the immediate environment are referred to as proximal processes.
>
> (Bronfenbrenner and Morris 1998: 996)

In relation to the use of the theory, Bronfenbrenner pointed out three essential considerations. First, ecological systems must be understood interdependently,

Table 1.1 Descriptions of Bronfenbrenner's ecological systems

Construct	Descriptor
Setting	'…a place where people can readily engage in face-to-face interaction.' (Bronfenbrenner 1979: 22)
Microsystem	'…a pattern of activities, roles, and interpersonal relations experienced by the developing person in a given setting with particular physical and material characteristics.' (Bronfenbrenner 1979: 22)
Mesosystem	'…the interrelations among two or more settings in which the developing person actively participates.' (Bronfenbrenner 1979: 25)
Exosystem	'…one or more settings that do not involve the developing person as an active participant, but in which events occur that affect, or are affected by, what happens in the setting containing the developing person.' (Bronfenbrenner 1979: 25)
Macrosystem	'…consistencies, in the form and content of lower-order systems that exist, or could exist, at the level of subculture or culture as a whole, along with any belief systems or ideology underlying such consistencies.' (Bronfenbrenner 1979: 26)
Chronosystem	'…the influence on the person's development of changes (and continuities) over time in the environments in which the person is living.' (Bronfenbrenner, 1986, p. 724)

such that what happens or fails to happen in any given environment depends to a large extent on events and relationships in other related environments. This means that researchers must consider the interaction of systems in which people participate, not only the influence of the developing individual's immediate setting. Second, development occurs via processes, or modes of interaction between people. Bronfenbrenner therefore argued that researchers conducting ecological research must consider more than one person in the setting of focus. Third, ecological environments are phenomenologically constructed and under-stood: they orient the developing person's actions and interactions. These ideas are observable and can be illustrated by an example that is pertinent to the discussion of disaster risk reduction. Emergency managers routinely send out warnings, communicated by radio, TV and the like, when a cyclone approaches the coast in Australia. The warnings are interpreted and acted upon in different ways, however, depending on whether individuals perceive a genuine danger and threat to self and property. It has been shown that some individuals who have lived through a natural hazard, such as flood or cyclone, do not heed emergency warnings to begin preparing themselves and their property for disaster impact, having instead a 'wait and see' attitude (Boon *et al.* 2012). Conversely, those who have never experienced a hazard, such as a fire or flood, might have a different response, such as panic or anxiety, and might be more likely to begin preparations to protect their property or even flee from the vulnerable location if they are able. The environment should thus be considered as it is perceived and understood by the individual. From a methodological perspective, a phenomenological analysis examines how each participant perceives the setting and the various elements contained within it. A critical aspect of the theory is therefore the concept of experienced relations: 'The term experienced is used to indicate that the scientifically relevant features of any environment include not only its objective properties but also the way in which these properties are perceived by the persons in that environment' (Bronfenbrenner 1979: 22).

An emphasis on the phenomenological view of the developing person means that people's perceptions of their environments constitute the most important influences upon their development, learning and behaviours. This implies that the aspects of the environment that have the most power to shape the an individual's psychological growth are those that have meaning to him or her in given situations. The theory also strongly suggests that relationships within contexts are important for learning and development, particularly for the development of resilience, as will be shown in forthcoming chapters. Realising the broad potential of the theory, Bronfenbrenner advocated specific research models or approaches for the study of developmental outcomes (Bronfenbrenner 1986). These, which he referred to as the person, process context and time (PPCT) models, he proposed to be used as a guide for any research using the bioecological theory. They are depicted and summarised in Figure 1.3, with illustrations of each possible design approach following.

To illustrate their application let us look at a question: how might extra-familiar conditions affect intra-familiar processes that lead to disaster resilience? Research to answer this question might take one of three possible approaches:

- Mesosystemic: for example, examining the influences of family and neighbours upon a person's disaster resilience through emotional and physical support strategies offered (e.g. Boon 2013).
- Exosystemic: for example, the effects of emergency management warnings upon preparedness and the subsequent disaster resilience that ensues from safely navigating through a hazard (e.g. Boon 2014b).

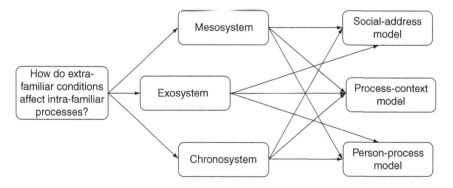

Figure 1.3 Research models conceptualised by Bronfenbrenner (1986).

- Chronosystemic: for example, the effects of environmental changes, such as climate change, and residential mobility or stability, in relation to changes in individuals' disaster resilience in context over time (Boon 2014a).

Further, in selecting a mesosystem, exosystem or chronosystem research approach to clarify the influences upon an individual's disaster resilience, an investigation might focus upon one of the three PPCT models to answer the research question. Specifically, using the mesosystem as the basis of the research, one could look at:

1   The social determinants of the context, a social address model: this might examine how social class, poverty or ethnicity moderates the amount of physical support that is offered.
2   The process context model might examine *qualitatively* the types of emotional and physical support processes that are proffered by family and neighbours within different socio-economic contexts.
3   A person process context model would focus on the moderation that individuals' personal characteristics have upon the types of emotional and physical support that are offered by family and neighbours within different socio-economic contexts.

Of course, Bronfenbrenner realised early on that the discovery of a relationship between social class and a particular expression of behaviour was a meaningless one until the sociological variable was reduced to psychological terms. For him, it was essential to examine thoroughly the intervening processes through which environmental influences exert their effects. Validation of this notion was obtained from evidence that children's behaviours were influenced more by what parents did in their interactions with them than by the parents' socio-economic status, in terms of income, education or profession. In other words, interpersonal processes were the key determinants of outcomes. This was the rationale that drove Bronfenbrenner's subsequent reformulations of his original ecological systems theory towards the bioecological theory (Bronfenbrenner 1986).

    This later bioecological systems theory stressed the role played by the individual, the impact of time and, most important of all, proximal processes. Crucial to the theory was Bronfenbrenner's emphatic assertion that stability and change occurs within a phenomenological perspective. Such a perspective considers not only the objective properties of the setting in which a person is acting and interacting but also its subjective properties, as experienced by the person (Bronfenbrenner and Evans 2000). Bioecological theory in its current form specifies that researchers should study the settings in which a developing individual spends time and his or her relations with others in those settings, as well as the personal characteristics of the individual (and those of the people with whom he or she typically interacts). A study of the individual's development over time must be teamed with due consideration of the historical time in which the individual lives, as well as the mechanisms that drive development (proximal processes). These later considerations by Bronfenbrenner echo his early recognition of the role of social interactions and networks in shaping development (Bronfenbrenner 1945); in fact he was a pioneer in the earliest days of social network research.

Bronfenbrenner's theory is an attractive one for research around disaster risk reduction and community resilience building because it is expansive, yet focused: one eye is trained on the complex layers of household, family and community relationships, and the other is sharply focused on individual learning and behaviour development. Through his bioecological theory, Bronfenbrenner accounts for the biological as well as environmental influences upon a person. He stressed that learning and subsequent behavioural profiles and belief systems are moulded by and develop within a complex system of interrelationships that are affected by differing aspects of the surrounding environment and biological dispositions of each person (Bronfenbrenner and Evans 2000).

Not only is this theory useful at the level of the individual but the same lens can also be applied to whole communities to examine their vulnerability and assess areas of resilience. Because of the intrinsic bidirectional effects inherent in the theory, whereby the individuals are effectively moderating their social and physical environment as the environment impacts upon them, it is possible to make accurate estimates for risks of natural hazards. At the same time it is possible to devise interventions targeted appropriately to help build stronger, more resilient communities. The chapters that follow will further illustrate applications of this theory to disaster prevention and social resilience.

Summary

Climate change is moderating the broader environmental conditions globally, and this has led to a focus of attention on the projected increase in natural hazards. These hazard events have led to socio-ecological disasters, but this is not an inevitable corollary of a natural hazard. To prepare for the impacts of hazard events, governments and emergency managers have set in motion a disaster risk policy that aims to reduce risk and community vulnerability and increase social and physical resilience.

Resilience, in its various and diverse definitions, is considered to be an adaptive state for individuals and communities to aim for when threatened with the prospect of impending hazard events.

In order to operationalise this policy, communities of all sizes need to be examined and assessed for risks and potential vulnerabilities to the specific natural hazards that could bear upon them.

One effective way to structure such an examination of communities and other social entities is through the use of a framework based upon Uri Bronfenbrenner's bioecological theory. This framework or theoretical lens permits an accurate examination of individuals, as well as larger entities such as communities and cities, both in terms of their organisation and the processes that take place within and between them. The theory offers a range of research designs that can be employed to measure the development of resilience, ranging from the more static and descriptive to more dynamic procedural applications.

References

ACECRC (Antarctic Climate and Ecosystems Cooperative and Research Centre) 2012, 'Report Card: Sea-level Rise 2012'. ACECRC, Hobart, Tasmania.

Back, E., Cameron, C. and Tanner, T.M. 2009, 'Children and Disaster Risk Reduction: Taking Stock and Moving Forward'. Children in a Changing Climate Report, Institute of Development Studies, Brighton, UK, 44 pp.

Berkes, F., Colding, J. and Folke, C. 2003, Introduction, in F. Berkes, J. Colding and C. Folke (eds), *Navigating Social-Ecological Systems: Building Resilience for Complexity and Change*. Cambridge University Press, Cambridge, pp. 1–32.

Boon, H.J. 2006, 'Students At-Risk: A Bioecological Investigation'. PhD thesis, James Cook University, Queensland, Australia.

Boon, H.J. 2013, 'Preparedness and Vulnerability: An Issue of Equity in Australian Disaster Situations', *Australian Journal of Emergency Management*, vol. 28, no. 3, p. 12.

Boon, H.J. 2014a, 'Disaster Resilience in a Flood-Impacted Rural Australian Town', *Natural Hazards*, vol. 71, no. 1, pp. 683–701.

Boon, H.J. 2014b, 'Investigating Rural Community Communication for Flood and Bushfire Preparedness', *Australian Journal of Emergency Management*, vol. 29, no. 4, pp. 17–25.

Boon, H.J., Millar, J., Lake, D., Cottrell, A. and King, D. 2012, *Recovery from Disaster: Resilience, Adaptability and Perceptions of Climate Change*. National Climate Change Adaptation Research Facility, Queensland.

Bronfenbrenner, U. 1945, *The Measurement of Sociometric Status, Structure, and Development*. Beacon House, New York.

Bronfenbrenner, U. 1977, 'Toward an Experimental Ecology of Human Development', *American Psychologist*, vol. 32, pp. 513–531.

Bronfenbrenner, U. 1979, *The Ecology of Human Development: Experiments by Nature and Design*. Harvard University Press, Cambridge, MA.

Bronfenbrenner, U. 1986, 'Ecology of the Family as a Context for Human Development: Research Perspectives', *Developmental Psychology*, vol. 22, pp. 723–742.

Bronfenbrenner, U. and Evans, G.W. 2000, 'Developmental Science in the 21st Century: Emerging Theoretical Models, Research Designs, and Empirical Findings', *Social Development*, vol. 9, pp. 115–125.

Bronfenbrenner, U. and Morris, P.A. 1998, 'The Ecology of Developmental Processes', in R.M. Lerner (ed.), *Handbook of Child Psychology* (fifth edn, vol. 1), pp. 993–1028. Wiley, New York.

Dale, A., Vella, K., Cottrell, A., Pert, P., Stephenson, B., Boon, H., King, D., Whitehouse, H., Hill, R., Babacan, H. and Gooch, M. 2011, 'Conceptualising, Evaluating and Reporting Social Resilience in Vulnerable Regional and Remote Communities Facing Climate Change in Tropical Queensland'. MTSRF Transition Project Final Report, Marine and Tropical Sciences Research Facility, Cairns, Australia.

Evans, G.W., Chen, E., Miller, G.E. and Seeman, T.E. 2012, 'How Poverty Gets Under the Skin: A Life-Course Perspective', in V. Maholmes and R. King (eds), *The Oxford Handbook of Poverty and Child Development*. Oxford University Press, New York, pp. 13–36.

Foresight 2012, 'Foresight Reducing Risks of Future Disasters: Priorities for Decision Makers, Final Project Report'. Government Office for Science, London.

ILO (International Labour Organization) 2011, 'Social Protection Floor for Fair and Inclusive Globalization'. ILO, United Nations.

McGuire, B. 2012, *Waking the Giant: How a changing Climate Triggers Earthquakes, Tsunamis, and Volcanoes*. Oxford University Press, Oxford.

McHale, S.M., Crouter, A.C. and Whiteman, S.D. 2003, 'The Family Contexts of Gender Development in Childhood and Adolescence', *Social Development*, vol. 12, pp. 125–148.

The National Academies 2012, *Disaster Resilience: A National Imperative*. The National Academies Press, Washington, DC.

NRC (National Research Council) 2015, 'Developing a Framework for Measuring Community Resilience: Summary of a Workshop'. National Academies of Sciences, Engineering, Medicine, Washington, DC.

Rose-Krasnor, L. 2009, 'Future Directions in Youth Involvement Research', *Social Development*, vol. 18, pp. 497–509. doi: 10.1111/j.1467-9507.2008.00506.x.

Szapocznik, J. and Coatsworth, J.D. 1999, 'An Eco-Developmental Framework for Organizing the Influences on Drug Abuse: A Developmental Model of Risk and Protection', in D. Meyer and C.R. Hartel (eds), *Drug Abuse: Origins and Interventions*. American Psychological Association, Washington, DC, pp. 331–366.

Uda, M. and Kennedy, C. 2015, 'A Framework for Analysing Neighbourhood Resilience'. Proceedings of the Institution of Civil Engineers, ICE Publishing, London. http://dx.doi.org/10.1680/udap. 14.00028.

UNISDR 2012, 'Making Cities Resilient Report'. United Nations Office for Disaster Risk Reduction, Geneva.

UNISDR 2013, 'Global Assessment Report on Disaster Risk Reduction'. United Nations Office for Disaster Risk Reduction, Geneva.

UNISDR 2014, Annual Report. United Nations Office for Disaster Risk Reduction, Geneva.

UNISDR 2015, 'Global Assessment Report on Disaster Risk Reduction'. United Nations Office for Disaster Risk Reduction, Geneva.

2 Rationale for the use of Bronfenbrenner's bioecological systems theory to examine resilience

Helen J. Boon

The context giving rise to natural hazards was detailed in Chapter 1. The chapter also outlined the rationale behind the focus on resilience and its use as a way to describe human activities that are sustainable in the context of climate change. The big questions of sustainability have been climate change, peak oil and biodiversity. Where sustainability was the focus for policy relating to interactions between the environment, societies and economies, resilience is now used as a framework to ensure that social and ecological entities are able to meet in sustainable ways in the face of potential hazards and shocks. Disaster risk reduction and recovery is now part of a global ongoing social sustainability and sustainable community development process. In sustainable development, interactions with the environmental, economic and social environments are balanced so that present-day populations and communities can prosper without compromising the well-being of subsequent generations. That balance aims for communities that are liveable, which means that they are built in a way that permits residents to live as they like. They must also be planned with a focus on equity so that policy decisions do not disadvantage any one community group, while the long-term view dictates that policies and community processes are flexible and able to adapt to changing demands without compromising the needs of future generations.

Chapter 1 also presented an essential preamble to the bioecological system theory: it described its origins and theoretical underpinnings. This chapter will illustrate the interconnectedness of community entities in supporting resilience to disaster and the effects of influences from proximal and distal organisations, policies and entities upon community or individual disaster resilience. It will also review the problematic issue of measuring community resilience, and demonstrate why measurement of a factor or attribute thought to contribute to resilience for an individual might not be useful for assessing resilience at community scale. In doing so it will highlight that the research question or purpose for a study dictates the method of analysis and drives the study design. Enhancing community or more generally social resilience is about places, networks, processes and society. The complexity of community structure demands complex pathways to disaster resilience.

Disaster logistics influencing policy formulation

Hurricane Katrina exposed massive deficiencies in the ability of one of the wealthiest countries in the world to prepare for and respond to disasters. 'Super storms' Sandy and Yasi, earthquakes in Haiti, New Zealand and Japan, floods in Britain and mega-typhoons in the Philippines demonstrate that natural hazards can and will continue to occur; however, they do not always have to have such catastrophic effects. Disasters are often followed by significant media attention and expert policy recommendations aimed at improving preparedness and preventing identified problems from recurring. Historically, scores of policy reforms are proposed immediately following a disaster but many are ignored, forgotten or shelved as other 'more pressing' issues come to the fore. Once the dust settles and the camera crews pack up and head home, nations must keep track of the implementation progress of these recommendations. However, to avoid a haphazard approach to policy implementation it is first necessary to assess exactly where reforms or interventions are required, so they that are carefully tailored to reduce vulnerability and risk and increase the resilience of residents and communities.

One of the problems besetting policy implementation for the preparedness and response capacities of emergency managers, government agencies, hospitals and public health agencies has been the difficulty of obtaining data during and immediately after a disaster. Important information that needs to be collected during and immediately following disasters can be missed because of barriers and obstacles to gathering such data (IOM 2015). These are put in place by institutional ethics review boards, and are also due to lack of sustainable funding and lack of knowledge about how best to integrate research into response and recovery frameworks (IOM 2015). After emergency groups, the armed forces and other volunteer crisis groups complete the first wave of rescue operations, the recovery period can be slow and, depending on the context, inefficient. The coordination of many organisations and government bodies must be timely and smoothly led. It is during this recovery period that most important lessons can be learnt about how to put in place interventions to prevent future disasters following a natural hazard. One important way to understand where vulnerability is most acute during this recovery period is through the work of aid agencies such as Oxfam and Save the Children. This work can also be problematic, however, if appropriate policy is not in place.

After a particularly deadly disaster, the earthquake that occurred in Haiti on 12 January 2010 and killed 225,570 people, a team of researchers compiled a list of nearly 200 aid agencies that were soliciting donations for Haiti relief. Observation of how such groups operate, how they distribute relief and the situation they find as first-hand observers can provide valuable information about specific vulnerabilities and concerns that arise through and immediately after a disaster. This information can in turn be used to formulate future policy. Since it was not possible for real-time collection and analysis of data to be conducted on the activities of the aid agencies, the Disaster Accountability Project (DAP 2010) conducted research to find and assess the availability and comprehensiveness of relief and aid organisations' situation reports and day-to-day activities of relief work. If correctly and appropriately documented these should contain detailed documentation of work that took place in Haiti. Otherwise concealed vulnerable groups, such as children or perhaps itinerant workers, can be highlighted this way, along with any infrastructure that has failed and the time it took to be restored. Reports of this kind potentially present snapshots of community needs, free of political bias and the misrepresentation that can sometimes emerge with later reporting. An equally if not more important reason for having access to these reports is that relief, from the USA and probably also from other wealthy countries, depends largely on the level of media coverage.

News biases relief in favour of certain disaster types and regions, regardless of need (Eisensee and Strömberg 2007). If a disaster occurs at the same time as other newsworthy events, such as the Olympic Games, relief will only flow if there are three times the number of casualties compared with a disaster that occurred when media pressure is at its lowest level. For example, in May 1999, a storm in India killed 278 people and affected 40,000 others. On the same day, a 15-year-old student shot and wounded six classmates at Heritage High School in Atlanta, Georgia, USA. Since this was just a month after the Columbine High School tragedy, the US television network news covered the events at Heritage High School extensively, but ignored the Indian storm (Eisensee and Strömberg 2007). Eisensee and Strömberg (2007) examined a range of disasters and news reports, and estimated that an African disaster would require 45 times as many deaths to achieve the same probability of media coverage as a European disaster.

Results of the DAP research about the Haiti relief work showed that of the near 200 aid organisations that were involved in relief operations only 10 per cent responded to the DAP research requests, and only seven offered detailed and easily accessible situation reports describing what had been accomplished. Relief organisations' sharing of information, such as their policies and day-to-day activities, not only demonstrates transparency (for public donations) but also helps to pinpoint the gaps in relief for government action and future responsiveness. Two points are noteworthy from the foregoing: first, all relief organisations should be held accountable not only for the consequences of their actions but also for maintaining a high level of transparency, so that the international community can monitor their activities; second, without documentation about how long aid organisations can maintain their relief efforts it is more difficult for government and other responders to mobilise their responses in a timely manner and plan for future disaster contingencies. This consideration arises in many disaster situations; to illustrate, where housing has been compromised or destroyed and aid organisations need to provide shelter for homeless people. While the specific circumstances of each aid operation vary, statements and policies covering how long aid organisations can and intend to accommodate people left without homes from disasters, for example, as well as how long the drip of essential supplies may last, are important factors in assessing community needs and governmental response efforts. The collaboration of different NGOs and government entities is imperative for effective response to disasters.

Essential interconnectedness of community organisations in responding to disasters

Government bodies, including medical services, relief organisations and service providers, along with infrastructure restoration, are all essential threads to mend a disaster-torn community. Moreover, responses that occur after disasters to repair the damage often mirror processes that can be set in place through careful risk assessments, to pre-empt conditions that lead to vulnerability. It is now generally accepted that effective disaster management depends on the implementation of a carefully planned sequence of actions that encompasses pre-disaster protection and resilience building and post-disaster recovery, which also builds resilience through learning and altering behaviour (Figure 2.1). When one step of this sequence is out of sync, dire consequences can ensue, as was the case with the tornado that hit central Florida on 2 February 2007. This tornado strike was sudden; it damaged 2,324 buildings, destroyed 602 buildings and caused the death of 21 people (*Orlando Sentinel* 2007). Although more than 50 warnings went out on TV and radio before the tornadoes struck, they were not received because the tornadoes hit between 3 a.m. to 6 a.m. when most people were sleeping.

If the recovery process to restore community functioning takes a long time after an emergency, this can also have an impact upon the resilience of the citizens involved. Two weeks after the category-5 Cyclone Larry hit the small

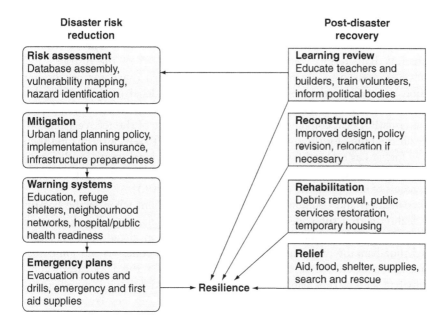

Figure 2.1 Disaster risk reduction and resilience building through pre-hazard preparation activities and post-disaster recovery activities.

town of Innisfail in North Queensland, Australia on 20 March 2006, the displaced residents still had nowhere to live, could not make phone calls and could not draw money from automatic teller machines or banks; as a result they were getting frustrated and very angry. Following the disaster, transport in and out of the town was severed and many of the standard providers of resources and services – such as medical services, retailers and child care providers – were shut down for weeks. Some resources and services, such as child care, were sometimes accessed through friends, family or neighbours, but these were only available to individuals with strong connections in the town. Compounding these problems was the issue of asbestos powder from ripped household roofs; it was flung across the town and dispersed though all the debris, rendering the whole area a contaminated site. Until it was effectively disposed of, an additional danger was faced by the residents and their children, one whose ramifications might not be fully assessed for years to come. A sizable proportion of individuals were so traumatised by the category-5 cyclone that they left the town permanently. More specifically, some children who lived through the event were still receiving counselling many years after they had moved away from Innisfail (personal communication from Innisfail refugees 2011).

Disaster recovery is a process of strategic community planning, replicating what happens in communities every day, except that what would normally occur over decades must happen over a short period of time. This time compression poses enormous challenges and therefore requires strong and trusted leadership. Leadership through the recovery process is a critical factor that can help build community resilience in the complex, post-disaster environment. Following what has become known in Australia as Black Saturday – where in the community of Strathewen, Victoria 27 people died and the primary school, community hall, tennis courts, cricket pavilion and 85 of the district's 130 homes were destroyed – community members reflected that good pre-disaster relationships both within the community and with local government had a strong influence on attitudes, relationships and the emergence of leadership in the aftermath. Local community members took charge of the recovery process. They allowed time for the town to regroup and begin to self-organise, and then moved forward using local knowledge and building on local strengths. Recovery agencies and government played a role later, by helping to address gaps through the process of rebuilding the community (Leadbeater 2013).

Preparedness and community cohesion are paramount when facing hazards and dealing with a subsequent disaster. Well before major earthquakes struck New Zealand in 2010 and 2011, the town of Lyttelton already had an established time-banking programme that had forged local cohesion and built trust among residents, enhancing their social capital. In 2005, the 3,000-strong community had set up a time bank whereby residents traded skills and earned credits for doing work for others that were then exchanged for services. For example, in return for transporting a neighbour to the doctor, a person could earn an hour of gardening on their property. Community currencies and other such programmes have been shown to increase levels of social capital and trust (Richey 2007).

Because this programme had been in place before the earthquakes struck, local residents in Lyttelton's various organisations had experience of working together in non-emergency situations. This built trust among residents with the result that emergency providers were able to work seamlessly after the disaster struck, using various focal points already in place, such as local cafés and recreation centres, as hubs for the recovery drive. The community's cohesion allowed it to move more effectively towards recovery, as has been shown in other disaster-impacted places (Boon *et al.* 2012). Once again, this highlights organisations' interdependence and interconnectedness, as well as the importance of relationships in disaster situations. These principles are reflected in national policies, which place a shared responsibility upon government and community members to address disasters (Commonwealth of Australia 2011).

To catalyse activities that build effective resilience to natural hazards, there is first a need to assess communities in context as shown in Figure 2.1. This will have to be an ongoing, periodic process to deal with changes in communities and populations as natural hazards induced by climate change multiply. Changes in communities can arise from the less frequent, sudden-onset natural hazards that trigger humanitarian disasters and lead to the mass movement of groups of people away from their homes, either as refugees to other countries or as internally displaced persons within their own borders. Though highly significant, these types of disasters may mask the equally important consequences of more chronic events, such as flooding, drought, famine and civil strife, all of which are also predicted to increase and intensify in the future due to climate change (IPCC 2013). The 2013 World Bank report on climate change impact and the necessity for building resilience has predicted that new clusters of vulnerable urban areas will mushroom as livelihoods in rural areas become unviable due to mounting pressure from droughts and floods. These new urban colonisations will primarily be in coastal cities, exposing a growing number of people to the impacts of sea-level rise. In addition, health impacts from heat waves will increase since they are felt more intensely in cities, where the built environment amplifies the warming effect. The majority of these effects are expected to strike the urban poor disproportionately. This is because new settlers concentrate in informal urban ghettos, where basic services and infrastructure tend to be lacking, increasing their vulnerability. Makeshift housing of substandard construction is prevalent in these types of settlements, increasing residents' exposure to storms, heat waves and flooding. Moreover, these informal settlements often provide conditions that are particularly conducive to the transmission of vector and water-borne diseases, set to become more prevalent as we head into the twenty-second century and the global temperature rises.

New and established cities often concentrate vulnerability, because of large and increasing populations (World Bank 2013) and complex social networks. More than half of the world's population now lives in cities. By 2050 the urban population will have nearly doubled, reaching an estimated 6.4 billion. Most of the increase in urban populations will be in middle and lower-income countries, which have more limited capacity to manage the new risks created – and

Figure 2.2 Settlement on edge of Phnom Penh, Cambodia (photo: Helen Boon 2007).

the existing exacerbated risks – by the global urban transition. For instance, the cities in developed and developing countries currently classified as high risk, measured by annual average losses due to floods, include: Guangzhou and Shenzhen in China; Miami, New York, New Orleans and Boston in the United States; Mumbai in India; Nagoya and Osaka-Kobe in Japan; and Vancouver in Canada (OECD 2013). Although Brisbane in Australia did not make the list based on the criteria for inclusion, it too suffered from devastating floods in 2010 and early 2011.

Taking past disasters into account, urban planners have an ethical obligation – and the opportunity – to increase significantly the future disaster resilience of urban populations. Careful urban planning that ensures efficient provision of basic services, as well as suitably designed and positioned housing developments, will assist large communities to cope with the adverse effects associated with climate change and concomitant hazards. To catalyse such activities it is necessary to obtain baseline snapshots of cities and communities, and to document and implement via policy the processes that have been shown to help communities and individuals through disasters.

Resilience revisited

Cutter, Burton and Emrich (2010), leading experts in the area of disaster mitigation, have rightly observed that for many resilience is considered the mechanism that will facilitate a movement to a more sustainable future. This is because it can save lives and money by taking action before a disaster occurs, and builds stronger, safer and more secure communities. Moreover, it can help communities and emergency managers to understand current levels of exposure and probable impacts from hazard events, thereby helping communities take responsibility for their own local disaster risks. These experts also pointed out that the policy community, at least in the United States, is somewhat ahead of the research community in pushing resilience as a means of mitigating disaster impacts.

To put in place interventions to strengthen entities so that they are resilient, a broad consensus across different key stakeholders and academic disciplines must be reached about the idea of resilience. Academics and the research community continue to debate the definition of resilience: whether resilience is a trait, an outcome or a process; what type of resilience is being addressed (psychological, economic systems, infrastructure systems, ecological systems or community systems); and whether it targets policy focused on climate change, emergency management, long-term disaster recovery or ecological systems. This has the led to many definitions from a range of academic perspectives, including ecological science, social science, human-environment system and natural hazards (Norris *et al.* 2008; Zhou *et al.* 2010). Zhou *et al.* (2010) identified at least 28 definitions of social resilience, while Norris *et al.* (2008) cited 21 definitions based at the individual, community and city scales, and from physical, social, ecological and psychological perspectives. Another confounding issue is that the terms 'community' and 'social resilience' have sometimes been used interchangeably in the research literature. An understanding of the term's meaning will be easier after reflecting on its history.

Resilience, a brief history of the concept

The word resilience is derived from the Latin term *resilio*, meaning 'to jump back'. Psychologists use the term to describe the capacity of a person to cope with trauma and other major life stresses (Bonanno 2004). Similar ideas characterise other disciplines' use of the term. In business management resilience denotes the capacity to use disruptive events to propel an organisation forward (Parsons 2010) and return to pre-disaster levels of performance (Sheffi 2006). The discipline in which the term was originally used is contested however, with some claiming it for ecology (Batabyal 1998), while others claim it for physics (Van der Leeuw and Leygonie 2000). It started to be used in ecology after Holling's 'Resilience and Stability of Ecological Systems' was published in 1973, when it was used to refer to an ecosystem's ability to adapt to environmental change while upholding optimal functioning (Holling 1973). Late in the 1980s, resilience in the ecological sense was applied to understand interactions between people and the environment (Janssen and Ostrom 2006). Nonetheless, a literature search reveals that the earliest studies referring to resilience are found in the disciplines of psychology and psychiatry in the 1940s work of Norman Garmezy, Emmy Werner and Ruth Smith, who focused on understanding the development of psychopathology in children deemed to be 'at risk' of psychopathological disorders due to persistent stressors such as parental mental illness, inter-parental conflict, poverty or a combination of structural and relationship problems (Werner 2000). These studies determined that, in the face of persistent stressors, some children and youths achieved resilience through processes involving adaptive behaviours and specific personality attributes.

As discussed above, resilience is now being applied across the field of disaster management. The adoption by the United Nations International Strategy for Disaster Risk Reduction (UNISDR) on 22 January 2005 of the 'Hyogo Framework for Action 2005–2015' has led to communities focusing sharply on what they can do to enhance their resilience. There is increasing consensus now among key stakeholders that apart from having an initial understanding of what resilience is, communities need to understand its determinants and how it can be measured, maintained and improved (Cutter et al. 2010). Empirical evidence has led to emerging agreement in research circles that resilience can be investigated either as a desired outcome(s) condition or state or as a process leading to a desired outcome(s) (Boon et al. 2012; Kaplan 1999; Winkworth et al. 2009). As a consequence, resilience can be investigated at diverse levels, including at the individual, community, organisation or ecosystem level. Which level is chosen for investigation depends on the issue or question of interest. Conceptually, the simplest level of investigation addresses the individual.

Personal resilience

Bonnano (2004) defined a resilient individual as one having the ability to maintain healthy psychological and physical well-being despite exposure to adversity. However, this definition does not take into account the wider community effects that appear to influence resilience. Therefore, resilience is better described as 'the capacity for successful adaptation, positive functioning or competence despite high-risk status, chronic stress, or following prolonged or severe trauma' (Egeland et al. 1993: 517). Echoing agreement, others put forward four indicators of resilience typically found in individuals:

1   absence of psychopathology;
2   healthy patterns of behaviour;
3   adequate role functioning at home, school and/or work; and
4   high quality of life.

(Norris et al. 2008: 133)

Additionally, Norris et al. (2008) stressed that the quicker a return to pre-stressor functioning is achieved, the greater the resilience. Of importance here is the term 'functioning' rather than 'state'. Resilience in this sense does not require a return to the status quo but rather healthy functioning, which might be different from pre-stressor functioning but is just as adaptive. In terms of time, Bonanno (2004) differentiated between recovery and resilience timelines in relation to psychological resilience. The former involves a period of dysfunction lasting several months or more, followed by a gradual return to pre-stressor functioning. Resilience, on the other hand, may involve transient difficulties lasting up to several weeks, but it generally involves a stable, short-lasting pathway back to healthy functioning.

An individual's resilience has been regarded as a personality trait, reflecting 'hardiness' or 'sense of coherence'. As a personality trait, resilience encompasses drives and characteristics, such as the will to live, perceiving a situation as challenging rather than threatening, a sense of commitment and control, a sense of meaning, a high level of confidence, resourcefulness, conscientiousness, toughness and self-reliance (Antonovsky 1987; Kobasa 1982). In addition to personal traits, social relations, such as social support, have been empirically identified as crucial to one's ability to cope with stressors (Boon *et al.* 2012). These findings also apply to resilient families (Walsh 2007).

Personal resilience is also believed to be a dynamic process rather than just a trait (Winkworth *et al.* 2009), and to potentially vary over a lifetime (Hegney *et al.* 2007). This is based on the psychological growth that develops as a result of living through adversity and which becomes activated when stressors are encountered. Research into stress, adaptation and coping has shown that resilient people are not only stoical individuals but that they display post-stress growth. This dynamic aspect of resilience – i.e. the interaction with the environment and the variation over the lifespan – has been measured empirically (Connor and Davidson 2003). In fact, research points to resilience as a process of struggle against hardship that can be learned and developed at any age (Gillespie *et al.* 2007), a critical and reassuring finding in the context of disaster resilience.

It seems that intrapersonal and environmental factors play a role in developing resilience (Tusaie and Dyer 2004). An individual's intelligence, optimism, humour and self-belief, as well as coping strategies and social skills such as involvement in collective action, help moderate environmental challenges found in the social and physical spaces. These personal attributes also influence how people interpret and perceive social interactions and social support. The key here is that resilience is dynamic and interactive, a choreography between individuals and their broader environment.

The challenge, of course, is to identify the underlying processes that strengthen resilience so as to ensure that interventions are firmly based on both theory and empirical findings. Protective factors from multiple levels of influence (structural, community, family and individual) that mitigate the negative effects of disasters and other adverse life events must be identified, so that interventions fit in with the 'life circumstances and everyday ecologies of the individuals served'. This is because resilience is based on the synergy between individuals, their environments and experiences (Luthar and Cicchetti 2000: 878–879), including factors that build economic resilience, such as employment opportunities and health services (Norris and Stevens 2007).

Individual resilience therefore appears to be entangled in community-level factors, as we have found in our own research (Boon *et al.* 2012). We also found that people must be informed and allowed to participate in mitigation efforts, with community-level system changes taking place through the preparedness stages as well as after disasters, to promote safety, calming, efficacy, hope and connectedness in the aftermath of a disaster situation. To summarise then, disaster resilience is an outcome emerging in individuals with the capacity to *adapt and learn* from the experience of a range of stressors over a period of time, so that they preserve healthy functioning. But does a population of resilient individuals constitute a resilient community?

Community resilience

Descriptions of resilient communities are not dissimilar to descriptions of resilient people. The ability to absorb perturbations, fast recovery from stressors and a capacity of the social fabric of the community to respond to adversity and reach a higher level of functioning are all connected to community resilience (Geis 2000; Adger 2000; Kulig 2000; Kulig and Hanson 1996). A recent case study conducted in the Wet Tropics of Northern Australia identified factors that were considered to build resilience in areas that suffered rapid economic and ecological changes (Maclean *et al.* 2014). A multi-disciplinary team of researchers who liaised with representatives from five key government and non-government agencies in the Wet Tropics of Northern Australia argue for six resilience characteristics at community level: (1) appropriate knowledge, skills and learning at individual and group level; (2) community networks linking local leaders and volunteers to support residents; (3) people-place connections showing an affective element that drives relationships between humans and the environment; (4) appropriate community infrastructure and services to help community residents; (5) diverse livelihood opportunities comprising a range of industries at different levels of size; and (6) governance based on collaborative approaches to decision making.

Community or social resilience is therefore clearly a function of its population and its stability. It is therefore inexorably linked to individual resilience. This raises the issue of mobility and migration, and whether a stable community population is an indicator of resilience. Population movement can be indicative of instability, or the converse, resilience, depending on the type of migration. In the face of external stress from a natural hazard impact, population movement is often an indicator of the breakdown of a town's resilience. As Adger points out:

> Displacement migration may be caused by a deleterious state of affairs in the home locality (such as loss of assets) and often has negative impacts on social infrastructure in both sending and receiving areas. Where migration is circular in nature and stimulated by the demand to move caused by attractive circumstances elsewhere, often in urban areas, the resource flows associated with remittances can often enhance resilience. Migration, whether circular or in the form of displacement, has both economic and social dimensions.

(Adger 2000: 355–356)

Population movement might therefore be evidence of community instability. In the IPCC study of 2007, migration in response to disasters induced by climate change is considered a failure to adapt. The IPCC (2007) authors emphasised that adaptation to a changing environment must take place *in situ*, and towns should not be abandoned. Significant external stress from the impact of a disaster leading to population displacement heralds the breakdown of a community's social resilience.

After the experience of Hurricane Katrina, researchers define community resilience as: 'a community or region's capability to prepare for, respond to and recover from significant multi hazard threats with minimum damage to public safety and health, the economy and national security' (Colten *et al.* 2008: 38). This goes beyond infrastructure issues to include the population's ability to maintain resilience. Perhaps this offers an opportunity to reflect on the way the bioecological systems theory framework can be superimposed upon community structure to see how different systems might correspond to those in the development of individuals' resilience.

The individual in the centre of Figure 1.2 (see Chapter 1) corresponds to the community itself, which is characterised by growth, change and development over time. The characteristics and features of the community are described by its geographical location, its infrastructure and assets, the demographic groups that comprise its population and its economic fabric. The community's microsystems are the various small organisational groups that operate within it, such as the administrative government (perhaps the local council), health facilities, education facilities, banks and other financial institutions, transport facilities and so on. The connections and collaboration between such entities correspond to the mesosystem, while administrative organisations located at national level comprise the community's exosystem. These might include the national bodies that govern from a location remote from the community and decree the policies that the community microsystems and mesosystems must uphold, such as as funding for education, health care and transport systems, but also the national policies that at federal government level decree regulations for building standards, the maintenance of armed forces, laws and whether a disaster is declared for a community after, for example, a cyclone has made landfall and destroyed part of it. The macrosystem influencing a community entity reflects the values, customs and international agreements and impacts that might affect its functioning, such as war, international diplomatic relations, trade laws and so on. The chronosystem retains the same function for a community entity as in the case of the individual. Of course the size and geographic location of a particular community will impose some variations in the way the different systems of the bioecological theory apply their influence.

Observing what happened after Katrina, Colten *et al.* (2008) urged communities to integrate emergency institutions and communications, make available formal disaster plans and train emergency responders. Following the experience of Hurricane Katrina they also recommend that communities have a reserve of personnel, material and financial resources and that they prepare residents through public education and information about risks and potential hazards, as well as long-term planning for recovery and vulnerability reduction. Fundamentally, the built environment infrastructure must be capable of withstanding the assault of severe hazards and have enough safe neighbourhood refuge shelters in public buildings, such as schools, community halls and the like.

Measuring community resilience: the landscape of resilience indicators

How can we know whether definitions of community resilience are accurate? To assess our ideas we must be able to measure them. Indicators can be about the population – that is, socio-economic indicators, developed from either question-naires or secondary data sources such as census data. They should be quantifiable, and able to be standardised for comparisons between places over time. The neces-sity for this kind of standardisation has been shown by a range of studies; for example, researchers created inventories to examine perceptions of health and well-being in samples of individuals (Andrews and Withey 1976; Campbell and Converse 1972). Respondents were asked to rate their health and well-being and satisfaction with their own lives. This work uncovered significant differences between perceptions of quality of life as conceived by the respondents in contrast to those defined by social indicators. Such a disconnect suggests the need to incorporate a sound theoretical model to underline the use of indicators designed to describe an idea, construct or theory about society. In addition, whether an indicator is causal or associative must be established when assessing the predictive potential of theoretical models. Of course an important aspect of measurement is whether temporal issues are addressed by the nature of the indicator, and whether adequate sampling techniques have been applied. The most rigorous assessments of resilience should include pre- and post-disaster (or any stressful event) snap-shots of individual or community resilience indicators. Longitudinal data yield best results for the purpose of prediction and direction of causality effects. A thorough representation of community resilience will require a mix of strategies and also a sound theoretical model, one that can represent the complexities of the object of research, in this case disaster resilience.

Community resilience can be assessed at the macro, sociological level through proxy indicators, like building-construction rates, growth domestic product, crime rates and demographic change. Economic growth, employment rates and economic diversity within a community are indicators of economic community resilience, a strong indicator of overall community resilience. Eco-nomic resilience depends not only on the capacities of individual businesses but also on the capacities of all the entities that depend and contribute to them and on which they depend, and hence it is a good indicator of overall community resilience (Boon et al. 2012).

A resilient community must be competent in managing its functioning. Com-petence is demonstrated through citizens' resilience and their collective action and decision making, problem-solving skills and creativity, based on collaboration at microsystem and mesosystem levels. None of this is possible though unless the microsystem contains functioning structures post disaster: reopening of grocery stores, health clinics and banks, so citizens regain their sense of community and start to recover. Stewart, Kolluru and Smith (2009) held that the economic system operates on micro, meso and macro levels before, during and after disasters, and argued that economic resilience must be developed on all three levels. At the microeconomic level, resilience is supported through, for example, reinforcing buildings to improve resistance to floods and storms and leveraging flexible technologies to ensure alternative sources of supply are available when local outlets are impacted. All levels of government can help businesses to improve microeconomic resilience, but meso and macroeconomic resilience focuses more on the interaction of economic sectors and markets. For instance, processes involved in dealing with imports represent intrinsic resilience at the meso and macro levels. Adaptive resilience at mesosystem and macrosystem levels involves measures to increase the accuracy and quality of information about impacted industries and markets (Stewart *et al.* 2009: 356).

To illustrate, dependency on a narrow range of natural resources can decrease community resilience because the resource might be at the whim of precarious weather patterns and sudden extreme hazards (Adger 2000; Zhou *et al.* 2010). For example, when severe flooding inundated the small North Queensland community of Ingham in 2009, the main industry of the town, sugar production, was ruined. This led to severe economic hardship for all the town's residents, not only the cane farmers, because of the interconnectedness of the economic flow from farming to services and commercial interests (Boon *et al.* 2012). The interconnectedness and interdependence of individual and community resilience creates a bidirectional effect that can be illustrated in several ways.

The interdependence and interconnectedness of individual and community resilience

Mere snapshot demographic measures or personal attributes such as wellness, hope, efficacy and the like are unlikely to yield a picture of whole-community resilience, even if estimated at a population level with representative samples. One of the reasons for this is the element of time as it plays out in resilience building. Two factors are important quantifiers for resilience:

1   Recovery rate: those who are resilient quickly regain equilibrium physiologically, psychologically and socially following stressful events, thus also supporting community resilience.
2   Sustainability: the capacity to maintain functioning in the face of adversity, which is a particularly important aspect of community resilience, especially in the face of hazards induced by climate change.

Even if a snapshot of demographic measures is obtained directly after a disaster, an improbable scenario, the litmus test of resilience is the test of time which cannot be effectively tested through a single extraction of data. Figure 2.3 demonstrates some of the interconnections between population health and well-being and community factors. It shows that climate change affects environmental hazards, which in turn have an impact upon the health of populations through an increase in diseases and injuries. The health of the population then stimulates policy formation, which aims to mitigate economic, social and environmental risks and vulnerabilities and also has an impact upon the potential for diseases and injuries.

Economic community resilience is a critical factor for supporting individuals' personal well-being and psychological resilience. This is because mental health issues can result from disaster experiences and can require formal ongoing support. Where there are insufficient economic community resources by way of government-funded health service supports the affected individual's resilience might be at risk. This is particularly crucial in the case where private income means are also lacking, as often occurs when employment ceases as a result of disaster. The link is also obvious in the case of an individual who has private funds, but the community infrastructure is so limited that medical care or counselling is unavailable. The resilience of a community is closely related to the resilience of its residents because a community that has a population of sick or unemployed people is not likely to remain viable over time unless resources from central government bolster it up. Conversely, a population of resilient

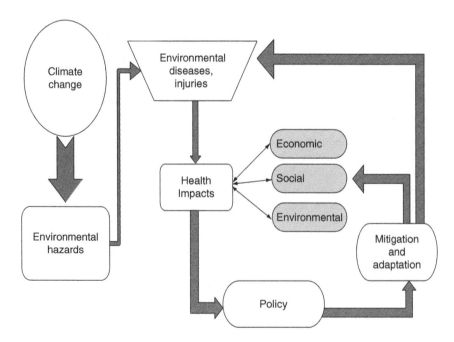

Figure 2.3 An illustration of the links between population health and well-being and community factors.

wealthy individuals may not support community resilience if the community is lacking facilities and opportunities for growth and recreation. Such communities often have an aging population and decline over time as the young move to more vibrant places.

Protection and preparedness behaviours and policies that support resilience are also subject to coordination between personal and community actions. A resilient community demonstrates competence through an ability to recognise, evaluate and address emerging issues via high levels of preparedness; it is composed of people who are willing to work together for the common good. In the case of rapid-onset events, such as impending hurricanes or fires, the cooperation of individuals with community mandates is important. For instance, if community evacuation plans are ignored by individuals or mandated mitigation (such as storm shutters for households) is not put in place, the community might have a large number of casualties that it cannot manage. Conversely, if effective infrastructure is not available, as was the case when Hurricane Katrina struck and the New Orleans levee system failed catastrophically leading to lethal flooding, the lack of community resilience causes individuals to perish. As for hazards that grow in intensity over time and befall a wide geographic area, like sea-level rise, drought or epidemics induced by climate change, resilience measures that reflect adaptive capacity also involve the coordination of both community and individual actions. One illustration of adaptation to drought in rural communities can be seen in north-east Brazil. Here the community adapted in two ways: individuals diversified their livelihood dependency and changed their agricultural risk management practices, and at the community scale various government groups tapped into records of prior drought events and put into place irrigation scheme projects (Nelson *et al.* 2007).

By contrast, the Big Dry or Millennium Drought that has affected southeast Australia since the mid-1990s has not led to significant changes in livelihood adaptation and management of the rural area in Victoria. As farmer debt in the Mildura region increased from AU$15 million in 2000–2001 to AU$275 million in 2007–2008, the numbers of farmers who received government assistance increased from about 9,000 in 2002–2003 to more than 25,000 in 2007–2008. The support that these farmers received from government might be connected to the stalemate observed in the region, with the drought being perceived as a crisis rather than as a sign of the uncertain availability of water into the future, which would have encouraged long-term adaptation through appropriate livelihood adjustments (Kiem *et al.* 2010).

In planning for the promotion of community resilience to disasters, Cottrell and King (2010) advocated attention to factors that help our understanding of the community at the micro, individual level – that is, psychological and demographic descriptors of – as well as at the macro, community level – aspects of the community that represent economic, built-environment, environmental and social infrastructure characteristics. Cottrell and King recognised that support for resilience to disaster can be conferred from various points in a geographical community and in doing so they invoked a model that closely parallels Bronfen-brenner's bioecological framework.

Others have reinforced the validity of Cottrell and King's assertions, claim-ing that the threat of natural hazards requires integration of resilience factors across interdependent systems and scales, since adaptation must originate from the community level (Keim 2008). Harney (2007) argued directly for the use of Bronfenbrenner's framework, because it can focus on the interrelationships between individuals and the contexts in which they participate, as well as the reciprocal interactive processes occurring between macro and micro-level con-texts. The macrosystem, which contains policies such as the relative freedoms permitted by the government, cultural values, religions, wars and historical memory, affects resilience either positively or negatively. Macrosystem charac-teristics centred on government orientation, the media, cultural biases, ethics and religions all inform the expectations, values, hopes, training and knowledge that shape people in communities. These are important facilitators of residents' know-how and collective understanding, which can assist the process of resili-ence and are therefore helpful in planning for disaster risk reduction.

In sum, since community resilience and individual resilience are inter-dependent and mutually supportive they are best examined using a theoretical lens, such as Bronfenbrenner's bioecological systems theory. One way of con-ceptualising the links between community and individual resilience using the bioecological systems theory is as depicted in Figure 2.4. Community resilience is the amalgam of its residents' personal resilience which links to the community itself; this in turn is subject to overlapping layers of influence from the different levels of the bioecological systems it is subject to. The suitability of the bioeco-logical systems theory for examining disaster resilience, vulnerability, wellbeing, or community adaptation to natural hazards at multiple levels of scale will be illustrated in the next chapter with two case studies which have been completed successfully.

Summary

Despite extensive theorising and literature about disaster resilience, there is still considerable disagreement about what precisely defines disaster resilience, the analytical frameworks for measuring it and the focus of measurement (indi-vidual, an individual organisation, households, infrastructure or community-wide systems). For each, there are variances in the methods, models and indicators employed based on the theoretical and epistemological alignments of the researchers. Conceptual orientations about the links between vulnerability, resilience and the more recent addition to this literature, adaptive capacity, are wide ranging and vary according to whether they are viewed from a socio-ecological systems perspective concerned with sustainability and global climate change research or from a hazards and disasters standpoint. There is consensus on disaster risk reduction as a strategy, however, and the enhancement of dis-aster resilience globally (UNISDR 2012).

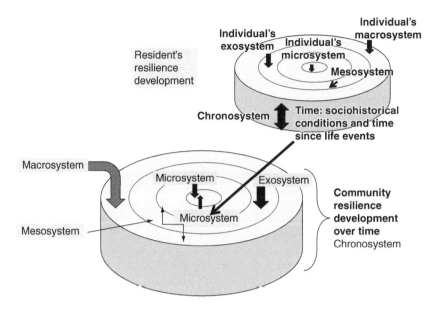

Figure 2.4 Interconnections between individual and community resilience.

Disaster risk reduction is most effectively implemented when the multiple and interconnecting organisations within particular communities are taken into consideration and baseline measures of their strengths and vulnerabilities are established. This is because a population of resilient individuals does not guarantee a resilient geographically defined community. It is quite feasible that resilient individuals will decide to abandon a disaster-impacted town to relocate to a community that is potentially safer. Such a move, *en masse*, could render a community vulnerable and subject to social and economic erosion.

Conversely, a vulnerable population might not disrupt a community's resilient state or equilibrium, as relief to support the community's vulnerable population might flow from the government, the macrosystem. Community resilience indicators therefore need to be carefully identified and thought out. Moreover, since the issue of time is an important one in terms of recovery and sustainability, longitudinal measures need to be available so that more accurate assessments can be made at the community scale.

An important matter for consideration in any examination of community or social resilience is to consider closely the purpose for observation or the research question. It is the purpose or aim of the investigation that should drive the type of examination undertaken: whether it is to assist the resilience of a particular group of people within a community in the face of a specific hazard, such as the risk of fire for rural residents near woodland in a dry, hot location (for example, the Murraylands, behind the Adelaide Hills, South Australia) or whether a whole township needs to be rebuilt as a result of fire destruction (for example, Slave Lake in northern Alberta, Canada).

Overall, the interconnectedness and interdependence of individual and community resilience points to a multi-level, multi-process model to help emergency managers, researchers and governments understand the mechanisms involved at the different stages of disaster risk reduction and disaster recovery. In this way policies targeted to support specific needs will be more easily implemented and resilience more easily achieved.

References

Adger, W.N. 2000, 'Social and Ecological Resilience; Are They Related?', *Progressive Human Geography*, vol. 24, no. 3, pp. 347–364.

Andrews, F.M. and Withey, S.B. 1976, *Social Indicators of Wellbeing: Americans' Perceptions of Life Quality*. Plenum Press, New York.

Antonovsky, A. 1987, *Unravelling the Mystery of Health*. Jossey Bass, San Francisco, CA.

Batabyal, A.A. 1998, 'The Concept of Resilience: Retrospect and Prospect', *Environment and Development Economics*, vol. 3, no. 2, pp. 235–239.

Bonanno, G.A. 2004, 'Loss, Trauma, and Human Resilience: Have we Underestimated the Human Capacity to Thrive after Extremely Aversive Events?', *American Psychologist*, vol. 59, pp. 20–28.

Boon, H.J., Millar, J., Lake, D., Cottrell, A., and King, D. 2012, *Recovery from Disaster: Resilience, Adaptability and Perceptions of Climate Change*. National Climate Change Adaptation Research Facility, Queensland, Australia.

Campbell, A. and Converse, P.E. 1972, *The Human Meaning of Social Change*. Russell Sage Foundation, New York.

Colten, C.E., Kates, R.W. and Laska, S.B. 2008, 'Three Years after Katrina: Lessons for Community Resilience', *Environment*, vol. 50, no. 5, pp. 36–47.

Commonwealth of Australia 2011, *National Strategy for Disaster Resilience*. Council of Australian Governments, Australia.

Connor, K. and Davidson, J. 2003, 'Development of a New Resilience Scale: The Connor Davidson Resilience Scale (CD-RISC)', *Depression and Anxiety*, vol. 18, pp. 76–82.

Cottrell, A. and King, D. 2010, 'Social Assessment as a Complementary Tool to Hazard Risk Assessment and Disaster Planning', *Australasian Journal of Disaster and Trauma Studies*, 2010–2011.

Cutter, S.L., Burton, C.G. and Emrich, C.T. 2010, 'Disaster Resilience Indicators for Benchmarking Baseline Conditions', *Journal of Homeland Security and Emergency Management*, vol. 7, no. 1, Article 51. doi: 10.2202/1547-7355.1732.

DAP (Disaster Accountability Project) 2010, 'July 12, 2010: Report on the Transparency of Relief Organizations Responding to the 2010 Haiti Earthquake'. Accessed 16 April 2015,   http://disasteraccountability.org/july-12-2010-report-on-the-transparency-of-relief-organizations-responding-to-the-2010-haiti-earthquake/.

Egeland, B., Carlson, E. and Sroufe, L.A. 1993, 'Resilience as Process', *Development and Psychopathology*, vol. 5, pp. 517–528.

Eisensee, T. and Strömberg, D. 2007, 'News Droughts, News Floods, and U. S. Disaster Relief', *The Quarterly Journal of Economics*, vol. 122, no. 2, pp. 693–728. doi: 10.1162/qjec.122.2.693.

Geis, D.E. 2000, 'By Design: The Disaster Resistant and Quality of Life Community', *Natural Hazards Review*, vol. 1, no. 3, p. 23.

Gillespie, B.M., Chaboyer, W. and Wallis, M. 2007, 'Development of a Theoretically Derived Model of Resilience through Concept Analysis', *Contemporary Nurse: A Journal for the Australian Nursing Profession*, vol. 25, nos 1–2, pp. 124–135.

Harney, P.A. 2007, 'Resilience Processes in Context', *Journal of Aggression, Maltreatment & Trauma*, vol. 14, no. 3, pp. 73–87.

Hegney, D.G., Buikstra, E., Baker, P., Rogers-Clark, C., Pearce, S., Ross, H., King, C. and Watson-Watson-Luke, A. 2007, 'Individual Resilience in Rural People: A Queensland Study, Australia', *Rural and Remote Health*, vol. 7, no. 4, p. 620. Available from www.rrh.org.au.

Holling, C.S. 1973, 'Resilience and Stability of Ecological Systems', *Annual Review of Ecology and Systematics*, vol. 4, pp. 1–23.

IOM (Institute of Medicine) 2015, *Enabling Rapid and Sustainable Public Health Research During Disasters: Summary of a Joint Workshop*. National Academies Press, Washington, DC.

IPCC 2007, 'Climate Change 2007: Impacts, Adaptation and Vulnerability. Contribution of Working Group II to the Fourth Assessment Report of the Intergovernmental Panel on Climate Change' (M.L. Parry, O.F. Canziani, J.P. Palutikof, P.J. van der Linden and C.E. Hanson). Cambridge University Press, Cambridge.

IPCC 2013, *Climate Change 2013: The Physical Science Basis*, in T.F. Stocker, D. Qin, G.-K. Plattner, M. Tignor, S.K. Allen, J. Boschung, A. Nauels, Y. Xia, V. Bex and P.M. Midgley (eds) *Contribution of Working Group I to the Fifth Assessment Report of the Intergovernmental Panel on Climate Change*. Cambridge University Press, New York.

Janssen, M.A. and Ostrom, E. 2006, 'Editorial: Resilience, Vulnerability, and Adaptation: A Cross-Cutting Theme of the International Human Dimensions Programme on Global Environmental Change', *Global Environmental Change*, vol. 16, pp. 237–239.

Kaplan, H.B. 1999, 'Toward an Understanding of Resilience: A Critical Review of Definitions and Models', in M.D. Glantz and J.L Johnson (eds), *Resilience and Development*. Kluwer Academic, New York, pp. 17–83.

Keim, M.E. 2008, 'Building Human Resilience. The Role of Public Health Preparedness and Response as an Adaptation to Climate Change', *American Journal of Preventive Medicine*, vol. 35, no. 5, pp. 508–516.

Kiem, A.S., Askew, L.E., Sherval, M., Verdon-Kidd, D.C., Clifton, C., Austin, E., McGuirk, P.M. and Berry, H. 2010, 'Drought and the Future of Rural Communities: Drought Impacts and Adaptation in Regional Victoria, Australia', National Climate Change Adaptation Research Facility, Queensland, Australia.

Kobasa, S.C. 1982, 'The Hardy Personality: Toward a Social Psychology of Stress and Health', in G.S. Sanders and J. Suls (eds), *Social Psychology of Health and Illness*, Erlbaum, Hillsdale, NJ.

Kulig, J. 2000, 'Community Resiliency: The Potential for community Health Nursing Theory Development', *Public Health Nursing*, vol. 17, no. 5, pp. 374–385.

Kulig, J. and Hanson, L. 1996, 'Discussion and Expansion of the Concept of Resiliency: Summary of Think Tank'. Regional Center of Health Promotion and Community Studies, University of Lethbridge, Alberta, Canada.

Leadbeater, A. 2013, 'Community Leadership in Disaster Recovery: A Case Study'. *Australian Journal of Emergency Management*, vol. 28, no. 3, pp. 41–48.

Luthar, S.S. and Cicchetti, D. 2000, 'The Construct of Resilience: Implications for Interventions and Social Policies', *Development and Psychopathology*, vol. 12, pp. 857–885.

Maclean, K., Cuthill, M. and Ross, H. 2014, 'Six Attributes of Social Resilience', *Journal of Environ Planning and Management*, vol. 57, no. 1, pp. 144–156.

Nelson, D.R., Adger, W.N. and Brown, K. 2007, 'Adaptation to Environmental Change: Contributions of a Resilience Framework', *Annual Review of Environmental Resources*, vol. 32, pp. 395–419.

Norris, F.H. and Stevens, S.P. 2007, 'Community Resilience and the Principles of Mass Trauma Intervention', *Psychiatry*, vol. 70, no. 4, pp. 320–328.

Norris, F.H., Stevens, S.P., Pfefferbaum, B., Wyche, K.F. and Pfefferbaum, R.L. 2008, 'Community Resilience as a Metaphor, Theory, Set of Capacities, and Strategy for Disaster Readiness', *American Journal of Community Psychology*, vol. 41, pp. 127–150.

OECD (Organization for Economic Co-operation and Development) 2013, www.oecd.org/newsroom/future-flood-losses-in-major-coastal-cities.html. Accessed 15 April 2015.

Orlando Sentinel 2007, various reports, 2–9 February.

Parsons, D. 2010, 'Organisational Resilience', *Australian Journal of Emergency Management*, vol. 25, no. 2, pp. 18–20.

Richey, S. 2007, Manufacturing Trust: Community Currencies and the Creation of Social Capital'. *Political Behaviour*, vol. 29, pp. 69–88.

Sheffi, Y. 2006, MIT Center for Transportation and Logistics', *Journal of Commerce*, 9 January.

Stewart, G.T., Kolluru, R.E. and Smith, M. 2009, 'Leveraging Public-Private Partnerships to Improve Community Resilience in Times of Disaster', *International Journal of Physical Distribution & Logistics Management*, vol. 39, no. 5, pp. 343–364.

Tusaie, K. and Dyer J. 2004, 'Resilience: A Historical Review of the Construct', *Holistic Nursing Practice*, vol. 18, pp. 3–8.

UNISDR (United Nations Office for Disaster Risk Reduction) 2012, 'Making Cities Resilient Report', United Nations Office for Disaster Risk Reduction, Geneva.

Van der Leeuw, S.E. and Leygonie, C.A. 2000, 'A Long-Term Perspective on Resilience in Socio-Natural Systems'. Paper presented at the workshop on System Shocks–System Resilience, Abisko, Sweden, 22–26 May.

Walsh, F. 2007, 'Traumatic Loss and Major Disasters: Strengthening Family and Community Resilience', *Family Process*, vol. 46, no. 2, pp. 207–227.

Werner, E.E. 2000, 'Protective Factors and Individual Resilience', in J.P. Shonkoff and S.J. Meisels (eds), *Handbook of Early Childhood Intervention*, second edn, Cambridge University Press, New York, pp. 115–132.

Winkworth, G., Healy, C., Woodward, M. and Camilleri, P. 2009, 'Community Capacity Building: Learning from the 2003 Canberra Bushfires', *Australian Journal of Emergency Management*, vol. 24, no. 2, pp. 5–12.

World Bank 2013, 'Turn Down the Heat: Climate Extremes, Regional Impacts, and the Case for Resilience'. Report by the Potsdam Institute for Climate Impact Research and Climate Analytics, World Bank, Washington, DC.

Zhou, H., Wang, J., Wan, J. and Jia, H. 2010, 'Resilience to Natural Hazards: A Geographic Perspective', *Natural Hazards*, vol. 53, pp. 21–41.

3 Methodology

An application of Bronfenbrenner's bioecological systems theory

Helen J. Boon

Chapter 2 described the complexities of investigating disaster resilience at diverse scales and outlined the rationale behind the need for the use of a more integrated analytical framework such as the bioecological systems theory.

Using two recently completed research projects, this chapter describes a method for measuring community or social resilience to disaster that is consistent with the bioecological systems theory. The studies focused on measuring community and individual resilience in two different regional Australian locations that sustained flood and fire respectively. Lessons learnt and implications from the findings are summarised, followed by limitations and caveats for future investigations, which are offered to guide future research and inform policy.

Measuring disaster resilience using the bioecological systems theory as a guiding framework: two case studies

As explained in preceding chapters, post-disaster community resilience cannot be determined from the evidence of personal resilience alone, even if a study sample is representative of the community population, because within a population a range of resilience levels will be evident. The research literature has shown that intrapersonal characteristics and traits such as resilience are influenced by social and economic factors at the individual level, whereas a range of infrastructure, economic and organisational features characterise resilience at the community scale. Between the two scales of resilience there will be connections via proximal processes.

Our exploration of the disaster literature from both theoretical and practical perspectives led us to the bioecological systems theory as a theoretical lens because it most closely approximates proposed models of other noted experts in the field (for example, the DROP – disaster resilience of place model – proposed by Cutter *et al.* 2008) and in our view it represents communities and their various nuances holistically. So we embarked upon a study that sought to test the model by investigating whether two disaster impacted towns in rural and regional Australia were resilient to disaster.

More precisely, our aim was to identify significant generic factors that supported community resilience in the context of two different types of disasters in two communities: Beechworth in Victoria and Ingham in Queensland, both regional Australian towns recovering from the impact of different types of hazard. Bushfire overwhelmed Beechworth in 2009 (the Black Saturday fires) and severe successive floods inundated Ingham in the same year (Figure 3.1). The disasters investigated were fast-onset ones, bushfire and flood, and they impacted similar-sized towns. As such, they were selected for investigation for their differences as well as their similarities.

The aim of the study was to link individual-level resilience factors with community-level factors. In the final analysis a triangulation of findings was sought to estimate and evaluate each community's resilience through a comparison of pre and post-disaster measures of community function, such as employment rates, numbers of businesses, rental rates and so on. In other words, the study was designed to examine individual and microsystem indicators and explore how these most proximal factors were linked to mesosystem, exosystem and macrosystem features of each community in the development of disaster resilience. The element of time, the chronosystem, was also an important consideration in the design of the project. The studies took place one to two years after the hazards had impacted each community and disaster status had been declared. This was an appropriate interval as it allowed each community time for the recovery and rebuilding processes to take place, so that communities had an opportunity to regain functioning. If resilience had

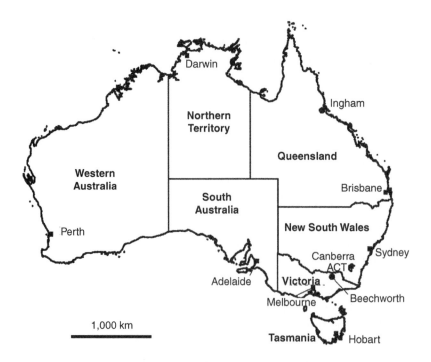

Figure 3.1 The location of the two study sites.

been achieved it would be possible for our studies to estimate it. At the same time, our research would examine the processes, or proximal influences, that led to recovery and resilience.

Methods

The theoretical and pragmatic considerations of community resilience described above led to a key hypothesis for the research: that individuals who remained in the disaster-impacted communities were likely to be resilient to disaster. Thus their personal characteristics, views and attitudes could be assessed to obtain a measure of their personal resilience, as well as a measure of generic indicators of personal disaster resilience, the innate trait. Moreover, their reports could be used to identify disaster-specific factors that helped them and their communities get onto a path of recovery and resilience. In other words, proximal influences and processes could be identified from the individual informants. To achieve the study purpose, a step-wise, mixed-method approach was adopted over the two-year research period.

The study design was by necessity non-experimental, cross-sectional and associative. To address the research questions, it was conducted sequentially by first implementing a qualitative phase, through focus group interviews. These were necessary to gather in-depth insights to the proximal process that took place before the impact of the natural hazard, throughout its duration and afterwards in the recovery and rebuilding stages. This stage was followed by a quantitative, survey-based phase, to generalise the findings from the qualitative phase. This is because an examination of social perceptions using traditional, quantitative strategies alone would have produced an incomplete, decontextualised picture. Perception is based on unique experiences filtering the wider, culture-specific experience of the individual. To contextualise the influences acting upon these cognitive constructs, an interpretive approach and qualitative data generation was required. This way, the overlapping ecological systems bearing upon an individual's perceptions could be distinguished (Bronfenbrenner 1979) (Figure 3.2).

Recapping Chapter 1, to examine and assess community resilience it is important to look at macro (community-level) and micro (individual-level) factors that promote resilience. While Bronfenbrenner's theory has been widely used in the context of child development, this was the first time it was used to model disaster resilience. This was done by organising our interviewees' response data about their experiences into categories: microsystem (where they participated directly), mesosystem (where networks operated between members of their microsystem), exosystem (comprising the facilities and organisations that were accessed by them), macrosystem (the nation-wide policies, mores and customs that helped them in their recovery and resilience) and chronosystem (time as it related to moderate the processes in their recovery and environment). Using this lens it was possible to structure the research so as to be able to extract both the most salient influences on resilience and their location within the

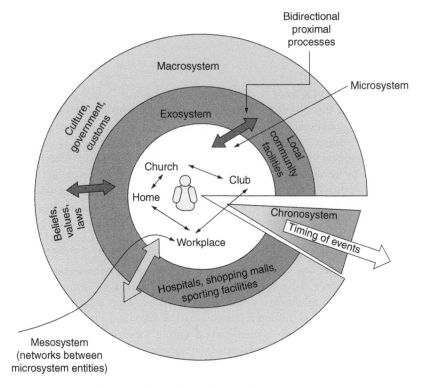

Figure 3.2 Bronfenbrenner's bioecological systems theory.

ecosystem, so that policy and interventions could be made to enhance future adaptation practices. Therefore, the observed factors within each community could be accounted for in context, to assess whether the disaster experienced had eroded the community as a whole, suggesting lack of resilience or, conversely, supported resilience.

To address our aims, we identified key local individuals in the case study sites and selected them for interview. Focus group interviews took place with key stakeholders from the emergency services, schools, hospitals and other health providers, local council recovery and response managers, insurance agents, philanthropic and volunteer organisations, church ministers, local industry and business personnel and local residents. This was necessary to help identify the behaviours and policies that promoted post-disaster resilience, and to populate Bronfenbrenner's bioecological theory model of resilience at the level of the microsystem, mesosystem, exosystem and macrosystem. These informants provided us with empirical variables that they held supported prevention, preparedness, response and recovery in each community. These comprised the *proximal* processes that the bioecological systems theory emphasises is critical. Their views, responses and identified processes were cross-checked to ensure that they were reported consistently in each relevant community context and then they were used to construct a range of survey items for a survey instrument. The survey instrument was important in order to test and generalise the views derived from the focus interview informants, since each community was comprised of several thousand citizens. After the survey was applied to a representative sample from each community, the variables we identified were measured and modelled using structural equation modelling (SEM) and Rasch analyses.

In order to satisfy the time elements important in resilience and macro-level community stability, demographic data were used to profile each community. These demographic analyses took place using data from national census collections before and after each disaster impacted the relevant community, to get a baseline level of understanding of community function. Extensive examination of 2006 and 2011 census data for each community indicated a stable population and economic picture, as measured by employment rates, population numbers, school enrolments, business entities and other socio-demographic indicators. The two communities did not appear to be significantly changed pre and post disaster, suggesting overall macro community resilience (Boon *et al.* 2012). This step was necessary, moreover, for between-community comparisons, to determine the representativeness of the samples we used and to compare community functioning, pre and post disaster, to assess disaster impacts and community-level resilience.

In order to gather empirical evidence to determine the factors that assisted with disaster resilience, individual and group interviews were conducted with 119 people across the two communities. The questions used in the interview schedules for both key informants and local residents were designed to elicit rich, descriptive answers. They were:

1 Tell me, did you know the event was coming?
2 How did you find out about the event?
3 When did you find out the event was coming?
4 Have you been through similar events in the past?
5 Tell me what helped you during the event.
6 Tell me your recollections post the event – how long were you back into your usual routines?
7 What sort of things helped you recover after the event?
8 Who do you think were most affected by the event? And why?
9 How do you think different people/groups coped with the event? And why?
10 Who do you think coped least during the event? And why?
11 In your view, has the community got better, got worse or remained the same as a result of the event? What sorts of things have made things better or worse?
12 Do you think you are now better prepared to face future similar events? Why or why not?

13   Do you think there is a risk of more disasters occurring?
14   What keeps you living in the community? Have you ever thought of moving from this community?

(Boon et al. 2012: 58)

Table 3.1 lists the various stakeholders who participated in the focus interviews in each community.

Before the main survey was administered, a pilot survey was constructed based on the interview data. The pilot survey included demographic questions and questions about each cluster of themes identified from the interviews, namely:

- preparedness at individual and microsystem scale (household preparedness and emotional preparedness);
- communications (from the media (exosystem) and the microsystem, more precisely family and friends, including the timeliness of these);
- microsystem positive influences (family, friends, neighbours);
- microsystem negative influences (family, friends, neighbours);
- macrosystem negative influences;
- exosystem influences;
- connectedness;
- sense of place;
- personal resilience (constructed from interview data and from validated surveys of resilience from the research literature);
- assistance from macrosystem;
- evaluation of pre and post-disaster community;
- climate change views and knowledge.

The pilot survey was trialled on 112 residents in Townsville and Cardwell and in the town of Yackandandah in Victoria. In both sites residents had experienced a disaster (Cyclone Yasi in 2011 and the 2003 bushfires, respectively) so they were qualified to respond to the questions about disasters to validate the survey instrument. The pilot survey was then Rasch analysed to ensure that the survey items were interpreted by respondents consistently and that they loaded to the underlying trait or construct; for example, sense of place. The results of these Rasch analyses permitted the final, main survey to be administered with few changes. After the final surveys were completed by the samples of interest in Ingham and Beechworth, the results were used to estimate the most parsimonious model of personal resilience, showing the influences impacting upon it.

The surveys comprised the same set of questions for the two communities, asking about issues that described their microsystem, their exosystem, their preparedness and their personal traits (for a full description of the survey questions, see Boon et al. 2012). A sample of 536 people from the two sites completed the survey approximately six months after the interview phase. The analysis steps are summarised in Figure 3.3. Respondents in the communities comprised:

Table 3.1 Focus group interview representatives from Ingham and Beechworth

Informants representing	Ingham	Beechworth
Macrosystem	Queensland Health; Queensland Police Service; Land and Refuse management; Emergency Management Queensland; governmental welfare providers; community health (incl. Indigenous health).	Government support (GFG) – representing Indigo Shire Council, Regional Development Victoria; emergency management; Department of Human Services Victoria; Community Health Service.
Exosystem	Local Chamber of Commerce; local community support organisation Hinchinbrook Shire Council; local government member; local aged care facility; local medical centre; hospital administration.	Beechworth Neighbourhood Centre; Carriage Motor Inn Beechworth; Beechworth Chamber of Commerce; Bushfire Youth Development Office Indigo Shire, also covering Alpine Shire; Emergency Management Planning Committee, Indigo Shire; Community Strengthening Project, Indigo Shire; Community Planning and Municipal Recovery, Indigo Shire.

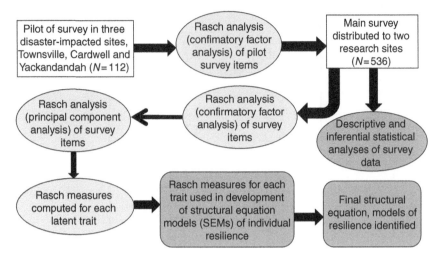

Figure 3.3 Overview of analytic process employed for quantitative phase of the research.

1   Ingham (pop. 10,259 in 2011) – 287 households;
2   Beechworth (pop. 12,826 in 2011) – 249 households.

As a result of all three phases of the research, it was possible to triangulate and generalise the interview participants' views, to construct a picture of each town's resilience and to develop an understanding of the factors that fostered resilience in the local residents. This was largely a result of the structural equation modelling (SEM), which was able to unveil the underlying interactions and influences upon individuals' disaster resilience using Bronfenbrenner's bioecological theory as a guiding framework.

The flood disaster of Ingham

> I do know a lot of people had sewerage through their house … You see the houses down at the Davidson Street area, which is sort of down that area [pointing]. I know a couple of people who had raw sewerage through their properties…
>
> (Key informant, in Boon *et al.* 2012: 399)

> In 2009 … there were people who had never been flooded in their lives, this flood screwed them raw … And they got water inside … 2009 … inundated places that had never been inundated before…
>
> (Emergency Management Focus Group, in Boon *et al.* 2012: 399)

Ingham is part of the Hinchinbrook Shire Local Government Area (LGA), located 110 km north of Townsville, 245 km south of Cairns and adjacent to Hinchinbrook Island (Boon *et al.* 2012). It enjoys a tropical climate, with a long wet season usually lasting five months, from November through to April. The town's main industries are based on sugar cane cultivation and milling, tourism, animal husbandry and aquaculture. In 2010, the Hinchinbrook Statistical Local Area (SLA) had an estimated population of 10,259 people (ABS 2012). Although the town is subject to annual floods and residents are accustomed to such occurrences, the two severe riverine floods that impacted the town in February 2009 took the residents by surprise because of their unprecedented nature. They reached the third-highest level recorded in Ingham's history and lasted for 10 days. The initial flood occurred on 12–13 January and the second between 29 January and 8 February. The peak of the floods presented on Tuesday 3 February, following heavy rainfall into the Herbert River catchment associated with category-1 Tropical Cyclone Ellie, which crossed the coast north of Ingham. It was possible to evacuate 40 residents from their homes; many others were isolated by flooding that trapped them in polluted waters for over a week. It has been estimated that 65 per cent of the Hinchinbrook Shire, comprising about 2,900 residences and businesses, was affected by the floodwaters, with initial estimates of infrastructure damage of AU\$120 million (Boon *et al.* 2012).

> What didn't help during the event was people being unprepared and not believing the flood would be bad. We [the police] had to go and tell people that they should pull their heads in and stop abusing volunteers and some were getting quite aggressive ... and they would say 'what are you going on about scaring people it is not going to flood' like armchair experts ... it wasn't right across the board but there were occasions where volunteers were accused of scare mongering ... historically floods only last 24–48 hours, this one lasted ten days so...
>
> (Police officer, Ingham, in Boon *et al.* 2012)

> Cordelia, Halifax, Macknade they do suffer badly and this last flood they did suffer badly but here in Ingham I would say it was the worst ... the longest flood, not the highest flood, the longest flood, and it was the worst flood that left so much bloody silt, the water we had here ... I don't know where the water come from, most likely the broken sewerage pipe.... He (A Lions Club volunteer) came back here and he gave a hand to clean a lot of the low block houses. He reckons the stink in the houses was unreal.... It (the effluent) comes from out the back from the cattle properties too.
>
> (Elderly gentlemen, Ingham, in Boon *et al.* 2012)

Results of the investigation on floods identified that resilience to flood events relied strongly on prior experience, preparedness, effective community leadership, strong cohesive social networks and individuals' sense of attachment to place. The Ingham people had just cleaned up after an initial flood only to do it again. This tested their stamina and caused more distress than had past floods. Nonetheless, Ingham residents reported that they well prepared to meet the flood disaster and as a consequence their community was resilient to the event.

This was verified by the demographic study that showed the stability of the population (Boon *et al.* 2012). Despite having the superimposed stress of the financial burden of the global financial crisis that beset the whole of Australia, the residents did not desert the town to flee to a safer location. This was considered a key attribute of a resilient community. Interviewees reported that they continued to live in Ingham in the face of the future risk of weather hazards because, although economic variables shaped their lifestyle choices, a sense of place and belonging bonded them to the town of Ingham. This exemplifies the importance of microsystem variables in shaping individuals' decision making.

The variables that were deemed to be helpful during and after the flood event, reflected in the responses of the vast majority of the participants, included:

1   Prior experience with floods that ensured appropriate preparedness (an individual-level factor, enhanced by exosystem influences that helped educate the residents and deliver timely warnings of the impending floods).

> Like my mother's generation, I grew up here, and we all knew, we live thirty-five ks out of town and we knew that come to wet season we were going to get cut off because we do ... we have a bridge across the road, so you stock up your food, you stock up your essentials, your dry essentials you do all of that, and if the flood doesn't come, no problem.
> (local resident, in Boon *et al.* 2012: 161)

> We were listening to the radio round the clock ... the television and the Internet were also helpful before we lost power ... we could monitor expected rainfalls and water heights of the local rivers ... you know we got the news 'word of mouth' too.
> (local elderly resident, in Boon *et al.* 2012: 161)

2   Strong, effective leadership by the local council and hospital provided appropriate help to meet the needs of all community members, but in particular those who were elderly, disabled or having mental health issues. The hospital, the mayor, council and essential services, such as electricity and water, were exemplary in their leadership and dedication to support the community, working round the clock (strong exosystem supports).

> A lot of the nursing staff stayed here (in the hospital) for ten days ... it was very humbling really because they had families at home themselves under water quite often but they were here with us. It was really strong community commitment.
> (local resident, in Boon *et al.* 2012: 162)

> The council here done a mighty job to give a hand in the clean-up, to get rid of all the stuff, they did that as hard as they could to repair the roads.
> (local resident, in Boon *et al.* 2012: 162)

3   Strong cohesive social networks ensured help was distributed across the community via volunteer groups and associations such as the Lions Club. These networks were also part of the local customs and nature of neighbourhood traditions. The community was very tightly knit through family and friend networks and through the Lions Club and other local associations that involved many of the residents (mesosystem effects and microsystem processes).

> …flood time is a really good time for me, it is a very social time, everyone goes around and looks at the water and chats to the neighbours … it pretty much defines our identity in this town. Anyway it really does. I have never been somewhere that is so frequently flooded, and is so accepting of flooding.
>
> (local businessman, in Boon *et al.* 2012: 163)

> I think having meetings for the whole town in the recovery phase and knowing that everyone can feed into that it just helps. We learn our shortcomings and we know how to improve on those shortcomings for the future instances … I did notice even among the businesses they were helping each other with staffing if somebody [a shop assistant] couldn't get through to their shop because they were trapped by flooding.
>
> (local shopkeeper, in Boon *et al.* 2012: 163)

4   Commitment to the community by local and national businesses and a sense of attachment to place that underlined the views of the local residents (individual developmental characteristic demonstrated in both focus interviews and survey results).

> Local and national businesses saw the needs of the community and remained open to supply the people with what they needed, even though they were also affected as individuals by the disaster. I guess I spent a lot of time at the local shop. It was still open. It was quite a good outlet because you could still get to talk to other people. I think people congregated at the pub [at Lucinda] or the shop. I guess it was a bit of a social outlet. Just sharing what was happening in their life at the time.
>
> (local resident, Boon *et al.* 2012: 162)

> But Ingham is a great place to live. It is a very good place to bring up kids, you know who you are … it's a lousy place if you're a young person who wants to run amok and sow your wild oats and that sort of mischief. It's like a gold fish bowl and everyone knows what you are up to, but it's a good town when you have gotten over that stage and raise a family.
>
> (local resident, Boon *et al.* 2012: 163)

There were also some lessons learnt for the future. The locals expressed a sense of powerlessness during the response phase of Emergency Management Queensland (EMQ). EMQ was seen to be inefficient because its personnel did not have local knowledge and did not liaise with locals, refusing to devolve power. The belief of local respondents was that if local knowledge and expertise had been utilised, EMQ's response efforts would have been more effective and timely. The local council noted these criticisms and responded in collaboration with EMQ with the implementation of a flood warden scheme. This scheme ensures that power devolves to local community members, who assume responsibility for safety and lead communications. Community members disseminate information and act as key points of contact in the case of future flooding events. The enthusiasm that met these efforts in the community is evidence of the strong social cohesion and sense of place shown by the individuals in this community. Extremely strong social networks were evidenced by these responses, illustrating mesosystem links.

Some mismanagement of macrosystem-instigated relief efforts was noted by various community representatives. The organisation of the response phase was too centralised and managed remotely. As a result of the lack of local knowledge the response and relief process was inefficient, taking an unnecessarily long time to reach those in need and wasting resources. For example, the helicopter used to deliver packages to those isolated by flood water, including essential medications and food, would make a single trip to a household and return to base. Liaising with locals would have ensured more efficient and timely distribution to needy residents. This is an example of macrosystem functions that should have been devolved to exosystem, community organisations.

> ...well the way it worked I feel wasn't the best way, because we had so many people sitting in rows of chairs all very traumatised, and the Department of Housing people, the Department of Communities people, and the other people sitting at the tables there at the other end of the high tower and these people they had to gradually, one seat by one seat, move up until they got to the front and they would shepherd them up to see these people to talk about their trauma. It was awful ... there was elderly people who couldn't walk and you had to help them moving. It was just traumatic for them and for myself, and it was hot and steamy.
>
> (Department of Communities respondent, in Boon et al. 2012: 163)

The state and federal governments offered financial relief via grants (a macrosystem intervention). But on the other hand, insurance companies, a macrosystem entity, were regarded as failing to support local businesses because in settling claims they did not use local businesses. This impacted upon the financial recovery of the community. Non-governmental organisations and charity groups provided significant financial support to local businesses, by contrast, as they purchased charity goods from them. This helped the town's financial recovery, which enhanced the sustainability and resilience of the community and highlighted the influence of proximal processes from the macrosystem to enhance community resilience.

In terms of individuals' disaster resilience, the survey analyses led to the construction of a model of resilience that incorporates elements inherent to an individual, that is, personal traits, as well as those emanating from various levels of the ecosystem. Figure 3.4 illustrates the interactions between various levels of influence and the development of individual disaster resilience in Ingham residents. The diagram might look complicated, but as Einstein remarked, everything should be as simple as it can be, but not simpler. This needs to be the case here, if the integrity of the bioecological systems theory is to be honoured.

A key finding from the survey analyses is that disaster resilience, as a trait, is strongly and directly linked to an individual's adaptability and sense of place or connectedness to the local community. These are all individual-scale factors. In addition, prior knowledge of climate change and financial capacity indirectly predicted disaster resilience through their effects on adaptability. Other *indirect* links to resilience were factors emanating from the microsystem, such as family and friends' support and communications about hazard events emanating from microsystem connections. Resilience negatively predicted a desire to leave the community, but family health problems or injuries and climate change knowledge were cited as factors that made people want to leave Ingham. However, the desire to leave was moderated by a sense of place and connectedness to the Ingham community. Important here too is the finding that resilience and adaptability strongly predicted preparedness, an expected result.

Was Ingham – the town as a whole – resilient to the flood disaster? Overall, two years after the flood events it was unclear whether recovery was complete and whether the community had been fully resilient to the disaster, even though demographic analyses showed no significant changes in community functioning (Table 3.2, Boon *et al.* 2012).

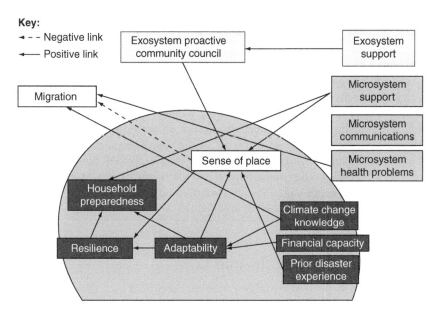

Figure 3.4 Factors and pathways empirically found to lead to resilience or a desire to leave Ingham (migration) ($N = 287$).

Table 3.2 Selected population characteristics of Ingham

Selected characteristics	2006 census	2011 census
	Person	Person
Total persons	12,071	12,201
Average household size	2.4	2.4
Median total household income (AU$/weekly)	752	908
Median mortgage repayment (AU$/monthly)	804	1,200
Median rent (AU$/weekly)	100	160
Total primary students	1,106	976
Total secondary students	913	867
Total number of families	4,795	4,894
Rental numbers	427	514
Owner-occupied dwellings	2,425	2,367
Unemployment rate	5.4%	4.2%
	Year 2008	Year 2010
Number of businesses	3,520	4,729

Source: Boon *et al*. 2012.

Certainly the macrosystem did a great deal of propping up, through proximal processes determined by policies. These policies offered financial support to affected residents, by way of financial grants for short-term recovery of individuals and cane farmers whose livelihood had been irretrievably damaged by the effects of the floods on their crops. Various reasons were proposed for the question mark about their recovery, including the global financial crisis. Another factor cited by interviewees in this context was the insurance companies' tendency to contract out community members' claims, excluding local businesses from the rebuilding effort. A reliance on sugar as the primary local industry clearly showed the risk of putting all the town's financial eggs into one basket, as those farmers who had 'forward sold' their crop were unable to meet contracts. Nonetheless, the community on the whole saw itself as more resilient than the Victorian community that was destroyed by fires shortly after the flood impacted Ingham. Ingham passed on relief money to the fire-affected Victorian community.

The bushfire disaster of Beechworth

An old gold rush town, Beechworth's settlement dates from the 1840s, with land used mainly for grazing. The gold rush led to its rapid growth from 1852 into the late 1860s, and since then Beechworth has been renowned for its alpine beauty and historical architecture. Located 200 km north of Melbourne, Beechworth has become a desirable destination for weekenders, overseas tourists and those seeking to retire or relocate to a pretty country town for a quiet life within reach of a major regional centre.

The Beechworth bushfires erupted at the same time as the more extensive Black Saturday fires on Saturday 7 February 2009. That day, and several preceding, had been categorised as absolute extreme fire weather spike days. The Black Saturday fires affected 78 towns and left about 7,500 people homeless. They claimed two lives in Beechworth, burnt through 30,000 hectares and destroyed several homes. The estimated overall cost of the Black Saturday fire disaster was AU$4.4 billion (Boon *et al.* 2012).

> It was a stinking hot day so we'd closed [the shop] early. There wasn't a lot of activity; no one was moving. So I was reading *The Age*, the front page of *The Age*: 'The Premier warns: bushfire – the state's a tinder box'. My son was sitting on his computer and at 6.13 the smoke came out of the gap and Aaron was one of the first who saw it…
>
> (local resident, in Boon *et al.* 2012: 315)

> …I don't think anyone else can understand the desperation you feel when it's your place. You'd do anything…. The wind changed and it [the fire] came back at us. We'd already lost two hundred and fifty acres of our farm … people say it's only grass…. It's not only grass … that grass is our life!
>
> (local resident, in Boon *et al.* 2012: 318)

Most interviewees from Beechworth concluded that the fire events built individual and community resilience at all levels of Bronfenbrenner's bioeoclogical systems theory. Lessons learnt included awareness of the need for self-sufficiency and the invaluable worth of prior experience. As a consequence, lack of prior experience with fires rendered newcomers to the town, as well as the elderly and children, particularly vulnerable. Microsystem support by way of neighbours, friends and family was critical to aid the recovery and essential to build resilience.

Prior experience with bushfires around Beechworth, those of 2003 for example, seemed to have taught residents valuable lessons and to have shown them the need to be self-sufficient and proactive, and that it was important to stay put to fight the fires. This is how resilience to such events is built at the individual and microsystem levels. Even if there was plenty of support from fire brigades, police, health services or other exosystem entities, individuals felt they could not rely on them being there at crucial life-and-death moments, because the fire spread so quickly. This required people to be prepared, resourceful and self-sufficient when utilities failed, and to keep reliable equipment to defend their properties. People had battery-operated radios, wired telephones, water supplies, protective clothing and boots. Adequate emergency warning of the fire gave people time to tidy up, move animals and generally take preventative action, and this was essential to tackling the fire with confidence. In other words, knowing what to expect gave people a self-efficacy to fight the fire and allowed them to stay calm. Experience of previous fires led most interviewees to claim that long-term farmers were resilient due to their prior experience and practical skills.

As already noted, the most vulnerable to fires were those lacking prior knowledge and experience, strength and self-efficacy to face the blaze: newcomers, the elderly, children and those in the direct path of encroaching fires. Community services interviewees identified as less resilient those who had difficulty in processing and coming to terms with their experiences:

> ...once the adrenalin rush is over they start to move into that second stage of coping, which is quite stressful. The first stage is just 'got to get something done', whatever you've got to do. Once you actually get out of that, it's got something to do with the long term focus on recovery. Some people stay in a much heightened sort of mind set, so their anxiety and everything stays quite heightened, and I think that those people don't start coping until that stops...
>
> (fire fighter, in Boon et al. 2012: 156)

As the fire event unfolded, the help and support of family, friends and neighbours (microsystem) was crucial. Proximal processes included not only physical help to save homes and farms from the blaze but also the presence of neighbours, friends and family, who enabled residents to rest, sleep, eat and share their anxieties during the days of watching and waiting before and after the fires.

The lessons learnt from prior experiences of fire had shown residents that their community had become stronger, with better communications, improved response and risk reduction strategies and a more determined and stronger community spirit. Mesosystem networks and exosystem support from community organisation provide physical and tactical support, and also emotional support: residents valued the knowledge that neighbours were available to lend a hand if need be. These proximal support processes included phone calls and messages of goodwill from far afield, outside the community (exosystem), which gave Beechworth residents a psychological boost.

The macrosystem had been proactive in providing interventions to reduce disaster risk as a result of lessons learnt from the previous fires. Many residents had attended state government-funded Fire Recovery activities, such as community barbeques, concerts or trips away. These activities brought people together, encouraging them to talk and share enjoyable experiences that built community spirit and a sense of place.

> I went on one of those weekends down to Lorne and it was lovely ... it was three hundred women and I enjoyed it very much, and it was very sobering for me because everybody I spoke to had lost their home...
>
> (focus group interviewee, in Boon et al. 2012: 157)

At the time of the study, community members noted that service provision following the 2009 fires had improved markedly, at the macrosystem and exosystem levels, since the 2003 fires. After the 2009 fires, the Bushfires Royal Commission legislated changes to planning and operations from the level of the Country Fire Authority to local, state and federal government levels. For example, to streamline operations, the Country Fire Authority (CFA) realigned its management boundaries to coincide with local government boundaries. Emergency management teams, including police and emergency services, local council and state agencies such as the Department of Human Services, now coordinated their responses, with responsibilities clearly defined.

The Vulnerable Persons Register was established by government agencies as an intervention to provide support for vulnerable people and their carers to plan and prepare for fire. This macrosystem strategy enabled a rapid response when, for example, evacuation was necessary.

There was unanimous agreement that individuals, communities and government agencies were better prepared for future fire events as a result of valuable lessons learnt from the 2009 (and 2003) fires. Lessons learnt through the recovery period meant that householders had become more resilient and determined to cope with a future fire, and to do so they had upgraded their firefighting equipment and their fire management plans. Moreover, the 2009 Black Saturday fires and the Bushfires Royal Commission inquiry led to improvements in protective community infrastructure: fire refuges and neighbourhood safe places were established, as well as funding to improve the equipment, operation and management of the CFA and its communications systems. The latter was a result of lobbying by community members to improve the telecommunications infrastructure, leading to a new communications tower. Thus the macrosystem and exosystem implemented interventions as a result of lessons learnt from the response and recovery period. These supports from the macrosystem and exosystem were instrumental in building community resilience. All in all, the Beechworth community saw itself as resilient to fires; the demographic profiles of the town did not contradict this impression (Table 3.3).

In terms of residents' personal disaster resilience, the survey analyses yielded a slightly different picture from the one in Ingham (Figure 3.5). While resilience was indeed predicted directly by adaptability and indirectly by microsystem factors, financial capacity and prior experience with fires, departure from the community was heralded by prior experiences of and problems connected to the macrosystem, such as poor emergency responses and recovery provision. On the other hand, sufficient financial means and a sense of connectedness to place negatively predicted leaving the town. Preparedness was a function of resilience, family support and financial capacity. However, resilience was eroded by climate change concerns in this community. Such a view would be based no doubt on the respondents' occupation, whether related to agriculture or tourism, since drought is much more likely in Beechworth in the wake of climate change compared to Ingham, which is located in the tropics.

Table 3.3 Selected population characteristics of Beechworth

Selected characteristics	2006 Census	2011 Census
	Persons	Persons
Total persons	14,358	14,790
Average household size	2.6	2.5
Median total household income (AU$/weekly)	957	1,059
Median mortgage repayment (AU$/monthly)	1,083	1,367
Median rent (AU$/weekly)	140	180
Total primary students	1,407	1,276
Total secondary students	1,224	1,189
Total number of families	3,944	4,105
Rental numbers	929	1062
Owner-occupied dwellings	4,260	4,473
Unemployment rate	3.7%	3.7%
Number of businesses	1,128	1,756

Source: Boon *et al*. 2012.

It is worth noting that climate change concerns and knowledge were factors that moderated the views of the residents in the communities in unique ways. The residents in the northern tropical region tended to be much more sceptical about climate change and its effects, more inclined to think that it was part of a natural cycle and that the natural hazards they were experiencing were not unusual. Those in the South Victorian community expressed more concern

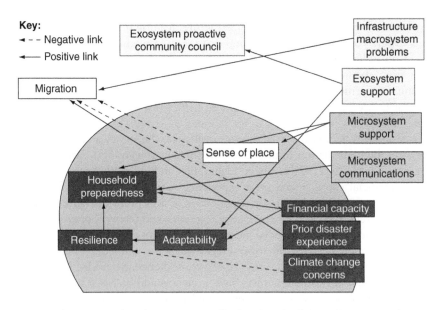

Figure 3.5 Factors and pathways empirically found to lead to resilience or a desire to leave Beechworth (*N* = 249).

about the future in a climate change scenario and were also more knowledge-able about climate change science, something that went hand in hand with their greater levels of formal education compared to the Queensland respond-ents. These differences are more fully discussed elsewhere (Boon 2014b).

As a result of combining all data from the two sites a generic model of per-sonal resilience (Figure 3.6) was developed via structural equation modelling (SEM). What seemed to be quite new to the disaster literature was the empiri-cal finding that resilience is not a single innate trait as had been thought but rather part of a process facilitated and predicted by adaptability and fostered by microsystem support, more precisely support emanating from family, friends and neighbours by way of both emotional and material support. Moreover, personal disaster resilience was further linked to perceived connectedness to place, or a sense of place, a microsystem and exosystem-derived influence. The drive to migrate out of each community, for the 5 per cent of individuals who indicated they wanted to leave, was increased when individuals had family members or friends who were injured or had other health problems. Out migration was also desirable when they felt no sense of place, or felt disconnected from the com-munity. In both communities a wish to migrate out was accompanied by very low measures of resilience and adaptability, an individual-level factor, by microsystem complicating factors such as family health issues and by lack of social connectedness to the exosystem. Those who received financial assistance from government and charities, that is, support from macrosystem entities, were also more likely to want to migrate. This was an expected finding, since the need for financial aid is linked to greater vulnerability and lack of personal fin-ancial means. These results highlighted the link between economic vulner-ability and mobility, which is tempered by an individual's capacity to leave: both vulnerability and capacity to leave dictate actual mobility, as has been reported elsewhere in the disaster literature (IPCC 2012).

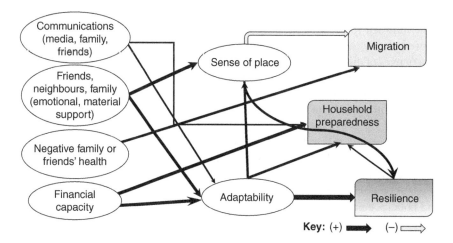

Figure 3.6 Empirically derived generic model of resilience.

Lessons learnt

Of the two study towns, the Ingham residents had the highest disaster resilience as reported through interviews and confirmed by the survey data. Residents there also had a higher level of employment, and respondents had been living in their community longer than the Beechworth sample. Most respondents from Ingham received financial assistance from the state or federal government as a result of the floods, unlike the Beechworth residents. They also had more experience of weather-related disasters over time than their Victorian counterparts, and were used to a higher level of economic disadvantage.

Disaster resilience for fast-onset events like flood, cyclone and fire is strongly predicted by adequate preparedness (e.g. Gissing et al. 2010; Cutter et al. 2008), which is in turn dependent on timely emergency communications (Cutter et al. 2008). Preparedness is essential for community and individual resilience (Kumagai et al. 2004). Accurate and trusted communications have been constantly cited as important in assisting the process of preparation (Colten et al. 2008). Neighbours, family and local community members were important communication conduits for those in Ingham, while the Country Fire Authority was more important for Beechworth residents.

Most respondents indicated that they were warned well in advance of the flood and fire. Queenslanders were significantly more emotionally prepared for the flood than were the Victorians for fire, and they reported higher levels of help from friends, neighbours and family than did the Victorians. This assistance was emotional as well as material, and included warnings, communications, emergency equipment, supplies and shelter. The Queenslanders reported a great deal of community cohesion.

Prior experience was also considered to be key to preparedness, a view endorsed by all. The survey results showed that it was also a precursor to disaster resilience. This shows the importance of learning for adaptation and behaviour change. Despite some focus interviewees' contentions that prior experiences sometimes led to complacency and a 'wait and see attitude', the survey results showed clearly that household preparedness was significantly predicted by prior experiences of disasters and other traumatic events.

What of community resilience? At the macro level, community stability pre and post-disaster, as shown by census data, was likely maintained because the macrosystem provided economic assistance to both communities. Measures of functioning at population level suggest that the communities were resilient. Nonetheless, does this indicate a truly resilient self-sufficient community? Paralleling individual resilience, which is both an inherent trait and a process fostered by the microsystem and the other consecutive layers of the bioecological system, community or social resilience seems also to be propped up by processes and policies emanating from the consecutive bioecological layers that surround it. This refers more precisely to the mesosystem, by way of the networks operating in the community, the exosystem, comprising state services such as emergency and infrastructure managers, and the macrosystem policies that permit communities to be given grants and financial assistance to rebuild themselves. Of note here is that community resilience in these two case studies was promoted by the resilience of residents who fought the disasters and remained in the towns to clean up and rebuild them. In some cases individuals might have been better served by leaving the community rather than staying put. Overall, those most likely to migrate were the newcomers to the town and those who lived in rented property, that is, those with fewer ties to the place.

Implications

Emergency managers and policy makers wishing to reduce disaster risk and enhance community resilience and adaptation to climate change should be aware that individual resilience supports community resilience. Since resilience is predicted by adaptability, it can be developed via community processes and activities that promote social cohesion. Of the two case studies, the Ingham residents proved to be most socially connected and also most resilient.

Policies must be tailored to community characteristics and needs. These must provide targeted assistance to the most vulnerable – the economically marginalised, those over 55 and the less well educated – so that they are more involved in the community (Field 2012).

Accurate and timely communications in advance of an impending weather event must be as precise as possible, both temporally and spatially, as they are critical to material and emotional preparedness. Community leadership for disaster preparedness, promoted through community activities, can use powerful social learning to motivate individuals to get ready with emergency kits, equipment and household preparedness. Since household preparedness was primarily a function of residents' financial capacity, defined by their ability to meet the costs of repairing the damage from the disaster as well as their insurance cover for the event's damage, policies must address these issues in the future. That can be achieved by providing specific assistance for subsidised insurance, low-cost subsidised emergency kits and the like, as appropriate for the type of hazard a community is most likely to encounter. That way, self-efficacy and confidence to meet a natural hazard can help prevent it from turning into a disaster at the level of the individual. It is also essential to recognise the importance of social connectedness in building both individual and community resilience. To enhance this aspect, programmes need to be organised by local councils to foster stronger connections between neighbours and increase residents' sense of belonging and place.

Finally, the most urgent way to move forward to promote adaptation to climate change and enhance disaster resilience is through education. Gaps revealed in awareness and understanding of climate change in the communities can prevent future adaptation to climate change risks. These gaps were revealed through the surveys. They were associated with respondents' level of education. Findings, therefore, highlight the need for educational interventions to be implemented at community level. Schools could be used as centres for information dissemination, with up-to-date evidence-based information about risks and responses needed for climate change. There is a corresponding need to ensure that current and future teachers are prepared and aware of climate change science (Boon 2010) by working with tertiary teacher training institutions to correct gaps in knowledge and understanding (Davis 2014; Boon 2014a).

Cutter et al. (2008) have repeatedly emphasised that the resilience of a community is based on macro-level population factors. If the community shrinks because of out migration as a result of a disaster, the community is not resilient. On the other hand, individuals who are unable to cope and adapt but who remain in a community with increased levels of hardship because they desire to display stoicism (Kiem et al. 2010) do not help their community to be resilient. True resilience is indicated by the capacity to adapt by learning from experience, ready for any potential new conditions and hazards (Arbon et al. 2012).

Limitations and caveats for future investigations

The most serious limitation of these studies is that we had no access to people who had left the community as a result of the disasters. They would have provided us with more insight into the recovery process, vulnerability and resilience, and helped to validate our findings from those who remained behind. Another potential limitation was the retrospective nature of the studies, since some important details relating to the response and recovery phases might have been forgotten. Finally, it could be argued that self-reports, which were the basis of the survey phase, might be inaccurate. However, given the phenomenological nature of perceived support and the ability to cope with disasters and traumas, a self-report could arguably be most valid. Certainly a wide range of personal resilience was found across the two samples, as measured by Rasch analyses, which also gives confidence to the self-reporting nature of the surveys.

Notwithstanding, the two cases studies presented are illustrations of the potential usefulness of the bioecological systems theory to measure disaster resilience. They highlight how to approach the issue with the theory in mind to try to extract both system-level factors that impact upon resilience as well as *proximal* influences, processes that are invaluable indicators of the types of processes that actually enhance individual and community-level resilience.

It is clear that with sufficient funding it would be possible to explore in much greater depth and with much more extensive sources of information the sorts of issues that emerge, the processes taking place and how they are perceived by residents, as well as how they are evaluated by organisations key to response, recovery and DRR. More notably, the types of connection between organisations and individuals in a range of occupational settings need to be examined, to produce a more detailed understanding of the processes that take place at different space and time coordinates of community functioning.

A longitudinal study that measures the development of resilience in a group of individuals and in a community entity would yield invaluable data to build policies that can support the needs of communities in situ, taking into account their local complexities and potential risks. For the sake of the safety of future generations, governments must employ a methodical and systematic approach to measuring the assets and vulnerabilities of specific geographic communities so that they can accurately target and implement disaster risk reduction strategies. This is especially needed when the focus is on cities, which are far more complex than smaller regional communities. They are more likely to be vulnerable when a hazard befalls them because of the large numbers of citizens who are members of vulnerable groups and because many of the large cities of the world have grown organically over time, with less than adequate attention on protecting their vulnerable neighbourhoods. This is especially the case in the face of climate change, which is altering weather patterns and shifting hazards like hurricanes, storms and wildfires to previously unaffected places.

When considering cities in developing countries, which usually do not have the infrastructure and economic wherewithal to meet the exigencies of a disaster, the pre-disaster planning phase is critical. Baseline studies and policies to protect communities from natural hazards will go a long way towards minimising the damage of hazards. The case of the massively destructive earthquake of April 2015 in Nepal is an example: citizens who survived it were outraged because the government had failed to implement building regulations that would have increased the strength and durability of the built environment against earthquakes that scientists had predicted would occur in the area.

Summary

This chapter has illustrated the application of bioecological systems theory in an examination of community and individual disaster resilience to two different types of disaster, flood and fire, both of which are predicted to increase in frequency as a result of climate change. The precise sequence and design of the research is of particular importance because it can focus and reveal proximal processes that occur at the micro, individual level, as well as zooming out to examine the community as a whole at the macro level.

The methods of analysis, the use of both qualitative and quantitative methods and the use of structural equation modelling as well as Rasch analyses yield an accurate picture of the nuances of individual resilience. At the same time, a demographic study of community functioning that examined pre and post-disaster community data can help governments and researchers understand how resilient to disaster a community actually is, and whether outside help is essential to prop the community up or whether it is self-sufficient and able to sustain function into the future.

The studies above show the interconnectedness of individual and community resilience in the case of small regional towns. The situation could be very different in a large city setting or in the case of a different type of disaster, such as drought or landslide. This serves to show that communities are unique, dependent on their ecological setting and geographical location, which often also drives economic development and dependencies. As such, each community will have different needs. Local residents should take ownership over their unique community needs. This approach has the twofold effect of strengthening community functioning and response to natural hazards and also building social cohesion and individuals' connectedness to place, a factor that feeds back to enhance personal disaster resilience.

In closing, the most important message of this chapter is that the research question must dictate the research design and methods adopted. If personal disaster resilience is the focus of the research, the method adopted will be quite different from the method adopted for social or community resilience. A research design focusing on the microsystem or individual might answer questions about personal resilience, as the next two chapters will describe.

References

Arbon, P., Gebbie, K., Cusack, L., Perera, M.D. and Becon, V.S. 2012, 'Developing a Model and Tool to Measure Community Disaster Resilience', report published by Torrens Resilience Institute. Available online: www.torrensresilience.org/images/pdfs/toolkit/trireport.pdf.

ABS (Australian Bureau of Statistics) 2012, 'Socio-Economic Indexes for Areas (SEIFA)', 2033.0.55.001, Commonwealth of Australia, Canberra.

Boon, H.J. 2014a, 'Climate Change Ignorance: An Unacceptable Legacy', *The Australian Educational Researcher*, vol. 42, no. 4, pp. 1–23. doi: 10.1007/s13384-014-0156-x.

Boon, H.J. 2014b, 'Perceptions of Climate Change Risk in Four Disaster-Impacted Rural Australian Towns', *Regional Environmental Change*, pp. 1–13, doi: 10.1007/s10113-014-0744-3.

Boon, H.J. 2010, 'Climate Change? Who Knows? A Comparison of Secondary Students and Pre-Service Teachers', *Australian Journal of Teacher Education*, vol. 35, no. 1, art. 9. Available: http://ro.ecu.edu.au/ajte/vol.35/iss1/9.

Boon, H.J., Millar, J., Lake, D., Cottrell, A. and King, D. 2012, *Recovery from Disaster: Resilience, Adaptability and Perceptions of Climate Change*, National Climate Change Adaptation Research Facility, Queensland.

Bronfenbrenner, U. 1979, *The Ecology of Human Development: Experiments by Nature and Design*. Harvard University Press, Cambridge, MA.

Colten, C.E., Kates, R.W. and Laska, S.B. 2008, 'Three Years After Katrina: Lessons for Community Resilience', *Environment*, vol. 50, no. 5, pp. 36–47.

Cutter, S.L., Barnes, L., Berry, M., Burton, C., Evans, E., Tate, E. and Webb, J. 2008, 'A Place-Based Model for Understanding Community Resilience to Natural Disasters', *Global Environmental Change*, vol. 18, pp. 598–606.

Davis, J.M. 2014, 'Climate Change, Sustainability and Science Education', *Queensland Science Teacher*, vol. 40, no. 4, pp. 5–11.

Field, C.B., ed. 2012, *Managing the Risks of Extreme Events and Disasters to Advance Climate Change Adaptation: Special Report of the Intergovernmental Panel on Climate Change*. Cambridge University Press, Cambridge.

Gissing, A., Keys, C. and Opper, S. 2010, 'Towards Resilience Against Flood Risks', *Australian Journal of Emergency Management*, vol. 25, no. 2, pp. 39–45.

IPCC 2012, 'Summary for Policymakers', in *Managing the Risks of Extreme Events and Disasters to Advance Climate Change Adaptation* (C.B. Field, V. Barros, T.F. Stocker, D. Qin, D.J. Dokken, K.L. Ebi, M.D. Mastrandrea, K.J. Mach, G.-K. Plattner, S.K. Allen,

M. Tignor and P.M. Midgley (eds)). A Special Report of Working Groups I and II of the Intergovernmental Panel on Climate Change. Cambridge University Press, Cambridge and New York, NY, pp. 1–19.

Kiem, A.S., Verdon-Kidd, D.C., Boulter, S.L. and Palutikof, J.P. 2010, *Learning From Experience: Historical Case Studies and Climate Change Adaptation*, National Climate Change Adaptation Research Facility, Queensland.

Kumagai, Y, Carroll, MS, & Cohn, P. 2004, 'Coping with interface wildfire as a human event: lessons from the disaster/hazards literature', *Journal of Forestry*, vol. 102, no. 6, pp. 28–32.

4   Individuals' disaster resilience

Helen J. Boon

In Chapter 3 we presented two case studies that illustrated the use of Bronfen-brenner's bioecological systems theory in the examination of disaster resilience, both at the individual and at the macro, community scale. This chapter will draw from the broad literature on resilience at the level of the individual to focus on what is known to date about individuals' resilience to disasters.

We will examine the indicators that have been shown to be characteristics of resilient individuals, and we will reflect on whether factors like gender, age, dis-ability, minority status, socioeconomic background, geographical location or disaster type shape and moderate resilience. The chapter will delineate a range of differences that exist in individuals' responses to disaster and their resilience, and some of the different ways that have been used in the field to assess such responses. The research that is described here in connection to disaster resili-ence is not based on Bronfenbrenner's bioecological systems theory, because we were the first researchers to apply this theory to the examination of disasters. Nevertheless, since this chapter focuses on individuals' responses to disaster it is still possible to make inferences about the research findings and how they reflect the bioecological systems theory. We will cross the intersection of psychologi-cal, environmental and sociological factors that impact upon individuals' resili-ence. The interlocking of these factors in producing their effects will become apparent to the reader, showing the relevance of the bioecological systems theory in understanding personal responses to disaster and how they can lead to resilience or sometimes leave the individual traumatised. The intention of the chapter is to make it easier for an interested researcher to design more robust research protocols to understand resilience to a range of disasters by taking into consideration prior findings and their limitations.

In a way, this chapter will be the kernel of the book, because it will show that even in the context of individuals the more distal effects of policy, services and the like can be just as important as more proximal, direct influences, such as physical location, protection from the elements and psychological preparedness for a natural hazard. All of these supports though are subject to the phenomeno-logical perspective of the individual, as Bronfenbrenner stressed (1986). In other words, the social, material and environmental influences on an individual are all filtered through a phenomenological lens that is uniquely personal and shaped by prior experience, as well as an individual's genetic and biological predispositions. The chapter will therefore connect the dots of the bigger picture view through the interpretive lens of the bioecological systems theory.

The need to protect all people, especially the vulnerable, from hazards

The aftermath of Hurricane Katrina highlighted how poorly the authorities had responded to the needs of the community's most vulnerable members (NMA 2005). Ten years later, the Asia and Pacific Disability Forum issued a press statement following the devastating earthquake in Nepal, which led to over 7,000 deaths (APDF 2015). This vehemently urged for increased focus on disaster risk reduction strategies across the world to protect all people, but especially those who are most vulnerable.

> Most importantly, however, for the APDF, especially for the persons with disabilities, children, women and senior citizens, there is always an extreme danger lurking in case of emergency. Recalling the Incheon Strategy Goal 7 (Ensure disability-inclusive disaster risk reduction and management) and UNCPRD article 11 (Situations of risk and humanitarian emergencies), we call on governments in every country to establish comprehensive plans for accessibility from all aspects in the situation of natural disasters. Also, we urge governments in every country to set forth safe, inclusive and accessible countermeasures against natural disaster for the vulnerable including persons with disabilities in the Sustainable Development Goals, to be declared in September 2015.
>
> (APDF 2015)

Those deemed vulnerable to natural hazards and extreme weather events include people living in low-income countries, those living in low-lying, flood-prone areas or close to the faults of tectonic plates prone to volcanic eruptions and earthquakes and, in addition, across all parts of the globe, a range of sub-populations: the homeless, children, women, the elderly and those with disabilities and other health impairments. Provision for those who are more at risk during natural hazard events should be improved because, as Stough (2015) maintains, when the vulnerability of one segment of the population is addressed, the resilience of the entire town or community is increased.

When Hurricane Sandy, America's second-most costly storm, smashed into the north-east and mid-Atlantic states in October 2012, uprooting trees and causing massive flooding, at least three large hospitals were forced to evacuate after emergency generators failed. Governors of 10 states declared emergencies and requested federal aid. One alarming consequence of the storm was its effect on people with special medical needs, those who were dependent on home nursing, personal care attendants or electric medical technologies such as kidney dialysis machines. Many people requiring ongoing respiratory care streamed into emergency rooms to receive respiratory treatments, refill oxygen tanks or recharge batteries. Some whose medical care needs had not escalated to emergency levels but who needed to recharge medical equipment were turned away from emergency shelters because operators believed their needs could not be met there (Jan and Lurie 2012).

Sobering disaster statistics from the Indian Ocean tsunami of 2004 demonstrate the vulnerability of women. An average of 77 per cent of the fatalities recorded were women, some having drowned because they had never been taught how to swim (Aglionby 2005). Anyone would have struggled against the massive tsunami, but these women's inability to swim made them vulnerable even in less ferocious waves. Not only are women vulnerable to the hazard itself but they are also vulnerable after the physical danger of the hazard passes, during the response phase and in the aftermath of disaster. To illustrate, after the 7.8-magnitude earthquake struck Nepal on 25 April 2015, many women whose husbands were migrant workers in wealthier countries such as Dubai found themselves homeless and at additional social and medical risk (Aryal 2015). The women staying in temporary camps were vulnerable to abuse, disease and neglect, and had no emotional or moral support. They had to take care of their children and aging in-laws and because communications were cut off they could not get in touch with their husbands abroad to let them know they were safe or ask for financial support to ease their desperate plight.

When women are less able to fulfil their duties as managers of the household, they are more vulnerable to domestic violence: in the aftermath of disasters there has been a marked increase in rates of sexual and domestic abuse towards women (Aryal 2015). Likewise, women are at increasingly greater risk of gender-based violence due to higher temperatures and shortages of natural resources induced by climate change. A 2011 report on Nigeria by the US Institute for Peace explained how additional heat resulting from climate change reduced rainfall, causing droughts and desertification that damaged the Nigerian economy, piling more social and psychological stress onto Nigerians. The report cites evidence in and outside Nigeria that suggests that as a result of drought, an insidious natural disaster, alienated young people who lack resources and economic opportunity are more likely to join rebellions. This gives fuel to the violent anti-establishment Islamic group Boko Haram, which attracts rafts of jobless young men displaced from their rural communities (Sayne 2011).

As for children, from an ecosystems perspective disasters erode the social fabric of communities, undermining the capacities of institutions that provide developmental support to children beyond their immediate caregivers. Emergencies disrupt the day-to-day routines that fill a child's life: formal and informal learning settings may be destroyed, seriously interrupting the opportunity for children's cognitive stimulation and critical thinking, as well as emotional well-being. In 2008 over 5,000 children were left without an adult caregiver in the immediate aftermath of the Sichuan earthquake (ReliefWeb 2008). Such separation from carers not only removes children's access to appropriate nurturing but it also leaves them susceptible to exploitation and abuse (Hepburn 2006).

Moreover, as a result of disaster children are likely to miss school, possibly for extended periods of time, especially in developing counties. After Bolivia's 2008 floods the education of 20,000 students was interrupted when 347 schools were damaged, and in Cambodia's disaster-prone areas principals report that floods cause 60 per cent of their schools to close for 2.5 months of every school year.

At the other end of the human lifespan, many, but not all, studies have found that older individuals are more likely to suffer adverse physical consequences as a result of disasters (Cherniack 2008). This is not surprising considering the elderly are more likely to be in worse health before disasters and less able to seek assistance afterward. The lack of agreement between studies is also unsurprising, because of the heterogeneity of disasters, populations and survey methods. This heterogeneity leads to ambiguity as to whether older individuals have a better or worse psychological outcome than younger ones. Several investigations have noted that people may become more resilient to some of the psychological effects of disasters with more frequent exposure, or with prior experience, as we found in our studies (Boon *et al.* 2012).

Socio-economic factors are enmeshed with the vulnerability of specific groups. An examination of 14 disaster studies that measured socioeconomic status concluded that 'lower [socio-economic status] was consistently associated with greater post-disaster distress' (Norris *et al.* 2002: 236). While the vulnerability associated with poverty has been consistently reported, the interplay

Figure 4.1 Cambodian village market (Helen J. Boon).

between financial status and risk can be as varied as are disasters themselves. Fundamentally, a lack of financial resources makes it more difficult to withstand the short and long-term demands imposed by disasters (Boon 2013); this becomes more acute, even a life-and-death issue, for those who are homeless (Every and Thompson 2014). For instance, survivors of the 1992 Hurricane Andrew reported that although people in low-income areas were aware of the emergency storm warnings, they lacked the money to buy storm-buffering supplies or to evacuate the area (Morrow and Enarson 1996). On a macro scale, the general lack of infrastructure in impoverished areas tends to impede the communication of warnings in advance of – and during – a disaster, as well as the ability of emergency response teams to provide aid (Chandrasekhar and Ghosh 2001). As a result, although developing nations experience natural hazards at about the same frequency as developed nations, the resulting death toll and damage vastly exceeds those experienced in wealthy nations (Kahn 2005). As will become evident, the physical and material impact of a natural hazard, along with loss of income and social support that are a frequent corollary, are the proximal processes that decrease individual resilience through the erosion of psychological well-being.

It is no surprise that, along with the social, physical and economic factors impacting upon a person's capacity to cope with natural hazards, psychological health can strongly moderate an individual's response to disaster, the ensuing personal loss and indeed to traumas in general. At one end of the spectrum are people with mental illness, whose symptoms can significantly affect their responses to disasters as well as the community's responses to them, sometimes with terrible consequences. Not only did people with a range of psychiatric health issues have difficulty following evacuation instructions and other essential messages during Hurricane Katrina but some were also treated harshly as a result: 'nine out of ten residents at one psychiatric facility in Mississippi still cannot be found', while some 'evacuees with psychiatric illnesses were arrested and jailed, sometimes dragged out of shelters and other times removed from the streets' (National Council on Disability 2006: 16, 19).

The incidence of mental health issues varies globally; in Australia, almost half the population experiences a mental illness at some time in their lives. This is a health problem that significantly affects how a person feels, thinks, behaves and interacts with other people (Department of Health and Ageing 2012). Most at risk are those with the more common mental maladies, depression and anxiety, as well as the roughly 3 per cent of adults who are affected by psychotic disorders such as schizophrenia and bipolar mood disorder (Department of Health and Ageing 2012). Clearly, if a natural hazard occurs when a person is suffering from a bout of mental illness, the impacts of the hazard are magnified. But it is important to remember that the often unexpected occurrence of natural disasters can in itself cause serious psychological anxiety, fear, uncertainty or even panic in a range of otherwise healthy people. Some researchers claim that the psychological effects of disaster – of drought, for example – are long lasting and even more detrimental than the physical effects (Ebi 2008).

Strong emotional regulation is critical in emergencies. When mothers from impoverished rural households experience debilitating anxiety, for example, it can obstruct their ability to regulate their own reactions and respond appropriately for the safety of their families in disaster scenarios. Aldana *et al.* (2013) examined the experiences of rural Mexican mothers who had survived the impact of a 7.2-magnitude earthquake in Mexico. The study sought to identify and describe levels of anxiety and capacity to respond to a natural disaster in mothers affected by the 2010 earthquake in the Valley of Mexicali, Baja California. A total of 100 mothers from the Mexicali Valley and the surrounding area of the earthquake's epicentre participated in the study. Aldana *et al.* (2013) measured the mothers' hypersensitivity, social concern and physiological anxiety via a series of cognitive indicators, using the Adult Manifest Anxiety Scale (AMAS-A) and self-reporting of emotional reactions. Results showed that fear was the most frequent emotion (24 per cent), followed by terror (10.9 per cent), with a total of 34.2 per cent of responding mothers demonstrating that they had two or more emotional reactions during the event. The AMAS-A questionnaire revealed symptoms of clinically significant physiological anxiety. The question is: does this sort of response during or just after a disaster always predict vulnerability to disaster, or is it a transient state, a temporary reaction that does not preclude disaster resilience? Social concern, hypersensitivity and physiological anxiety have a high probability of manifesting in most people after a natural hazard.

Proximal and distal effects of experienced disaster

A preliminary caveat must be flagged before this discussion develops further. It is important not to lose sight of the fundamental role of the disaster, the stressor. There are horrific disasters from which even the most resilient, resourceful individuals would struggle to recover. What is more, the higher the exposure to the disaster, that is, the closer a person is to the impact, the greater the distress and psychological impairment demonstrated. Overall, irrespective of degree of exposure to a disaster event and its impacts, research has led most experts in the field to conclude that globally, disasters involving mass violence such as war, genocide or terrorism result in more severe levels of psychological distress than technological disasters, for example a nuclear power-plant meltdown or a train derailment, which in turn lead to more psychological impairment than disasters resulting from natural hazards, such as floods, hurricanes and the like (Norris, Friedman *et al.* 2002). The basis for this is likely to be the level of control that people perceive in these disasters. Greater levels of control are associated with more malicious intent, negligence or power to prevent the disaster. Therefore anger, disbelief and blame are entangled with powerlessness, and these feelings are superimposed upon the damage or impairment sustained through the disaster, leading to escalating distress.

Yet regardless of exposure factors, the number of resilient individuals does not fall below a third of the sample under consideration, even after being exposed to extreme danger in close proximity (for example, being inside the World Trade Center at the time of the September 11 terrorist attacks (Bonanno et al. 2006)). Apart from the emergence of a group of stalwart individuals who can maintain their functioning even in the face of unspeakable danger, another curious finding was noticed. When comparing two locations, one directly hit by hazard with another less affected by the same hazard, individuals in the most severely hit site appear to be more resilient than the ones in the less impacted site. This effect has been demonstrated several times, both in developed and developing countries (Bonanno et al. 2010).

A longitudinal survey and interview study was conducted after the impact of an earthquake in north Hebei province, North China. The earthquake, measuring 6.2 on the Richter scale, took place at 11:30a.m. on 10 January 1998: it affected an area of 2,000 square km, left 49 dead and over 10,000 injured and rendered 44,000 people homeless at a temperature below −20°C. The study compared two village groups: one located 10km away from the epicentre with a loss of 4.4 per cent of their dwellings; the other located 0.5km from the epicentre where 80 per cent of houses had been destroyed. The survey covered all households in the two villages, which were similar in all demographic categories. At both three and nine months after the earthquake, the village most severely impacted had significantly fewer cases (19.8 per cent) of post-traumatic stress disorder (PTSD) than the one further away from the epicentre (30.3 per cent). Because the most severely impacted village was assessed by government relief authorities as having suffered greater damage, it was given a greater amount of immediate disaster relief and subsequent reconstruction support than the less directly impacted village. These resources, and the solicitude that the villagers received from a range of sources, helped buffer the villagers from developing chronic PTSD reactions (Wang et al. 2000).

A federal government's recognition of disaster is key for individuals who might otherwise be blocked from disaster-related programmes. For those who are impacted by a natural hazard, the declaration of disaster can be critical for raising the economic means necessary to rebuild or even to get sufficient relief work to the damaged site. This was the case for the 2006 Cyclone Larry, which impacted the small town of Innisfail in North Queensland, Australia. The poor US government handling of the response to Hurricane Katrina the previous year ensured that the Australian government had learnt some valuable lessons: it was proactive, immediately declaring the site a disaster, and responded with timely support for the impacted community. As a result, relief flooded into the town and rebuilding efforts were timely and sustained. In the US a declaration of disaster can lead to federal income tax assistance, which can make a difference because it allows for emergency access to retirement funds and adjustments in tax schedules and loss declarations. Disaster was not declared in the case of Idaho's Charlotte Fire, which raged during June 2012, burning 60 homes to ashes, consuming 1,038 acres and leading to the evacuation of 1,000 people. Residents' ensuing difficulties were compounded by the response of insurance companies. Claims for replacement homes were denied or quoted at considerably higher rates, because residents were held individually responsible for a 'total loss claim' (Stamm 2015). This would clearly affect future insurance cover, which can further impact a household's security and the householders' resilience in a fire-prone community. Stamm (2015) concluded that resilience and psychological equilibrium are attainable with counselling and social support, but obviously the reinforcement from federal government edicts hastens the recovery process. The relevance of Bronfenbrenner's bioecological systems theory is clearly illustrated by these studies. They also parallel our studies in Ingham and Beechworth (Chapter 3) to some degree.

Transience of post-disaster distress and the reinstatement of resilience

The roots of individual or personal resilience are found in two bodies of literature: the psychological aspects of coping and the physiological aspects of stress (Tusaie and Dyer 2004). A large number of studies have shown that the majority of those who survive a natural disaster report some degree of distress soon after, but most symptoms will resolve a year or so after the traumatic event (Bonanno and Mancini 2008; Kazantzis *et al.* 2009; Norris *et al.* 2008). While a range of conditions can be found in above-average rates in post-disaster populations – that is, depression, anxiety disorders, complicated grief, substance abuse and somatic or physiological responses – only 10–12 per cent of disaster victims develop a chronic condition (i.e. one lasting longer than three months) consistent with a diagnosis of post-traumatic stress disorder (Friedman *et al.* 2006). Moreover, the disaster experience can represent an opportunity for personal growth in some individuals, resulting in positive psychological outcomes. These might be the development of deeper relationships, greater compassion or spirituality, as well as enhanced appreciation of life (Tedeschi and Calhoun 2004). Attributes of this kind are thought to be typical of more resilient individuals.

George Bonanno (2004) further argued that adult resilience to loss and trauma is different from the process of recovery. He noted that the term *recovery* implies a time during which normal functioning is replaced by temporary threshold or sub-threshold psychopathology (e.g. symptoms of depression or PTSD); this might last for several months, but functioning gradually returns to pre-event levels. Full recovery may be relatively rapid or may take as long as one or two years. *Resilience to disaster and trauma, on the other hand, reflects an ability to maintain a stable equilibrium, that is, healthy levels of psychological and physical functioning.* Resilience is not just the absence of psychopathology, Bonanno argues, because resilient individuals, while they might experience temporary distress such as several weeks of restless sleep or heightened alertness and sensitivity, generally display healthy functioning across time. In short, resilience is widely considered to be an ability to thrive in the face of stress and other adversity. At the individual level, resilience is thought to be determined by many factors. Existing research suggests that *genetic* (Caspi *et al.* 2003; Jabbi *et al.*

2007; Jang *et al.* 2007; Tannenbaum and Anisman 2003), *biological* (Charney 2004; Ozbay *et al.* 2008), *psychological* (Campbell-Sills *et al.* 2006; Tugade and Fredrickson 2004) and *environmental* (Haskett *et al.* 2006; King *et al.* 1998) factors all play significant roles.

Researchers have also speculated about personality characteristics and their contribution to resilience. They have attempted to tap into personality aspects that might carry a survivor through a disaster and out the other side as a resilient traveller. Milojev *et al.* (2014) examined longitudinal changes in the Big Six personality markers (extraversion, agreeableness, conscientiousness, emotional stability, openness to experience and honesty-humility) before and after the 2010–2011 Christchurch earthquakes in a study of 3,914 New Zealand residents. Their findings showed overall stability and robustness in personality characteristics. The only exception was that those who were directly affected by the earthquakes developed a slight decrease in emotional stability over the two-year test–retest period in comparison to those unaffected by the disaster. The researchers concluded that most aspects of personality are constant following a major natural disaster, although the slight decrease in emotional stability could flag a possible increase in vulnerability to depression and anxiety for those who experienced the earthquakes.

A common method to measure disaster impacts at the level of the individual is to examine extreme or dysfunctional reactions, with their absence assumed to signify resilience. The reasoning behind this approach from a public health perspective is that psychopathology is a straightforward and practical way to identify and potentially treat psychological distress in individuals. This approach also helps to facilitate the planning of interventions and recovery efforts. One of the problems associated with this focus on psychopathology, however, is that its diagnosis can be influenced by social and cultural factors while its precise symptomatology is not of a simple categorical nature, but rather of a more complex spectrum of overlapping or comorbid conditions, such as depression and post-traumatic stress disorder (Broman-Fulks *et al.* 2006). Notwithstanding, this line of research persists in the study of individual resilience to disaster.

Resilience as a process rather than a fixed innate trait

In addition to the various characteristics that have been recognised as fitting into the profile of resilience, rather like a jigsaw puzzle, individual resilience is thought to be a process rather than a steady state (e.g. Winkworth *et al.* 2009). Findings from our research on Australian disaster-impacted individuals have shown that personal resilience is not simply a fixed personality trait, but rather a malleable character attribute that is predicted by adaptability and lessons learnt over time, such as comprehension and appreciation of climate change (Boon *et al.* 2012). A person's level of resilience can potentially vary over the course of a lifetime (Hegney *et al.* 2007). This is because research has revealed that psychological growth occurs as a result of living through adversity, and this growth can be tapped into when future stressors are encountered (Aldwin 2007; Polk 1997). Accordingly, resilience is more than stoicism or survival: it assumes post-stress growth. This dynamic aspect of resilience, its moderation by environment and its variation over the lifespan, has regularly been highlighted (Garmezy and Rutter 1983; Connor and Davidson 2003) but rarely researched longitudinally (Masten and Obradovic 2008). A study of the resilience literature by Gillespie *et al.* (2007) led them to argue that resilience is a process of struggle against hardship, and as such it can be learned at any age. This presents the notion of resilience as an acquired skill, one that is promoted by prior disaster experience, as our research has found (Boon *et al.* 2012). For this reason, resilience is likely to be complex: not a single trait or process but a 'complex family of concepts' (Masten and Obradovic 2006: 22). Masten and Obradovic (2008) described several adaptive patterns to acute-onset disasters, including resistance and positive transformation from a range of base levels of adaptive functioning, as well as a response and recovery that is typical for the type of disaster, one that does not involve prolonged psychological distress.

Another track of research pointed to the importance of *intrapersonal* and *environmental* factors in the development of resilience (Tusaie and Dyer 2004). Intrapersonal factors include intelligence, optimism, creativity, humour and self-belief or confidence in one's own abilities to cope, as well as competencies such as adaptive coping strategies, good social skills, above-average memory and higher educational attainments. Environmental factors include perceived social support, or the phenomenological aspects that Bronfenbrenner referred to in his theory. Since there are aspects of resilience that are developed via a range of processes, Luthar and Cicchetti (2000) emphasised the need to identify the underlying proximal processes or mechanisms of resilience development so that government bodies can establish policies and resilience-enhancing interventions that are soundly based on theory and empirical findings. To do so, researchers must first identify protective factors from multiple levels of influence (community, family and individual) that can alleviate the negative effects of trauma and disaster experiences. Bonanno and Mancini (2008) found that protective factors include an individual's characteristics – for instance, an easy-going temperament, adaptive coping strategies, problem-solving ability, optimism – along with some demographic variables, such as being male or having more educational attainments, and social structural factors, such as supportive relations, community resources and the like. Combinations of these factors have been found to be instrumental in promoting positive trajectories in relation to post-traumatic stress disorder for populations exposed to trauma (Atkinson *et al.* 2009). Norris and Stevens (2007) also endorsed these attributes, but with the caveat that economic resilience, by way of physical capital, employment opportunities and health services, is essential to support resilience. Their contentions have achieved greater credibility through longitudinal evidence derived from research with Hurricane Katrina survivors.

Empirical evidence to support claims about personal disaster resilience

In general, empirical evidence to support ideas about disaster resilience is a little patchy and difficult to interpret accurately. The quantification and establishment of the precise nature of personal resilience is difficult because of variations in the definitions used in studies, variations in the samples used and the contexts studied, as well as a preponderance of qualitative and cross-sectional studies (Atkinson *et al.* 2009). In addition, there are several survey instruments that have been used with various samples to measure resilience, but none have been consistently used across different population types and contexts (Ahern *et al.* 2007). Another major limitation in many disaster studies is the reliance on convenience samples. Convenience samples might not adequately represent the exposed population but rather only those individuals interested in participating in the research. Sometimes, convenience samples have led to inaccurate estimates of pathology, greater than is found in population-based samples (e.g. Neria *et al.* 2007). Further, convenience samples often have a restricted range and underestimate variability in post-disaster functioning. Care must be exercised when interpreting research results, even when longitudinal studies are conducted to assess how survivors of a disaster have fared over time as was the case in a study of Italian earthquake survivors. This study observed that 10 years after the disaster, 30 per cent of the most highly exposed survivors 'still reported symptoms' of PTSD (Bland *et al.* 2005: 420). Such data are not meaningful in and of themselves, in the absence of normative data on the distribution of PTSD symptoms in this population. Several symptoms included in the PTSD diagnosis are nonspecific in relation to the earthquake (e.g. difficulty sleeping). Routine clinical interviews on populations that have not experienced a disaster have shown that even in the absence of a recent traumatic event, many people report one or two PTSD symptoms (Bonanno *et al.* 2006). The research design of a study reporting on disaster-impacted victims' resilience is obviously critical if meaningful information is to be derived.

Several studies based on cross-sectional survey designs have examined individuals' self-reported perceptions of coping self-efficacy (i.e. perceived capability for managing post-traumatic recovery demands). These studies have shown that such psychological assets are important in psychological recovery, and hence resilience, in the wake of a range of natural disasters (Benight and Bandura 2004; Benight *et al.* 1999a; Benight *et al.* 1999b; Benight *et al.* 2000; Benight and Harper 2002; Masten and Obradovic 2008). But once the maelstrom of the initial response passes and people find themselves in safe circumstances, there are additional needs that must be met for a resilient state to be achieved. When aid and donated supplies dwindle away after the response phase of a disaster, coping self-efficacy might not be enough, more material aid might be required. Extra help from the exosystem by way of governmental grants helps buoy resilience during the recovery period (Regehr *et al.* 2008). Tobin and Whiteford (2002) found links between an individual's resilience and his or her economic capacity. More notably, they found that perceptions of risk and actual health status were strongly connected to economic capacity, with disease being more prevalent in those evacuated from their homes, whose losses were great. Similar findings about economic capacity and resilience emerged from our studies of disaster resilience to flood, cyclone, fire and drought (Boon *et al.* 2012).

The importance of a *perceived reality* and the phenomenological construction of support were demonstrated by a study conducted by Benight (2004), which showed that belief of high collective efficacy serves as a buffer to stress and vulnerability under conditions of high resource loss. The study went beyond assessing personal coping self-efficacy; a disaster community's collective self-efficacy perceptions were also explored. The study was based on the hypothesis that a perception that a community would not be able to effectively respond – that is, if people had low collective efficacy in the face of a natural hazard – that could lead to a heightened sense of personal vulnerability, lower adaptive capacity and lower resilience. Conversely, communities judged to have higher levels of collective efficacy would be perceived as more effective at exerting appropriate informal social control in order to coordinate available resources in the most effective manner (e.g. emergency supplies, human capital). Collective efficacy perceptions are therefore considered to be related to psychological distress levels. The results of the study were based on a sample of 50 participants from a community that had experienced fire and flash flooding. In conclusion, when resource loss is high, individuals who perceive low collective efficacy report significantly higher distress levels compared with those who have a strong faith in community efficacy. Sampson *et al.* (1997) also found communities' perceptions of high collective efficacy corresponded with constituents' high resilience.

The way a person *perceives* a situation – the phenomenological mental construction of a disaster as determined by personal characteristics such as optimism, self-confidence and other psychological filters – is critical to their resilience post disaster. This is evidenced by studies that have looked at perceived and received support. Received support is not always predictive of resilience. For example, in some cases received support has been shown to be positively linked to adjustment (e.g. Bolin 1982; Joseph *et al.* 1992), whereas in other studies it has not been connected to resilience characteristics (e.g. Morgan *et al.* 1995; Murphy 1988). Yet perceived support has been consistently positively associated with post-disaster resilience among adults and children (Bonanno *et al.* 2005; La Greca *et al.* 1996; Norris and Kaniasty 1996; Ruggiero *et al.* 2009). Likewise, perceived social support has been shown to be predicative of resilience after controlling for a range of demographic variables. Using quantitative research designs and respectively large samples of US residents who had experienced the 9/11 disaster and Hong Kong residents after a SARS epidemic, it was found that perceived support was instrumental in resilience across all demographic groups and this held even in groups that have been found to be more susceptible to disaster impacts: women, those with lower educational attainments, those whose income was reduced by the disaster and those who had experienced traumas and stressors or chronic disease besides the disaster in question (Bonanno *et al.* 2007; Bonanno *et al.* 2008).

Indigenous and ethnic minority conceptions of resilience also demonstrate that individuals' resilience is a composite of personal and social factors. Survivors of the so-called 921 Earthquake in the Tung Shih areas of Taiwan participated in a qualitative study to explore their disaster resilience. The Hakka people, comprising about 15–20 per cent of the population, originate mainly from Guangdong, China. They are the second-largest ethnic group on Taiwan Island. Residents are repeatedly exposed to natural hazards: from 1959 to 2007 the island has been battered by 196 typhoons, 49 floods and 22 damaging earthquakes. On 21 September 1999, the devastating 7.6-magnitude earthquake, which Taiwanese people refer to as the 921 Earthquake, struck central Taiwan. It resulted in 2,415 deaths, 11,306 injuries and made 110,000 people homeless. Researchers Jang and Wang (2009) used purposive sampling strategies to select information-rich participants for an in-depth study. A total of 15 interviewees and eight focus group members participated in the research. Findings from qualitative data analyses indicated that acceptance, preparedness, self-reliance, spirituality, a Hakka spirit, resource availability, social support networks and serving others were positively connected with disaster resilience by the Hakka people. The study affirmed the importance of government support and of re-establishing social support networks, but only on the basis of an understanding of culture and its meaning for the local people.

The sample of studies described above highlights the contextual and integrated nature of resilience development, and supports Bronfenbrenner's framework in assessing resilience to be a developing process. The next question that arises pertains to the specificity of disasters: when looking at specific types of disaster is there evidence that different resilience characteristics or indicators come to the fore or do the same characteristics sustain resilience in different disaster contexts?

Are there disaster-specific resilience indicators? Some examples for consideration

Fires

A qualitative study investigated six residents' bushfire experiences in Darlington, Western Australia (Pooley *et al.* 2010). Resilience after the fire was thought to be assisted by a sense of community, individuals' adaptive coping and self-efficacy, perceived community competence and social support forming spontaneously as needed. In rural Australian communities fire preparedness tends to be left to the males of the household to manage (Eriksen *et al.* 2010; Eriksen and Gill 2010). The relative monetary and time costs of preparing for potential fires make preparedness a low priority item for rural landholders. This makes them vulnerable to fire hazards since effective preparedness goes some way towards facilitating household and individual resilience.

Research has shown that women who rely on their husbands for knowledge and protection during fires are less resilient during bushfires, particularly if their partner is not at home on the day (DeLaine *et al.* 2008). Winkworth *et al.* (2009) examined the recovery of people affected by the Australian Capital Territory (ACT) bushfires (known as the Canberra Bushfires) to glean information about what helped or hindered community disaster recovery. Survey responses from 482 individuals cited that strong family, friend and neighbourhood support networks served as an important informal communication network. Correct information during a bushfire is imperative in enabling people to make informed decisions about what actions should be undertaken and when.

During the Bitter Root Valley fires in Western Montana, USA, residents responded to confusion about whether to evacuate by monitoring various conditions to judge the level of risk and then disseminating this information, which was tailored to the needs of others in the community, through various information networks (Halvorson 2002). The Bitter Root Valley fires provide an example of community members working together and using social ties for support independent of outside groups. For example, many evacuated residents did not utilise the Red Cross shelter because they sought accommodation with friends and family or camped with other families by the river (Halvorson 2002). While the study does not report the respondents' personal attributes, such as their coping self-efficacy, it is probably safe to assume that most residents *perceived* strong community self-efficacy, which would have augmented any personal resilience attributes.

The hardiness and resilience of fire-impacted groups has been found elsewhere. Papanikolaou *et al.* (2011) examined the resilience of Greek villagers on the Peloponnese Peninsula after the widespread fires that occurred in 2007. Adult (18–65 years) inhabitants of villages affected by the wildfires were selected randomly and compared with a demographically similar group living in neighbouring fire-free villages. The sample sites were chosen based on the extent of fire damage in that area, as Greece is frequently impacted by fires. The research design involved a comparison of two groups: 409 participants in the fire group and 391 in the control group. They were assessed on their psychological status, subjective health evaluation, personal attitudes and values and trust in different institutions. The survey instrument consisted of a range of questions tapping into: (1) demographic information; (2) views on general problems in the region and trust in institutions; (3) locus of control; (4) psychological distress using the SCL-90-R (a self-report symptom checklist with 90 items) designed to provide an overview of an individual's psychological symptoms and their intensity over a specific period, typically the last seven days; (5) self-perception of health; and (6) stressful life events. Data collection took place six months after the cessation of the fires. Results showed that although the fire-impacted villagers reported a higher level of psychological distress than the control group, this was only slightly above the standardised T score mean for the instrument used and the scores of both groups were within the normal range. Of interest was the fire-impacted villagers' external locus of control, that is, the belief that events impacting an individual are outside his or her personal control. These attributions were considered psychologically adaptive in the context because the fires and associated devastation were indeed out of the villagers' control, and as such there were no feelings of blame associated with the disaster. The participants expressed a focus on the presence of dialogue communication and mutual assistance, reflecting other findings in connection to fire experiences.

Floods

Floods are the most common type of global natural disaster, and were responsible for almost 53,000 deaths in the last decade (Alderman *et al.* 2012; Doocy *et al.* 2013). In Australia alone floods cost on average over AU$300 million annually (Group NFRA 2008). Fernandez *et al.* (2015) conducted a systematic review of flood research studies focusing on individual responses to floods. In the final 83 studies included in their review, they identified the main issues connected with the impacts of the floods were mental health impacts rather than factors supporting survivors' resilience. While the survey-based and interview studies showed consistent findings, Fernandez *et al.* (2015) concluded that very few studies included controls of potential confounders and only short-term follow-up was reported. In connection to flood resilience the review was not particularly illuminating.

Armaş and Avram (2009) used a correlational predictive study to examine resilience to floods in a sample of 153 Romanian (Danube Delta) residents. They used a survey instrument to extract attitudes and perceptions in order to reveal conscious and unconscious attitudes towards flood risk and predict

Figure 4.2 Mortlock surge, Papua New Guinea, 2008 (Scott Smithers).

resilience to the impact of floods. The study was based on the hypothesis that different degrees of psychological vulnerability set the stage for behavioural patterns which in turn generate specific adjustment mechanisms and strategies. They found that those who had greater inner control had significantly reduced general anxiety level in comparison to those who placed the control factor externally. A greater locus of external control was also associated with lower educational and income levels, which tended to make people rely on external variables for support and have stronger beliefs that floods would leave a major blot on their life. These individuals also believed the recovery of their losses would be harder and were more fearful about the security of their family. Armaş and Avram (2009) suggest that such an external focus of control leads to lower resilience, characterised by non-action and non-adaptive behaviours. Endfield's work has supported Armaş and Avram's (2009) proposals. Using archival data from flood records in Mexico, Endfield (2007) showed that the degree of impact of a flood is a function of an external locus of control in terms of expectations that others, namely the government, had a responsibility to protect and prepare the community. This study, too, identified specific socio-economic structural variables as moderating prospective resilience responses.

Many areas of Queensland, Australia are prone to floods, with the floods of 2013 being the most recent and notable. This flood, which deluged south-east Queensland in the wake of tropical Cyclone Oswald, proved to be the largest and most significant since European settlement. Rainfall in excess of 1,000 mm was recorded over 96 hours. Prior to that, Apan *et al.* (2010) investigated flood-prone Charleville and Mackay, to understand the communities' resilience and viability. They aimed to identify the characteristics of resilience and adaptive capacity to flooding among households, businesses and institutions, and to that end they used a mixed-method approach to target household residents, businesses and government institutions with structured questionnaires and semi-structured face-to-face interviews. They concluded that individual residents' resilience in Charleville was enhanced by strong personal networks, high levels of a sense of belonging in the community and high participation rates in community activities. Charleville residents also believed that the onus was on them to prepare for floods. In other words, they did not have an external locus of control for flood preparedness, as had been noted in the Romanian and Mexican studies. Mackay householders were also found to have a high sense of belonging to the community, which was considered to enhance their resilience to flood.

Drought

Dean and Stain (2010) conducted a study in New South Wales with 111 adolescents using a mixed-method research design. Findings suggest that the ongoing economic impact of the drought, entangled with the emotional effects that this had on family functioning, filtered down to the adolescents and acted as a stressor, eroding their resilience. In contrast to previous studies, Dean and Stain (2010) found drought had a cumulative effect on adolescents' ability to cope with the stress of a natural disaster. These adolescents showed significantly higher levels of distress and behavioural difficulties than those in the general population. Higher levels of problematic behaviour, worse peer relationships and hyperactivity were associated with drought-related variables, such as family concerns, financial stress, climate change, mental health impacts and an environment where death and loss were perceived and anticipated. Distress levels for older adolescents were related more to a loss of friends from the area than was the case for the younger adolescents. Resilience for rural adolescents was supported by and included strong positive feelings about communities and family connections. For rural residents in general, being able to sustain a rural lifestyle is a major factor for individual (and community) resilience. Residence within small towns is associated with a strong attachment to place (Boon 2014). Dean and Stain (2010) also found these strong positive feelings associated with living in a small rural community, but the reported levels of distress strongly imply that the long duration of the drought was challenging this resilience. Adolescents in the study connected the drought to the context of more global influences such as climate change.

Cyclones, hurricanes and typhoons

A number of studies have been conducted to assess the impacts of hurricanes and cyclones on individuals and their resilience. Many have focused upon the devastating 2005 Hurricane Katrina, partly because in the aftermath of Hurricane Katrina evidence emerged of the authorities' poor response to the needs of the most vulnerable community members (NMA 2005). Inadequate

Figure 4.3 Cyclone Yasi impact in Queensland home (David King 2011).

emergency planning for children, for example, and the rapid pace of evacuation for Hurricanes Katrina and Rita of 2005, led to over 5,000 children being displaced from their families. A nongovernmental US agency, the National Center for Missing and Exploited Children, had to step in and help reunite families, a process that lasted for 18 months (Chung *et al.* 2008). Pfefferbaum *et al.* (2008) conducted focus group interviews with children and adolescents aged 9–17 years who had been displaced by Hurricane Katrina. They determined that family attitudes, economic support and positive community perceptions were proximal processes that were instrumental in helping to build children's adjustment and resilience after relocation, while acknowledging that individual resilience attributes were strongly implicated in this adjustment.

Intrapersonal (within-person) variables are critical determinants of resilience, as already noted. These variables are moderated by development. Changes in children's cognition fine tune their interpretation of the world, emotions and emotional understanding, self-regulation skills, social relationships, and many other aspects of their processing of everyday life, including traumatic experiences. For example, La Greca *et al.* (1998) obtained accurate measures of anxiety and behavioural problems on a sample of fourth-grade through sixth-grade children, using triangulated data from self-reports, peer reports and teacher reports, 15 months before the area was struck by Hurricane Andrew. Assessments three and seven months after the hurricane showed that children's pre-disaster levels of general anxiety predicted post-disaster PTSD symptoms, after controlling for actual disaster exposure and demographic variables. Children's pre-disaster levels of inattention and academic difficulties, a developmental indicator, also predicted greater PTSD symptoms at three months post disaster. Additional evidence of more immature developmental attributes compounding the stress of the disaster was obtained when analyses were conducted of peer ratings of children. Children who were rated higher by peers on anxiety measures before the hurricane were less likely to reduce their PTSD symptoms three to seven months post disaster than those with low pre-disaster anxiety. These findings were comparable to results reported by Asarnow *et al.* (1999), who conducted phone interviews with children for a study of childhood-onset depression at the time of the 1994 Northridge earthquake in Southern California. Finally, it is known that gender is implicated in the resilience of children and adolescents. For example, it was found that two years after the 2005 Hurricane Katrina, school-based assessments of young people aged nine to 18 revealed that females were more susceptible to symptoms of depression and PTSD symptoms than males (Kronenberg *et al.* 2010).

In earlier longitudinal research centred upon adult populations, Norris and Kaniasty (1996) examined the impact of receiving social support on subsequent levels of perceived social support and psychological distress in two independent samples of victims of severe storms Hurricane Hugo and Hurricane Andrew. Waves of survey data collected 12 and 24 months after Hurricane Hugo and six and 28 months after Hurricane Andrew provided strong evidence that disaster victims need active mobilisation of social support to sustain their resilience and stave off the negative stress sequelae and psychopathology that can ensue. Perceived support, moreover, was a positive mediator for enhanced resilience in the longer term. Once again, evidence points to the phenomenological aspects important for promoting resilience, as Bronfenbrenner's bioecological systems theory predicted.

Summary of empirically derived personal resilience indicators

In 2013, Rodriguez-Llanes, Vos and Guha-Sapir embarked on a project to extract evidence-based indicators of psychological resilience, because psychological resilience is now understood to be a critical component of societal resilience to disasters. The rationale behind the study was based on the differentiation of resilience as an outcome measure and as an indicator. Community resilience as an outcome post facto, that is, after the impact of a hazard, is assessed via low mortality and low injury rates, along with absence of or low PTSD symptoms in the impacted community members or high rates of timely mobility of displaced individuals. Resilience as an indicator generally refers to baseline conditions measurable in a community ante facto. Those resilience indicators can predict a community's resilience before a disaster occurs.

Rodriguez-Llanes et al. (2013) reviewed 58 studies conducted from 1969 to 25 January 2013, and distilled 53 indicators of psychological resilience obtained from empirical evidence that focused exclusively on disaster settings. The most consistent indicators of psychological resilience were social support and gender. High levels of social support from relatives and friends increased all studied resilient outcomes, whereas women were consistently found to be at higher risk of suffering psychological distress after a disaster. Other indicators empirically derived by the study were degree of exposure to the disaster, which if low positively predicted resilience; whereas predictors of erosion to an individual's resilience included previous traumatic experiences (economic or psychosocial), along with resource or human loss (of friends or relatives) and poor physical and mental health.

In short, individual resilience can be distilled into a psychological attribute that is moderated by material (and economic) environmental and social factors, as we found with our studies across flood, fire, cyclone and drought-impacted Australian communities (Boon et al. 2012). The proximal processes that appear to influence personal resilience are perceived and received support from other community members, family and friends. The importance of social ties and relationships in the development and sustenance of disaster resilience, as predicted by Bronfenbrenner's bioecological systems theory, is therefore verified.

Conclusion

One of the matters considered in this chapter is the question of disaster vulnerability. Is it situated at the opposite end of a continuum that terminates in resilience? Or is it distinct from structural factors that typically lead to the classification of individuals as vulnerable? Are there generic attributes that render individuals resilient to disasters? How might governments help those most in need of support during the response and recovery periods?

The research literature shows that resilience is strongly predicted by intraperpersonal (within person) psychological factors, which are themselves refined and moderated by external social and economic variables. As such, there is scope for interventions and policies to make disaster resilience a real possibility, even for those most at risk of post-disaster distress. Studies cited above demonstrate this. For example, the study comparing Chinese villagers close to and further removed from the epicentre of a destructive earthquake and the study examining comparable groups of Greek villagers, either exposed to fire or more distant from it, show that although these groups were all potentially vulnerable because of structural demographic variables such as poverty, they were nonetheless resilient to the disasters because of perceived social support, in the case of the Chinese villagers, or because of an inherent hardiness and social connectedness in the case of the Greek villagers.

In general, it appears that disaster resilience is a function of psychological, intrapersonal factors, which are malleable and enhanced by perceived social support that is both emotional and material, through and in the aftermath of disasters. Those individuals who have mental health impairments and maladies and those with physical impairments appear to be most vulnerable to negative disaster experience outcomes. To date, however, there have been insufficient appropriately designed studies comparing the resilience of those with mental health maladies with others, while controlling for other factors, such as gender, socio-economic status and disaster impact, and including baseline measures. It is not known precisely how the resilience of such individuals is eroded under disaster circumstances, or what factors potentially improve their responses and resilience. Some research suggests that it is likely that a return to baseline functioning after disaster will be delayed for these individuals. For instance, the mental health and case management needs of Hurricane Katrina child victims persisted for four years after the disaster, and showed no signs of abating. The study sample of 296 children investigated by Olteanu *et al.* (2011) was severely affected by the hurricane; most were from homes whose income was below the federal poverty level. Many of the studied children who received mental health services and showed developmental or learning problems had also shown signs of psychological distress prior to the hurricane. The researchers (Olteanu *et al.* 2011) who followed the children longitudinally could not make any causal links between the hurricane experience and their psychiatric disorders.

Summary

Disaster risk reduction makes it imperative that all people, including the most vulnerable in society, are protected when facing natural hazards and disasters. Disasters have led to some horrific problems and those who are impacted most are the poor, physically or mentally frail, socially unconnected, women, the elderly or young children. The severity and extent of hazard exposure is an important and serious moderator of the effects upon those impacted, with some hazards leaving extreme and long-lasting psychological imprints upon their victims. However, most disaster survivors are hardy and distress symptoms are generally transient. Of course when a disaster experience is an additional stressor, as is the case when the victims are already suffering from mental maladies or other medical conditions, its effects might be multiplied.

There is evidence that the nature of personal disaster resilience is a multifaceted amalgam of innate qualities that have the potential to be further developed by experience and learning. Psychological indicators of distress are those used most often to measure personal resilience and, time after time, these show that social support factors, as perceived by the individual (that is, as they are phenomenologically constructed) are critical enhancers of resilience. As Bronfenbrenner predicted through the bioecological systems theory, proximal processes taking place between social agents in a person's environment or between the social milieu and the person are stimulators of resilience to disaster, strengthening and developing it. Because of these social proximal processes, even those who are rendered vulnerable because of poverty or other structural factors can be resilient to disaster.

Research conducted on specific disasters indicates that different types of natural hazard do not require different resilience attributes, although human-induced disasters, such as wars or terrorism, leave stronger and more long-lasting influences upon victims than either technological disasters, for instance industrial accidents, or disasters caused by nature. Limitations of research to date make it difficult to be precise about the nature of personal resilience. Studies have not been sufficiently robust to determine the full array of possible responses to disasters or to make causal inferences. Few studies have been designed to take into account individuals' baseline attributes. Fewer still have been designed with Bronfenbrenner's bioecological systems theory in mind, which, if applied judiciously, could tease out relevant influences upon resilience as delineated in Chapter 1 (Figure 4.4).

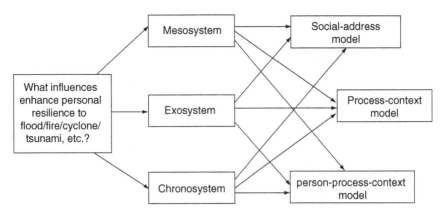

Figure 4.4 Conceptual model to direct research questions using Bronfenbrenner's bioecological systems theory.

Similarly, few studies have followed individuals longitudinally in the context of different disasters to tease out the possible nuances of resilience of diverse groups in situ. There is great scope for future studies to close this research gap by pursuing more controlled longitudinal research, so that in the future disaster impacts can be diminished by appropriate pre-disaster interventions based on empirical evidence.

References

Aglionby, J. 2005 'Four Times as Many Women Died in Tsunami', *Guardian*, 26 March. Available: www.theguardian.com/society/2005/mar/26/internationalaidanddevelopment. indianoceantsunamidecember2004.

Ahern, N. R., Kiehl, E.M., Lou Sole, M. and Byers, J. 2006, 'A Review of Instruments Measuring Resilience', *Issues in Comprehensive Pediatric Nursing*, vol. 29, no. 2, pp. 103–125.

Aldana, G., Camarillo Sánchez, J., Pérez, R., Sandoval Lugo, G. and Padilla López, A. 2013, 'Anxiety in Mothers of Family after Natural Disaster in a Rural Community', *International Journal of Advances in Psychology*, vol. 2, no. 3, pp. 172–177.

Alderman K., Turner, L.R. and Tong, S. 2012, 'Floods and human Health: A Systematic Review', *Environment International*, vol. 47, pp. 37–47. doi: 10.1016/j.envint.2012.06.003 PMID: 22750033.

Aldwin, C.A. 2007, *Stress, Coping, and Development: An Integrative Perspective*, second edn. The Guilford Press, New York.

Apan, A., Keogh, D.U., King, D., Thomas, M., Mushtaq, S. and Baddiley, P. 2010, 'The 2008 Floods in Queensland: A Case Study of Vulnerability, Resilience and Adaptive Capacity', Report for the National Climate Change Adaptation Research Facility, National Climate Change Adaptation Research Facility, Queensland.

APDF (Asia and Pacific Disability Forum) 2015, *Press Statement on Earthquake in Nepal*, 4 May. Available at: http://nodl.or.kr/nodeuledu_freebbs/2213.

Armaş, I. and Avram, E. 2009, 'Perception of Flood Risk in Danube Delta, Romania', *Natural Hazards*, vol. 50, no. 2, pp. 269–287.

Aryal, M. 2015, 'No Husband, No Home: Migrant Wives Struggle in Nepal', IRIN. Available online: www.irinnews.org/report/101446/no-husband-no-home-migrant-wives-struggle-in-nepal#.VUr8u3pjW8Y.twitter.

Asarnow, J., Glynn, S., Pynoos, R.S., Nahum, J., Guthrie, D., Cantwell, D.P. and Franklin, B. 1999, 'When the Earth Stops Shaking: Earthquake Sequelae among Children Diagnosed for Pre-Earthquake Psychopathology', *Journal of the American Academy of Child and Adolescent Psychiatry*, vol. 38, pp. 1016–1023.

Atkinson, P.A., Martin, C.R. and Rankin, J. 2009, 'Resilience Revisited', *Journal of Psychiatric and Mental Health Nursing*, vol. 16, pp. 137–145.

Benight, C.C. 2004, 'Collective Efficacy Following a Series of Natural Disasters', *Anxiety, Stress and Coping*, vol. 17, no. 4, pp. 401–420.

Benight, C.C. and Bandura, A. 2004, 'Social Cognitive Theory of Posttraumatic Recovery: The Role of Perceived Self-Efficacy', *Behaviour Research and Therapy*, vol. 42, pp. 1129–1148.

Benight, C.C. and Harper, M. 2002, 'Coping Self-Efficacy as a Mediator for Distress Following Multiple Natural Disasters', *Journal of Traumatic Stress*, vol. 15, pp. 177–186.

Benight, C.C., Freyaldenhoven, R., Hughes, J., Ruiz, J.M., Zoesche, T.A. and Lovallo, W. 2000, 'Coping Self-Efficacy and Psychological Distress Following the Oklahoma

City Bombing: A Longitudinal Analysis', *Journal of Applied Social Psychology*, vol. 30, pp. 1331–1344.

Benight, C.C., Ironson, G., Klebe, K., Carver, C., Wynings, C., Greenwood, D., Burnett, K., Baum, A. and Schneiderman, N. 1999a, 'Conservation of Resources and Coping Self-Efficacy Predicting Distress Following a Natural Disaster: A Causal Model Analysis where the Environment Meets the Mind', *Anxiety, Stress and Coping*, vol. 12, pp. 107–126.

Benight, C., Swift, E., Sanger, J., Smith, A. and Zeppelin, D. 1999b, 'Coping Self-Efficacy as a Mediator of Distress Following a Natural Disaster', *Journal of Applied Social Psychology*, vol. 29, pp. 2443–2464.

Bland, S.H., Valoroso, L., Stranges, S., Strazzullo, P., Farinaro, E. and Trevisan, M. 2005, 'Long-Term Follow-Up of Psychological Distress Following Earthquake Experiences Among Working Italian Males: A Cross-Sectional Analysis', *Journal of Nervous and Mental Disease*, vol. 193, pp. 420–423.

Bolin, R. 1982, *Long-Term Family Recovery from Disaster*. University of Colorado Press, Boulder, CO.

Bonanno, G.A. 2004, 'Loss, Trauma, and Human Resilience: Have We Underestimated the Human Capacity to Thrive after Extremely Aversive Events?', *American Psychologist*, vol. 59, pp. 20–28.

Bonanno G.A. and Mancini, A.D. 2008, 'The Human Capacity to Thrive in the Face of Potential Trauma', *Pediatrics*, vol. 121, no. 2, pp. 369–375.

Bonanno, G.A., Brewin, C.R., Kaniasty, K. and La Greca, A.M. 2010, 'Weighing the Costs of Disaster: Consequences, Risks, and Resilience in Individuals, Families and Communities', *Psychological Science in the Public Interest*, vol. 11, no. 1, pp. 1–49.

Bonanno, G.A., Galea, S., Bucciarelli, A. and Vlahov, D. 2006, 'Psychological Resilience after Disaster: New York City in the Aftermath of the September 11th Terrorist Attack', *Psychological Science*, vol. 17, pp. 181–186.

Bonanno, G.A., Galea, S., Bucciarelli, A. and Vlahov, D. 2007, 'What Predicts Psychological Resilience after Disaster? The Role of Demographics, Resources, and Life Stress', *Journal of Consulting and Clinical Psychology*, vol. 75, pp. 671–682.

Bonanno, G.A., Ho, S.M., Chan, J.C., Kwong, R.S., Cheung, C.K., Wong, C.P. and Wong, V.C. 2008, 'Psychological Resilience and Dysfunction among Hospitalized Survivors of the SARS Epidemic in Hong Kong: A Latent Class Approach', *Health Psychology*, vol. 27, no. 5, p. 659.

Bonanno, G.A., Rennike, C. and Dekel, S. 2005, 'Self-Enhancement Among High Exposure Survivors of the September 11th Terrorist Attack: Resilience or Social Maladjustment?', *Journal of Personality and Social Psychology*, vol. 88, pp. 984–998.

Boon, H.J. 2014, 'Disaster Resilience in a Flood-Impacted Rural Australian Town', *Natural Hazards*, vol. 71, no. 1, pp. 683–701.

Boon, H.J. 2013, 'Preparedness and Vulnerability: An Issue of Equity in Australian Disaster Situations', *Australian Journal of Emergency Management*, vol. 28, no. 3, pp. 12–16.

Boon, H.J., Millar, J., Lake, D., Cottrell, A. and King, D. 2012, *Recovery from Disaster: Resilience, Adaptability and Perceptions of Climate Change*. National Climate Change Adaptation Research Facility, Queensland.

Broman-Fulks, J.J., Ruggiero, K.J., Green, B.A., Kilpatrick, D.G., Danielson, C.K., Resnick, H.S. and Saunders, B. 2006, 'Weighing the Costs of Disaster Taxometric Investigation of PTSD: Data from Two Nationally Representative Samples', *Behaviour Therapy*, vol. 37, pp. 364–380.

Bronfenbrenner, U. 1986, 'Ecology of the Family as a Context for Human Development: Research Perspectives', *Developmental Psychology*, vol. 22, pp. 723–742.

Campbell-Sills, L., Cohan, S.L. and Stein, M.B. 2006, 'Relationship of Resilience to Personality, Coping, and Psychiatric Symptoms in Young Adults', *Behaviour Research and Therapy*, vol. 44, pp. 585–599.

Caspi, A., Sugden, K., Moffitt, T.E., Taylor, A., Craig, I.W., Harrington, H., McClay, J., Mill, J., Martin, J., Braithwaite, A. and Poulton, R., 2003. 'Influence of life Stress on Depression: Moderation by a Polymorphism in the 5-HTT Gene', *Science*, vol. 301, no. 5,631, pp. 386–389.

Chandrasekhar, C.P. and Ghosh, J. 2001, 'Information and Communication Technologies and Health in Low Income Countries: The Potential and the Constraints', *Bulletin of the World Health Organization*, vol. 79, pp. 850–855.

Charney, D.S. 2004, 'Psychobiological Mechanisms of Resilience and Vulnerability: Implications for Successful Adaptation to Extreme Stress', *American Journal of Psychiatry*, vol. 161, pp. 195–216.

Cherniak, E.P. 2008, 'The Impact of Natural Disasters on the Elderly', *American Journal of Disaster Medicine*, vol. 3, no. 3, pp. 133–139.

Chung, S., Danielson, J. and Shannon, M. 2008, 'School-Based Emergency Preparedness: A National Analysis and Recommended Protocol', Agency for Healthcare Research and Quality, Rockville, MD, December.

Connor, K. and Davidson, J. 2003, 'Development of a New Resilience Scale: The Connor Davidson Resilience Scale (CD-RISC)', *Depression and Anxiety*, vol. 18, pp. 76–82.

Dean, J.G. and Stain, H.J. 2010, 'Mental Health Impact for Adolescents Living with Prolonged Drought', *Australian Journal of Rural Health*, vol. 18, no. 1, pp. 32–37.

DeLaine, D., Pedler, T. and Probert, J. 2008, '"Fiery Women": Consulting, Designing, Delivering and Evaluating Pilot Women's Bushfire Safety Skills Workshops'. Paper presented at the International Bushfire Research Conference, Adelaide Convention Centre, Australia, 1–3 September.

Department of Health and Ageing, 2012, *What is Mental Illness?* Department of Health and Ageing, Canberra.

Doocy, S., Daniels, A., Murray, S. and Kirsch, T.D. 2013, 'The Human Impact of Floods: A Historical Review of Events 1980–2009 and Systematic Literature Review', *PLoS Currents*, 5.

Ebi, K.L. 2008, 'Healthy People 2100: Modeling Population Health Impacts of Climate Change', *Climatic Change*, vol. 88, pp. 5–19.

Endfield, G.H. 2007, 'Archival Explorations of Climate Variability and Social Vulnerability in Colonial Mexico', *Climatic Change*, vol. 83, no. 1–2, pp. 9–38.

Eriksen, C. and Gill, N. 2010, 'Bushfire and Everyday Life: Examining the Awareness-Action "Gap" in Changing Rural Landscapes', *Geoforum*, vol. 41, pp. 814–825.

Eriksen, C., Gill, N. and Head, L. 2010, 'The Gendered Dimensions of Bushfire in Changing Rural Landscapes in Australia', *Journal of Rural Studies*, vol. 26, pp. 332–342.

Every, D. and Thompson, K. 2014, 'Disaster Resilience: Can the Homeless Afford It?', *Australian Journal of Emergency Management*, vol. 29, no. 3, pp. 52–56.

Fernandez, A., Black, J., Jones, M., Wilson, L., Salvador-Carulla, L., Astell-Burt, T. and Black, D. 2015, 'Flooding and Mental Health: A Systematic Mapping Review', *PLoS ONE*, vol. 10, no. 4, p.e0119929.

Friedman, M., Ritchie, E. and Watson, P. (eds) 2006, *Overview, Interventions following Mass Violence and Disasters: Strategies for Mental Health Practice*. Guilford Press, New York.

Garmezy, N. and Rutter, M. 1983, *Stress, Coping and Development in Children*. McGraw-Hill, New York.

Gillespie, B.M., Chaboyer, W. and Wallis, M. 2007, 'Development of a Theoretically Derived Model of Resilience through Concept Analysis', *Contemporary Nurse: A Journal for the Australian Nursing Profession*, vol. 25, no. 1–2, pp. 124–135.

Group NFRA 2008, *Flood Risk Management in Australia*. Contract No. 4.

Halvorson, S.J. 2002, 'The Fires of 2000: Community Response and Recovery in the Bitter Root Valley, Western Montana'. Quick Response Research Report No. 151, Natural Hazards Research and Applications Information Center, University of Colorado, Boulder, CO.

Haskett, M.E., Nears, K., Ward, C.S. and McPherson, A.V. 2006, 'Diversity in Adjustment of Maltreated Children: Factors Associated with Resilient Functioning', *Clinical Psychology Review*, vol. 26, pp. 6–812.

Hegney, D.G., Buikstra, E., Baker, P., Rogers-Clark, C., Pearce, S., Ross, H., King, C. and Watson-Watson-Luke, A. 2007, 'Individual Resilience in Rural People: A Queensland Study, Australia', *Rural and Remote Health*, vol. 7, no. 4. Available online: www.rrh.org.au.

Hepburn, A. 2006, 'Running Scared: When Children Become Separated in Emergencies', in N. Boothby, A. Strang and M. Wessells (eds), *A World Turned Upside Down: Social Ecological Approaches to Children in War Zones*. Kumarian, Bloomfield, CT, pp. 63–88.

Jabbi. M., Kema, I.P., van der Pompe, G., te Meerman, G.J., Ormel, J. and den Boer, J.A. 2007, 'Catecholomethyl Transferase Polymorphism and Susceptibility to Major Depressive Disorder Modulates Psychological Stress Response', *Psychiatric Genetics*, vol. 17, pp. 183–193.

Jan, S. and Lurie, N. 2012, 'Disaster Resilience and People with Functional Needs', *The New England Journal of Medicine*, vol. 367, no. 24, pp. 2272–2273.

Jang, K.L., Taylor, S., Stein, M.B. and Yamagata, S. 2007, 'Trauma Exposure and Stress Response: Exploration of Mechanisms of Cause and Effect', *Twin Research and Human Genetics*, vol. 10, pp. 564–572.

Jang, L.J. and Wang, J.J. 2009, 'Disaster Resilience in a Hakka Community in Taiwan', *Journal of Pacific Rim Psychology*, vol. 3, no. 2, pp. 55–65.

Joseph, S., Andrews, B., Williams, R. and Yule, W. 1992, 'Crisis Support and Psychiatric Symptomatology in Adult Survivors of the Jupiter Cruise Ship Disaster', *British Journal of Clinical Psychology*, vol. 31, pp. 63–73.

Kahn, M.E. 2005, 'The Death Toll from Natural Disasters: The Role of Income, Geography, and Institutions', *Review of Economics and Statistics*, vol. 87, pp. 271–284.

Kazantzis, N., Flett, R.A., Long, N.R., Macdonald, C., Millar, M. and Clark, B. 2009, 'Traumatic Events and Mental Health in the Community: A New Zealand Study', *International Journal of Social Psychiatry*, vol. 56, no. 1, pp. 35–49.

King, L.A., King, D.W., Fairbank, J.A., Keane, T.M. and Adams G.A. 1998, 'Resilience-Recovery Factors in Post-Traumatic Stress Disorder Among Female and Male Vietnam Veterans: Hardiness, Post-War Social Support, and Additional Stressful Life Events', *Journal of Personality and Social Psychology*, vol. 74, pp. 420–434.

Kronenberg, M.E., Hansel, T.C., Brennan, A.M., Lawrason, B., Osofsky, H.J. and Osofsky, J.D. 2010, 'Children of Katrina: Lessons Learned about Post-Disaster Symptoms and Recovery Patterns', *Child Development*, vol. 81, no. 4, pp. 1240–1258.

La Greca, A.M., Silverman, W.K., Vernberg, E.M. and Prinstein, M.J. 1996, 'Symptoms of Posttraumatic Stress in Children after Hurricane Andrew: A Prospective Study', *Journal of Consulting and Clinical Psychology*, vol. 64, pp. 712–723.

La Greca, A.M., Silverman, W.K. and Wasserstein, S.B. 1998, 'Children's Pre-Disaster Functioning as a Predictor of Posttraumatic Stress Following Hurricane Andrew', *Journal of Consulting and Clinical Psychology*, vol. 66, pp. 883–892.

Luthar, S.S. and Cicchetti, D. 2000, 'The Construct of Resilience: Implications for Interventions and Social Policies', *Developmental Psychopathology*, vol. 12, pp. 857–885.

Masten, A.S. and Obradovic, J. 2008, 'Disaster Preparation and Recovery: Lessons from Research on Resilience in Human Development', *Ecological Society*, vol. 13, no. 1, art. 9. Available online: www.ecologyandsociety.org/vol 13/iss1/art9/.

Masten, A.S. and Obradovic, J. 2006, 'Competence and Resilience in Development', *Annals of the New York Academy of Science*, vol. 1,094, pp. 13–27.

Milojev, P., Osborne, D. and Sibley, C.G. 2014, 'Personality Resilience Following a Natural Disaster', *Social Psychological and Personality Science*, vol. 5, no. 7, pp. 760–768.

Morgan, I., Matthews, G. and Winton, M. 1995, 'Coping and Personality as Predictors of Post-Traumatic Intrusions, Numbing, Avoidance and General Distress: A Study of Victims of the Perth Flood', *Behavioural and Cognitive Psychotherapy*, vol. 23, pp. 251–264.

Morrow, B.H. and Enarson, E. 1996, 'Hurricane Andrew through Women's Eyes: Issues and Recommendations', *International Journal of Mass Emergencies and Disasters*, vol. 5, pp. 5–22.

Murphy, S.A. 1988, 'Mediating Effects of Intrapersonal and Social Support on Mental Health 1 and 3 Years After a Natural Disaster', *Journal of Traumatic Stress*, vol. 1, pp. 155–172.

Neria, Y., Gross, R., Litz, B., Maguen, S., Insel, B., Seirmarco, G., Rosenfeld, H., Suh, E.J., Kishon, R., Cook, J. and Marshall, R.D. 2007, 'Prevalence and Psychological Correlates of Complicated Grief Among Bereaved Adults 2.5–3.5 Years After September 11th Attacks', *Journal of Traumatic Stress*, vol. 20, no. 3, pp. 251–262.

NMA (National Medical Association) 2005, 'NMA Calls Response to Hurricane Katrina a "National Disgrace"', *Journal of the National Medical Association*, vol. 97, no. 10, pp. 1334–1335.

Norris, F. and Kaniasty, K. 1996, 'Received and Perceived Social Support in Times of Stress: A Test of the Social Support Deterioration Deterrence Model', *Journal of Personality and Social Psychology*, vol. 71, pp. 498–511.

Norris, F.H. and Stevens, S.P. 2007, 'Community Resilience and the Principles of Mass Trauma Intervention', *Psychiatry*, vol. 70, no. 4, pp. 320–328.

Norris, F.H., Friedman, M.J., Watson, P.J., Byrne, C.M. and Kaniasty, K. 2002, '60,000 Disaster Victims Speak: Part I. An Empirical Review of the Empirical Literature, 1981–2001', *Psychiatry*, vol. 65, pp. 207–239.

Norris, F., Phifer, J. and Kaniasty, K. 1994, 'Individual and Community Reactions to the Kentucky Floods: Findings from a Longitudinal Study of Older Adults', in R. Ursano, B. McCaughey and C. Fullerton (eds), *Individual and Community Responses to Trauma and Disaster: The Structure of Human Chaos*, Cambridge University Press, Cambridge, pp. 378–400.

Norris, F.H., Stevens, S.P., Pfefferbaum, B., Wyche, K.F. and Pfefferbaum, R.L. 2008, 'Community Resilience as a Metaphor, Theory, Set of Capacities, and Strategy for Disaster Readiness', *American Journal of Community Psychology*, vol. 41, pp. 127–150.

Olteanu, A., Arnberger, R., Grant, R., Abramson, D. and Asola, J. 2011, 'Persistence of Mental Health Needs Among Children in New Orleans Affected by Hurricane Katrina Four Years Later', *Prehospital and Disaster Medicine*, vol. 26, no. 1, pp. 3–6.

Ozbay, F., Fitterling, H., Charney, D. and Southwick, S. 2008, 'Social Support and Resilience to Stress Across the Life Span: A Neurobiologic Framework', *Current Psychiatry Reports*, no. 10, pp. 304–310.

Papanikolaou, V., Leon, G.R., Kyriopoulos, J., Levett, J. and Pallis, E. 2011, 'Surveying the Ashes: Experience from the 2007 Peloponnese Wildfires Six Months After the Disaster', Prehospital and Disaster Medicine, vol. 26, no. 2, pp. 79–89.

Pfefferbaum, B., Houston, J.B., Wyche, K.F., Van Horn, R.L., Reyes, G., Jeon-Slaughter, H. and North, C.S. 2008, 'Children Displaced by Hurricane Katrina: A Focus Group Study', *Journal of Loss and Trauma*, vol. 13, no. 4, pp. 303–318.

Polk, L.V. 1997, 'Toward a Middle-Range Theory of Resilience', *Advances in Nursing Science*, vol. 19, p. 13.

Pooley, J.A., Cohen, L. and O'Connor, M. 2010, 'Bushfire Communities and Resilience: What Can They Tell Us?', *Australian Journal of Emergency Management*, vol. 25, no. 2, pp. 33–38.

Regehr, C., Roberts, A.R. and Bober, T. 2008, 'On the Brink of Disaster: A Model for Reducing the Social and Psychological Impact', *Journal of Social Service Research*, vol. 34, no. 3, pp. 5–13.

ReliefWeb, 2008, 'More than 10,000 Children, Elderly "Alone After Quake"', Available online: http://reliefweb.int/rw/RWB.NSF/db900SID/RMOI-7EYKC5?OpenDocument. Retrieved 12 June 2008.

Rodriguez-Llanes, J. M., Vos, F. and Guha-Sapir, D. 2013, 'Measuring Psychological Resilience to Disasters: Are Evidence-Based Indicators an Achievable Goal?', *Environmental Health*, vol. 12, p. 115.

Ruggiero, K.J., Amstadter, A.B., Acierno, R., Kilpatrick, D.G., Resnick, H.S., Tracy, M. and Galea, S. 2009, 'Social and Psychological Resources Associated with Health Status in a Representative Sample of Adults Affected by the 2004 Florida Hurricanes', Psychiatry, vol. 72, pp. 195–210.

Sampson, R.J., Raudenbush, S.W, and Earls, F. 1997, 'Neighborhoods and Violent Crime: A Multilevel Study of Collective Efficacy', Science, no. 277, pp. 918–924.

Sayne, A. 2011, 'Climate Change Adaptation and Conflict in Nigeria'. Special Report 274, www.usip.prg.

Stamm, B.H. 2015, 'A Personal–Professional Experience of Losing My Home to Wildfire: Linking Personal Experience with the Professional Literature', *Clinical Social Work Journal*. doi:10.1007/s10615-015-0520-y.

Stough, L.M. 2015, 'World Report on Disability, Intellectual Disabilities, and Disaster Preparedness: Costa Rica as a Case Example', *Journal of Policy and Practice in Intellectual Disabilities*, vol. 12 no. 2, pp. 138–146. doi: 10.1111/jppi.12116.

Tannenbaum, B. and Anisman, H. 2003, 'Impact of Chronic Intermittent Challenges in Stressor Susceptible and Resilient Strains of Mice', *Biological Psychiatry*, vol. 53, pp. 292–303.

Tedeschi, R. and Calhoun, L. 2004, 'Post-Traumatic Growth: Conceptual Foundations and Empirical Evidence', *Psychological Inquiry*, vol. 15, pp. 1–18.

Tobin, G.A. and Whiteford, L.M. 2002, 'Community Resilience and volcano Hazard: The Eruptions of Tungurahua and Evacuation of the Faldas in Ecuador', *Disasters*, vol. 26, no. 1, pp. 28–48.

Tugade, M.M. and Fredrickson, B.L. 2004, 'Resilient Individuals Use Positive Emotions to Bounce Back from Negative Emotional Experiences', *Journal of Personality and Social Psychology*, vol. 86, pp. 320–333.

Tusaie, K. and Dyer, J. 2004, 'Resilience: A Historical Review of the Construct', *Holistic Nurse Practitioner*, vol. 18, pp. 3–8.

Wang, X., Gao, L., Shinfuku, N., Zhang, H., Zhao, C. and Shen, Y. 2000, 'Longitudinal Study of Earthquake-Related PTSD in a Randomly Selected Community Sample in North China', *American Journal of Psychiatry*, vol. 157, pp. 1260–1266.

Winkworth, G., Healy, C., Woodward, M. and Camilleri, P. 2009, 'Community Capacity Building: Learning from the 2003 Canberra Bushfires', *Australian Journal of Emergency Management*, vol. 24, no. 2, pp. 5–12.

5 The microsystem in disaster resilience

Helen J. Boon

Disaster resilience at the level of the individual was the subject of Chapter 4. Its scope has by no means been exhausted since there are few robust studies examining individuals' disaster resilience and fewer still using Bronfenbrenner's bioecological systems theory as their guiding research design. The chapter showed how individual or personal resilience is intertwined with community-level factors. This chapter will zoom in to a more circumscribed area of influence upon individuals' disaster resilience, the microsystem.

The microsystem comprises the elements that an individual is in direct contact with or is directly influenced by. As such, it involves an individual's family, work place, immediate neighbours and all the organisations that he or she is involved with. The microsystem, then, is an influential part of a person's social and physical milieu, since it contains all those variables and conditions of the immediate environment that impact resilience.

First, the chapter will review the possible influences emanating from microsystem entities in response to natural disasters. This will be followed by research findings that are available from the international research literature and our own research.

The importance of support from microsystem entities, leading to a sense of place and resulting in disaster-resilient individuals, will be illustrated by our research findings. Conversely, the tendency for communities to become depleted as a result of out migration or relocation will also be discussed. The definition of community resilience will be strongly considered in this section, and out migration will be examined through our bioecological lens as a result of microsystem deficiencies at the individual level. The reason for this stems directly from our research findings.

An important section of this chapter will focus on the disaster resilience of children and adolescents, a vulnerable section of the population when disaster strikes. Studies highlighting the role of children in disaster response in the context of their microsystem, the school, will be outlined, along with an important function that schools can potentially play in supporting disaster preparedness, resilience and well-being in children and adolescents.

The microsystem and its importance in disaster resilience

As described in Chapter 4, the microsystem that envelops a person is instrumental in making him or her feel that there is emotional and material support available should it be needed, and that is one of the mitigating factors in promoting disaster resilience. To date, few examples of research-based resilience literature use a design that examines the microsystem. However, as it is understood that microsystem entities are instrumental in promoting individuals' resilience, it is possible to extract and examine sample studies that show the influence of microsystem proximal processes upon disaster resilience. In theorising about human development, Bronfenbrenner described these proximal processes as follows.

> Human development takes place through processes of progressively more complex reciprocal interaction between an active, evolving biopsychological human organism and the persons, objects, and symbols in its immediate external environment. To be effective, the interaction must occur on a fairly regular basis over extended periods of *time*. Such enduring forms of interaction in the immediate environment are referred to as *proximal processes*.
>
> (Bronfenbrenner and Morris, 1998: 996, original italics)

These processes, bound as they are by the element of time in that they need to be enduring to be influential, are very difficult to derive empirically from the disaster literature. This is because most of the literature is based on post-disaster studies, which mainly examine disaster impacts and their effects rather than what has sustained individuals and kept them healthy and functioning optimally. However, research does suggest that certain types of pre-disaster activities and processes enhance individual disaster resilience. Moreover, it has long been accepted that disaster resilience at the community level is a combination of community-wide preparedness, infrastructure effectiveness and the resilience of the individuals that comprise communities and manage emergency responses and resources. Underpinning all this, at the individual level, microsystem activities and processes are vital.

A critical proximal process that builds disaster resilience is preparedness for the hazard (Monnier and Hobfoll 2000), as we found empirically (Boon *et al.* 2012). That entails emotional as well as physical preparedness. Preparedness might involve a number of things, depending on the type of impending natural hazard: putting together emergency kits; clearing property to avoid dangerous flying debris in the case of a hurricane or cyclone (this is often the howling winds' instrument of destruction); preparing property for an encroaching fire by clearing flammable vegetation around the perimeter; preparing for encroaching floodwaters by lifting furniture or other property to a higher part of the house; and so on. These domestic activities implicitly involve the cooperation of other household members and very often neighbours since loose materials from adjacent properties can cause damage to neighbouring households in a variety of ways. Physical preparedness follows warning messages that can be sourced from the media, but in many instances these emanate from friends and neighbours (Boon et al. 2012; Boon 2014a). These sorts of preparedness activities become increasingly instrumental in building resilience if they have been enacted several times, so that the anticipation of the hazard is built upon prior experiences that have not left the individual severely traumatised.

The instrumentality of family or household members in preparedness can be illustrated by a case study. When the super category-5 Cyclone Yasi struck the North Queensland coast on February 2011, residents up and down the coast prepared for its impact as the media fired warnings of its enormous size and destructive power. A study that looked at the impact of Yasi on the communities along the North Queensland coast reported that 37.5 per cent of residents began their preparations three or more days before Yasi made landfall, and they did so with help from other household members (Woods et al. 2012). The value of preparation and coping skills positively affect survivors or victims of disasters and provide some level of protection from psychological stress, thus enhancing resilience.

> My family and I prepare for cyclones at the start of every cyclone season …
> this means that when a cyclone does come what we have to do is minimal.
> Hence I feel we are always well prepared.
> (Respondent from North Queensland, in Woods et al. 2012: 17)

> Generally, as a family we are always basically prepared with a kit supply of
> necessities such as first aid kit, radio, batteries, insect repellent etc.
> (Respondent from North Queensland, in Woods et al. 2012: 17)

In the aftermath of disaster the help that neighbours and family members can provide cleaning up, supporting essential needs and reassuring victims is invaluable. Neighbours and friends – more often than government agencies or NGOs – provide the necessary resources for recovery after disaster. When power is disrupted, as often happens after a severe cyclone or storm, neighbours with a range of emergency equipment and supplies can provide a life-line for survival until emergency services or government support arrives. Very often transport systems are blocked by fallen trees and debris and so essential goods cannot flow to the disaster-impacted places for up to several days. In such instances neighbours and friends are the best source of short-term assistance. Borrowing a dynamo to charge cell phones or restore internet facilities and other communication devices can be vital for those living alone and seeking to communicate with loved ones or call for emergency medical help. Neighbours often provide such help, particularly in small, tight-knit rural and regional communities (Boon 2014b).

Another vital microsystem entity is the work place. The importance of an individual's work place in supporting his or her disaster resilience is critical, but this area has not been much studied. It is through deficits in work place provisions, which have been documented in the literature, that the potential importance of the work place in disaster resilience is revealed. For example, Drabek (2001) compared 12 communities' responses in the US after seven different disasters impacted various states: the 1995 Hurricane Felix, the 1996 Hurricane Fran and five different floods that impacted several states in 1997. The research used a comparative case study design, using field observations, interviews with businesses and mail surveys of individuals within a range of business organisations. The firms studied varied considerably in their degree of disaster preparedness and support for their employees – whether, for example, the business was one that provided essential supplies or shelter in the wake of the disaster – as well as by type of business. Results showed that employees would have benefitted from a number of work-related adjustments and concessions to cope with work–family tensions that arose as a result of the disasters' impacts. For example, many said they would have liked to be allowed to go home to deal with their families and home emergency contingencies; they would have liked to be paid while the they were evacuated from their work place; they would have appreciated better emergency communications, evacuation drills and preparedness information provided by their employers; they wanted earlier closing times to get home; and they felt the need for clear and unambiguous return-to-work procedures. Dissatisfaction with management was more acute within disaster-relevant companies, such as lumberyards and retail shops that stayed open to supply residents with emergency equipment for the predicted events. There was also dissatisfaction with some hotel managers who delayed closure or even remained open during the impact period in order to serve the community and those who might be caught on the road and need shelter. Those employees who had received no on-the-job disaster training and those with children at home were particularly dissatisfied with their employers. Findings like these have been endorsed by many studies that have reported relief worker and other aid and medical emergency worker burnouts as a result of operating for long hours under unavoidably stressful conditions during and after a disaster event. To illustrate with an example, school nurses after Hurricanes Katrina and Rita in 2005 not only had to deal with an increased workload, but also had the additional emotional burden of dealing with displaced children and families while facing their own personal losses and providing care to children with no available medical records (Broussard *et al.* 2008).

On the other hand, Drabek (2001) documented some well-received efforts by managers in support of their employees. These ranged from pay advances to ensure that employees would not be left without their weekly pay if pay day fell after the impact of the disaster, to time off to allow employees to repair their damaged homes, to offers of accommodation for employees in inland, more protected areas than their usual residence. In one case, an employer offered an employee a room in his own house, knowing that the employee was living in a trailer that would be subject to the full impact of the hazard. These sorts of initiatives are obviously not always practicable from the point of view of an employer. But it is clear how much influence they can potentially have upon the resilience of employees and their families, and in the long term upon the resilience of the business, by way of employee loyalty. All this has a flow-on effect upon community resilience.

During a natural disaster, many need help from their microsystem to survive. The May 2015 floods that ravaged Texas and took the lives of 19 people offer a good example of how isolation renders people vulnerable, while the converse – social support – saves lives. One death, that of a 14-year-old who was found with his dog in a storm drain, occurred while the boy was alone, away from his family. Another death resulted from solitude: a high school senior student was alone in her car when it was caught in high water. A resort on the banks of the Blanco River was almost totally destroyed by the raging flood waters, but on the night of the flood the owners were able to get all 100 guests out safely after they received warnings that the river was rising (Robbins and Lozano 2015). Of course many others, such as tourists, were particularly vulnerable because emergency services sent the first wave of warnings to the cell phones of registered users, once again highlighting the dangers of social isolation and dislocation in the face of disaster.

Dislocation and isolation caused by the impact of a natural hazard can lead to tragedy. Furthermore, when disasters remove significant individuals from survivors' networks, through death, injury or relocation, the long-term post-disaster picture alters dramatically. Once again, the importance of microsystem support for individuals' resilience – and by association community resilience – is highlighted. This is because community resilience can be measured by the attitudes of its members (King and MacGregor 2000). Drabek and Key (1984) conducted an early study of post-disaster adaptation at the family level, looking at trauma imprints left by the experience of the 1966 Topeka Tornado in Kansas. The rigorous study included pre-disaster baseline psychological and social-functioning data, and compared families exposed and unexposed to the tornado. The primary research questions concerned the impact of the disaster on family functioning, including interactions with social contacts like neighbours, friends and others in the community. A mixed pattern of results was discovered. Affected families reported poorer relationships within their marriages and frayed bonds with their neighbours, but stronger connections with relatives and friends. They interacted with fewer neighbours and fewer of their exchanges were based on providing assistance or help. Affected families also reduced their participation in a wide range of social and civic groups, ranging from fraternal organisations or lodges to hobby or political action groups, although for those who were religious church attendance increased. Such responses to serious disaster impact are not difficult to understand. The central dyad, the husband and wife, are likely struggling to recover from losses and the trauma of the disaster experience, and as a result expectations within the marriage become greater. Greater expectations can result in greater disappointment, guilt and blame between spouses, and the need for more support expresses itself in stronger relationships with friends and family until the marital relationship heals. Even where aid agencies provide timely support there are often delays and frustrations before household members' lives are restored to anything like they had been before the disaster. These experiences are likely to exacerbate individual psychological problems, making the development of new relationships or even sustaining existing ones problematic.

A number of forces combine to produce social support deterioration within survivors' immediate social networks and community. Disasters remove significant supporters from survivors' networks through death, injury and relocation, and even if they return to their original place of residence to rebuild, many find that old neighbours and friends have moved away, thus permanently changing the structure of the community (Hutchins and Norris 1989). Besides, victims' expectations for support may be unrealistic in post-disaster conditions: potential support providers are likely to be victims themselves, and as a result the support needs of disaster victims exceed available resources. Often even the influx of support from external aid sources is not enough to fulfil a community's needs in the immediate disaster aftermath. Profound disappointment is consequently experienced by survivors, because help from relatives, friends or neighbours is not provided as readily as expected (Kasapoglu *et al.* 2004).

Many studies confirm similar findings about the quantity and quality of interpersonal relationships after disasters. For example, Mexican survivors of floods and mudslides scored below the population mean on number of household connections with family and friends at six months after the disasters, using measures of social support normed for the population (Norris *et al.* 2005), and these figures remained lower for two years after the disaster. A longitudinal study of flood survivors in south-west Poland in 1997, which used multivariate analyses to control for potential confounding variables such as the influence of sociodemographic factors and direct disaster exposure measures, found that a greater involvement in the immediate post-disaster altruistic communities, measured mainly by the amount of social support received, predicted more favourable appraisals of interpersonal and community relationships 20 months after the disaster. Conversely, indicators of post-disaster social bitterness, that is, dissatisfaction with aid and a range of interpersonal and community animosities and disagreements, predicted lower levels of subsequent social psychological well-being (Kaniasty 2012).

Social support, either from microsystem entities or others, is an important factor in maintaining psychological well-being following exposure to natural hazards. For example, older adults with access to higher levels of social support experienced lower levels of depressive symptoms in the wake of floods (Tyler and Hoyt 2000). Negative mental health effects following survival of a disaster are indicators of frayed disaster resilience, as already discussed in Chapter 4. These can be exacerbated by the breakdown of community functioning and the social support systems that communities provide for the most vulnerable, for example the elderly, who are often relatively more dependent on social systems in developed countries (Saniotis and Irvine 2010). Older adults in particular tend to have fewer microsystem support networks and have to rely more on the support of doctors, support workers or psychologists rather than close friends and family (Tyler 2006). Lack of immediate microsystem support not only affects resilience but it can also place individuals of all ages in grave danger. The mortality rates during and immediately after the 2005 Hurricane Katrina and subsequent flooding peaked in the elderly (Adams et al. 2011). The over 60s, 15 per cent of the New Orleans population at the time, comprised approximately 75 per cent of all deaths. In the year following Hurricane Katrina, the health of elderly survivors declined at a rate of four times the national average for older adults not affected by the disaster (Burton et al. 2009).

Structural changes in the disaster-impacted neighbourhoods change the social dynamics of a locale. When whole neighbourhoods are destroyed or damaged victims may not want to return and rebuild their lost homes, and so their ties with old neighbours and friends may break, further adding to the disruption of social interchanges in the shorter term. Such results point strongly to complex neighbour relationships, developed over time, and the necessary trust placed upon those relationships. A place-based community spirit or sense of place that prevails is likely an important factor that also plays a part in the development of post-disaster relations with microsystem entities, and by implication in disaster resilience. This notion is suggested from results of another tornado study in Texas, which investigated family functioning post disaster (Bolin 1982). Here too post-disaster interpersonal dynamics examined 12 and 18 months after the tornado impact were mixed. Social interchanges between victims and their families and friends increased, though the same held for control respondents who were unaffected, while their involvement with neighbours waned.

Sense of place and disaster resilience

The actual physical space where people spend the majority of their time, a microsystem entity, has a strong influence upon their emotional and psychological functioning. The effects that a town or neighbourhood or other geographical space have on the human psyche have been considered under the broad banner of sense of place. A sense of place has been theoretically discussed by considering the social and geographical context of place bonds and the sensing of places, such as aesthetics and a subjective feeling of dwelling. Insider status, sometimes linked to local ancestry, imparts a perceived connection to place and helps develop what is thought of as a sense of place (Hay 1998). The study of sense of place has been taken up by a range of disciplines, including social anthropology, environmental and social psychology and human geography, and these have fostered various understandings and conceptual measures (Graham et al. 2009). Notwithstanding these different approaches to the concept, a sense of place has commonly been thought to emerge from the perceptions of individual residents. Empirical data from an Israeli study concluded that:

> In residential environments the sense of place is established mainly by the residents themselves and is formed at the inter-subjective level, connecting

between the behaviour of the individual and that of the other residents. The sense of place of the residential environment will thus be affected by perceptions of its physical characteristics, by the feeling and behaviour of its residents, and by the interactions between them.

(Billig 2005: 118)

In the context of disaster resilience, sense of place has been identified as binding people to place despite hardship. Chamlee-Wright and Storr (2009), for instance, looked at sense of place in examining the return of residents to an impoverished neighbourhood of New Orleans following Hurricane Katrina. According to their findings, sense of place was composed of place attachment, place identity and place dependence. They argued that it was the residents' sense of place that influenced their return to New Orleans. In Queensland, Australia, Hegney *et al.* (2007) identified sense of place as supportive of rural community resilience, while community cohesion was reported as a significant factor in supporting the recovery and resilience of Britons inundated by the floods that devastated Carlisle in 2005 (Chang 2010), in an event that led to three rivers meeting as one. Our study of a double flood disaster in Ingham, Australia (Figure 5.1) also showed that 'sense of place' strongly predicted residents' disaster resilience after the February 2009 floods (Boon 2014b).

Our study, which used multiple methods to assess community resilience to an event of severe flooding classified as a national disaster by the Australian Federal Government in 2009 (Queensland Government 2009), showed that those residents who felt a strong emotional connection to Ingham were most likely to want to stay in the town after the flood disaster, thus enhancing overall community resilience. Their sense of place in Ingham was the strongest predictor of their individual resilience even after controlling for the number of years they had lived in the town (Figure 5.2). The model shows that sense of place is a strong predictor of resilience (standardised regression $\beta = 0.41$). Sense of place was also protective of negative health impacts in our sample (standardised regression $\beta = -0.09$) and of wanting to leave or migrate out of the town (standardised regression $\beta = -0.23$). Health problems, on the other hand, eroded individuals' resilience ($\beta = -0.09$) and strongly predicted their desire to migrate out ($\beta = 0.28$). The model accounted for 18 per cent of the variance in individual resilience ($R^2 = 0.18$) and 15 per cent of the variance for those who indicated they wanted to migrate out of the town ($R^2 = 0.15$), both significant empirical results given the myriad of possible factors that might influence an individual's resilience and desire to stay or migrate out of a place. The structural equation modelling results based on 287 residents' survey results also showed that, for some, the number of years living in the community were not necessarily linked to sense of place. All results were statistically significant at least to $p < 0.05$.

In relation to a sense of place it is of interest to consider why people opt to relocate or migrate out of a community following a disaster. Our studies of disaster-resilient individuals across four disaster-impacted communities in Australia (Boon *et al.* 2012) showed quite clearly that personal resilience was

Figure 5.1 Ingham, Queensland, Australia.

incompatible with a desire to leave the disaster-impacted community. Those who measured high on disaster resilience were not the same people who had thought of leaving the community or who indicated a desire to leave the community. Of course, our interviews and survey only included residents who remained in the community post disaster, and therefore by default they were unlikely, in the main, to wish to relocate or migrate out of those communities.

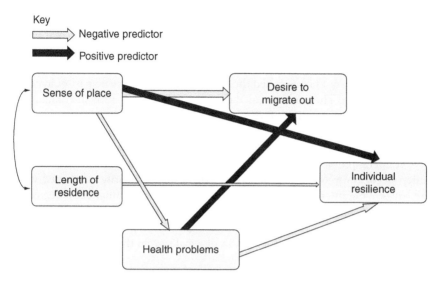

Figure 5.2 Model of links between sense of place, number of years living in Ingham, health impacts, resilience and desire to leave (*N* = 287).[1]

Had we surveyed a number of individuals who had left the communities after the disasters we might have found that they too were resilient.

In this context, during the data-gathering period of that research, we interviewed two families who had left the town of Innisfail after Cyclone Larry had decimated it and the surrounding areas. The themes that came through from those two interviews were that the families had lost all sense of place in the community of Innisfail and the experience was so traumatic that they never wanted to go through a similar one again. There was much talk about how there was nothing left there for them, in terms of employment opportunities and social connections with family or friends. More significant, for one of the families interviewed, was the terrible psychological trauma that their two young boys continued to suffer from the cyclone experience, a trauma that necessitated the constant attendance of a psychologist for the boys five years after the event. That particular family had lost all their business assets, a tourist campsite and café, during the cyclone. The other family relocated because their business interests could no longer be served in Innisfail. They too found the experience harrowing but their main reason for moving was an economic one. These two examples are supportive and illustrative of the case made by King *et al.* (2014): that migration out of hazard-prone areas might signify individual resilience and adaptation to a hostile global landscape affected by climate change. According to our findings (Boon *et al.* 2012) then, those who remain in as well as those who leave a hazard-prone location may both demonstrate disaster resilience at the individual level. From the perspective of community resilience, however, out migration is likely to corrode the social and economic fabric of a place and is therefore unlikely to be supportive of resilience.

Another recent study also examined sense of place and its influence upon resilience. Brown (2015) identified sense of place and community cohesion as instrumental in promoting community and individual resilience through what Bronfenbrenner would have called the proximal process of participation in community gardening. The study revealed the process of participating in community gardens led to the formation of social connections and enhanced sense-of-place feelings and social cohesiveness perceptions, both indirect contributors to disaster resilience. The community gardeners grew food, worked with others to solve common problems, and developed friendships with fellow gardeners. Some garden networks were very social, while others were primarily concerned with problem-solving interactions directly associated with gardening, but a degree of each element was present. Brown (2015) concluded that disaster resilience building can be aided through community garden programmes, which when regarded through Bronfenbrenner's bioecological system theory comprise proximal microsystem processes.

Why is it, then, that people in some places recover from disaster more quickly than others? Why do some places seem to nurture resilience? For instance, across the Big Easy, New Orleans, in some neighbourhoods, such as the Vietnamese neighbourhood of Village de L'Est, there was strong evidence of ties among residents who cooperated to clean up damaged housing, whereas in others there was little if any broad-scale cooperative activity (LaRose 2006; Faciane 2007). Physical infrastructure, such as field hospitals, water and food distribution, certainly provides important, often life-saving resources for disaster survivors, but without social cooperation and support these programmes and other schemes that focus on infrastructure do not guarantee community or individual resilience. Village de L'Est recovered quickly due to its dense community networks and high levels of trust between residents, while other even adjacent neighbourhoods that lacked these characteristics deteriorated (Chamlee-Wright 2010). These types of voluntary reciprocal microsystem interactions are proximal processes that act on each person's psychological and emotional compass to generate a stronger sense of support which in turn enhance individual resilience. Over the last 30 or so years neuroscience research has pointed to the changes that take place in a person's neural matter as a result of experiences and learning (e.g. see Davidson and McEwen 2012; Howard-Jones 2014) and therefore resilience – which was once thought to be an inherited biological predisposition, a trait – can now very likely be demonstrated to develop as a result of enhancing experiences. Microsystem interactions that lead to feelings of social support and sense of place regarding a particular geographical location are such moulding proximal processes that promote individual resilience.

These notions about resilience as a process are now well established. They have already been adopted by the US National Center of Disaster Medicine and Public Health (NCDMPH), which supports national resilience by providing education and training resources for the disaster health workforce. Its slogan,

'Resilience through Learning', heads many NCDMPH and outside resources designed to help emergency responders, educators and health trainers gain specific all-hazard knowledge and understanding so as to improve preparedness for any emergency event.

Children and adolescent disaster resilience

Nowhere is the promotion of disaster resilience more evident than in children who have suffered disasters but have managed to come through with minimal negative effects as a result of microsystem assistance. Children are among the most vulnerable victims of disaster. A review of 160 studies of disaster victims worldwide concluded that children experience the adverse effects of disasters more acutely than adults or the elderly. Many children have died in disasters (Save the Children 2007); children aged four and under are most likely to die of exposure to extreme heat, while 5–14-year-olds are most likely to die in cyclones and floods as a consequence of inappropriate conduct (FitzGerald *et al.* 2010). Children's and youths' vulnerability can manifest in three different ways: psychologically, via the development of PTSD, depression, anxiety, emotional distress, sleep disorders, somatic complaints and behavioural problems; physically, through injury, illness and disease, malnutrition, heat stress, physical and sexual abuse; and educationally, because of missed school, poor academic performance or delayed progress due to psychological and structural impediments post disaster (Peek 2008). It is therefore imperative that young people are prepared – given armour – to sustain the impacts of any natural hazard, as well as being taught coping skills post disaster to avert potential adverse psychological effects.

Recalling that the social environment in which a child develops is characterised by both structural and functional properties, it is worth remembering that all are relevant when considering the impact of a disaster on the child. Apart from unique child structural factors (e.g. demographics, temperament, coping, prior trauma), structural variables include the characteristics of the family microsystem (e.g. family structure, socio-economic status), the school microsystem, other significant interacting adults, the neighbourhood microsystem including the child's religious affiliations and participation in organisations and the peer group microsystem. The more distal effects of health and mental health care, social services, public resources, social policy, economics, the media, politics and emergency management also contribute to the development of resilience or its absence. Functional impacts as a result of disaster can interrupt a child's social environment via direct loss or harm, reduced responsiveness from significant adults, decreased communications and barriers to resources and services, all of which are liable to be disrupted to varying degrees by disasters. The most salient contexts for young children and adolescents, however, are those illustrated in Figure 5.3. This shows the links and overlaps between two of the most important microsystems in young children's lives, the home and school microsystems.

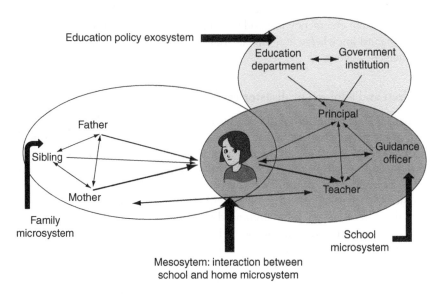

Figure 5.3 The home and school microsystems.

The impact that a disaster can have upon a child's life might be as simple as blocked access to the local playground, as shown in the photo below, taken after category-5 Cyclone Yasi made landfall north of Townsville, Australia, or as tragic as the loss or injury of a loved one, parent, sibling or friend.

Across the range of possible disaster impacts, the ecology of the family and the competence of family functioning are strong predictors of children's and adolescents' resilience. Children and adolescents are particularly sensitive to transmission of secondary trauma following disasters. Family mental health, separation from parents in the immediate aftermath of disaster or troubled family functioning are thought to be important determinants and moderators of a child's response to disaster (McFarlane 1987a). Results from a disaster study of children and parents exposed to an Australian bushfire linked enduring maternal distress and subsequent changes in parenting to children's persisting distress, even more so than children's direct exposure to the disaster (McFarlane 1987a). In a study of adolescent survivors of Hurricane Katrina, it was found that the more a family relied on external help in the aftermath, the greater the likelihood of a negative impact on adolescent mental health. Young people whose families relied heavily on relief agencies displayed lower self-esteem, greater psychological distress and worse symptoms of depression (Vigil and Geary 2008). Of course these are associative rather than causal factors and it is possible that those who relied heavily on aid agencies were already more vulnerable because of structural socio-demographic variables. Nonetheless, family ecology seems significant in supporting a developing young person's resilience, because healthy family functioning predicts children's healthy functioning. Weems and Overstreet (2008) examined various influences

Figure 5.4 Playground after Cyclone Yasi impacted Townsville, February 2011, Hodell
St (photo courtesy Dr Sally Cavalieri).

on children's disaster adjustment in the specific context of Hurricane Katrina, and found parental mental health factors that negatively affected their disaster recovery. Another Hurricane Katrina study examined the responses of preschool children and their caregivers. Children of parents who had no pre-existing adverse mental health symptoms, such as anxiety, depression or alcohol abuse, but who developed PTSD symptoms as a result of the hurricane also developed post-traumatic stress symptoms (Scheeringa and Zeanah 2008). In their 20-year review of disaster research, Norris and colleagues (2002) concluded that parental stress is among the robust predictors of children's distress following disasters.

Children are dependent on significant adults to meet their needs and to help them prepare for and respond to disasters. There are thought to be three types of 'coping assistance' children might receive following a disaster: processing emotions; reinstitution of familiar roles and routines; and help with distraction. Research that surveyed school children seven months after Hurricane Andrew showed that reinstitution of roles and routines was reported most frequently, followed by distraction and emotional processing (Prinstein 1996). These kinds of supports to help children and youth to be resilient can be provided by a range of significant adults. Pina *et al.* 2008 found that as perceived support from extra-familial sources (e.g. teachers, friends, church members) increased, post-traumatic stress reactions in youth decreased (i.e. PTSD, anxiety and depression) after the impact of hurricane exposure.

Churches and other religious institutions can often provide tangible as well as spiritual relief to disaster victims, including children. These can range from running programmes to help provide stability, such as childcare for affected families, through to providing shelter, access to medical care, transportation, communication services and even help completing disaster-related paperwork following Hurricane Katrina (Pant et al. 2008). Churches in the Baton Rouge area provided food, financial aid, clothing, counselling, transportation, child care and shelter for Hurricane Katrina evacuees. They helped evacuees access federal and state resources and helped reunite family members (Cain and Barthelemy 2007). These kinds of supports are the proximal processes that Bronfenbrenner would identify as instrumental in raising the developmental outcomes of children and adolescents.

The other critical column of the microsystem for children is the school. Schools are well placed for coordinating and delivering mental health services for children following trauma (e.g. Jaycox et al. 2009), and disaster (e.g. Stuber et al. 2002). School-based services promote the recovery and resilience of students following disasters mainly through the help provided by teachers and peers. Through the provision of accessible mental health services, the school environment plays an essential role in fulfilling children's and families' post-disaster needs (Jaycox et al. 2006). School-based disaster interventions normalise the trauma experience and reduce the stigma associated with mental health care. Moreover, interventions set at school, as compared to those conducted in settings less familiar to children and their parents, are more likely to be accessed by students. For example, Jaycox et al. (2010) compared interventions delivered at school with those in a clinical setting following Hurricane Katrina, and found that while children benefitted from both treatments participation was greater in the school-based intervention. A wide range of services can be implemented in schools. These include school-based screenings, which can be used to assess children's disaster reactions and identify those at risk. Information like this can aid parents and teachers in understanding the extent of student distress and guide clinicians in helping at-risk students. School-based assessments can also be used to evaluate available and needed resources for preparedness and debriefing activities, and help government agencies determine how to allocate resources by applying health promotion strategies in schools, particularly for the most vulnerable children, those with disabilities (Boon et al. 2014).

Other possible school-based interventions include psycho-education, which can be used to help children address and accept common emotional reactions to the disaster and promote positive coping skills. Schools can also promote positive student coping by re-establishing normal routines and extracurricular activities, such as band rehearsals or athletics, which can help reconnect students with peers and provide normative activities to distract them from disaster-related rumination. An example is given in the news clip below, which documents an initiative organised by the local Queensland Alliance for Mental Health branch after Cyclone Yasi made landfall on the Queensland town of Tully in 2011. Effective classroom interventions provide factual information about the disaster and model appropriate responses, while dispelling myths; they also aid class cohesion, encourage mutual support and facilitate help-seeking behavior (Pynoos *et al.* 1995).

Children's resilience is demonstrably increased when they are given access to resources and information, empowering them to participate in disaster preparedness and response activities (Back *et al.* 2009). The importance of the school's role in helping children prepare for possible disaster, and hence avert post-disaster

Figure 5.5 Reproduced with permission from the *Tully Times*, Thursday 12 July 2012, p. 19.

problems, was demonstrated by an Australian research study that focused on 131 children (aged 5–12 years) living in high bushfire-risk areas in south-eastern Australia (Towers 2015). Towers found that children understood 'evacuating' in terms of deciding what to take, choosing a destination, identifying triggers and contingency planning; they also understood 'staying to defend' property. While the children understood sophisticated ideas associated with both 'evacuating' and 'staying to defend', the study found they also held misconceptions that influenced how they interpreted information and instructions to do with bushfire safety. Schools are well situated to dispel such misconceptions, by identifying them and supplanting them with more accurate understandings. Indeed, many studies confirm that school interventions by way of education are helpful not only in promoting preparedness, and by corollary resilience, in the young person but also in raising the level of household preparedness, as they alert parents to take precautionary emergency measures (Back et al. 2009). These effects were found to be particularly strong in developing countries (Back et al. 2009).

The role of peers in supporting disaster resilience in youth has not been well investigated to date (Noffsinger et al. 2012). Friends and peers constitute an important microsystem for children and youth and they can potentially cushion the trauma of disaster and help peers' resilience through emotional and even physical support. Such support can be mediated by the sharing of entertainment artefacts and resources. Children are usually able to reconnect with friends and peers at school because schools tend to reopen quickly after a disaster, so classmates and peers could provide valuable relief to each other. Unfortunately, knowledge about the role of peers in children's disaster reactions is limited. The available research conducted with Hurricane Katrina victims only shows that negative peer interactions exacerbated post-traumatic stress symptoms among adolescents (Noffsinger et al. 2012).

Summary

In considering the microsystem and its influence upon disaster resilience, it is reasonably clear that family, friends and neighbours are instrumental in building individuals' disaster resilience. In addition, other microsystem entities such as the workplace, churches and schools can, though a range of interventions, build up resilience by providing salient supports before, during and after disasters.

Information about an impending natural hazard and any processes that help to prepare households and individuals to withstand the physical impact of a hazard are invaluable. Not only are these imperative to avoid physical harm, they are also critical for emotional preparedness, so that people are less likely to be traumatised by the hazard event. The saying 'forewarned and forearmed' takes on a very serious meaning in this context for all individuals, including children and adolescents.

Positive perceptions and emotions about a town or a city are a microsystem factor that raises a person's subjective feelings of connectedness or sense of place. These perceptions in turn enable or compel people to remain in a town even after it has been ravaged by disaster; moreover to remain and help rebuild the town even if it is likely to be repeatedly struck by a natural hazard.

Implications and gaps

There is an urgent need to conduct research to understand the role of the microsystem of individuals in building resilience. This research needs to be appropriately designed, utilising Bronfenbrenner's bioecological systems theory and the process-person-context-time model, in order to decipher the precise processes that are effective in promoting disaster resilience. We need to know how, for example, workplaces actually lift levels of resilience rather than what has not been done and what might be wished for by employees. It is possible that what employees believe they need does not significantly raise their level of resilience from base levels, or, conversely, it might be that in fact small changes in conditions and expectations from workplaces or better consultative processes and emergency plans are all that is needed for a measurable effect in disaster resilience.

Similarly, we need to know to what extent peers influence children's and adolescents' resilience, as well as how these proximal processes exert their influences. The role of the organisations that people participate in – churches, sporting clubs, local neighbourhood hubs such as libraries and the like – and residents' neighbourly relationships also need to be unpacked and examined in terms of pre-disaster, emergency response and post-disaster effects. In this way more effective policies and advice can be disseminated by local government authorities in both developed and developing countries to enhance community cohesion at the neighbourhood level. It is possible that the creation of municipal spaces or community gardens might be a simple yet effective way to promote cohesion and disaster resilience at the individual and, by default, at the community level.

Note

1 There is one R squared (R^2) or squared multiple correlation (smc) for each dependent variable in the model. It is the percentage variance explained in that variable. $R^2 = 0.4$ may be interpreted as follows: approximately 40 per cent of the variation in the response variable can be explained by the explanatory variables. The remaining 60 per cent can be explained by unknown variables or inherent variability (Norusis 2003).

References

Adams, V., Kaufman, S., Van Hattum, T. and Moody, S. 2011, 'Aging Disaster: Mortality, Vulnerability, and Long-Term Recovery Among Katrina Survivors', *Medical Anthropology*, vol. 30, no. 3, pp. 247–270.

Back, E., Cameron, C. and Tanner, T.M. 2009, 'Children and Disaster Risk Reduction: Taking Stock and Moving Forward'. Children in a Changing Climate Report, Institute of Development Studies, Brighton.

Billig, M. 2005, 'Sense of Place in the Neighborhood, in Locations of Urban Revitalization', *GeoJournal*, vol. 64, pp. 117–130.

Bolin, R. 1982, *Long-Term Family Recovery from Disaster*. University of Colorado Press,
Boulder, CO.

Boon, H.J. 2014a, 'Investigating Rural Community Communication for Flood and Bushfire
Preparedness', *Australian Journal of Emergency Management*, vol. 29, no. 4, pp. 17–25.

Boon, H.J. 2014b, 'Disaster Resilience in a Flood-Impacted Rural Australian Town',
Natural Hazards, vol. 71, no. 1, pp. 683–701.

Boon, H., Brown, L. and Pagliano, P. 2014, 'Emergency Planning for Students with Disabilities: A Survey of Australian Schools', *Australian Journal of Emergency Management*,
vol. 29, no. 1, pp. 45–49.

Boon, H.J., Millar, J., Lake, D., Cottrell, A. and King, D. 2012, *Recovery from Disaster:
Resilience, Adaptability and Perceptions of Climate Change*. National Climate Change
Adaptation Research Facility, James Cook University, Queensland, Australia.

Bronfenbrenner, U. and Morris, P.A. 1998, 'The Ecology of Developmental Processes',
in W. Damon and R.M. Lerner (eds), *Handbook of Child Psychology, Volume 1: Theoretical Models of Human Development*, 5th edn, pp. 993–1023. Wiley, New York.

Brown, N. 2015, 'Building Disaster Resilience: Why Community Gardens Improve Community Resilience'. Dissertation, California State University, Long Beach, CA.

Broussard, L., Myers, R. and Meaux, J. 2008, 'The Impact of Hurricanes Katrina and Rita
on Louisiana School Nurses', *Journal of School Nursing*, vol. 24, pp. 78–82.

Burton, L.C., Skinner, E.A., Uscher-Pines, L., Lieberman, R., Leff, B., Clark, R., Yu, Q.,
Lemke, K.W. and Weiner, J.P. 2009 'Health of Medicare Advantage Plan Enrollees at
1 Year after Hurricane Katrina', *The American Journal of managed Care*, vol. 15, no. 1,
pp. 13–22.

Cain, D.S. and Barthelemy, J. 2007, Tangible and Spiritual Relief after the Storm: The Religious Communities' Response to Katrina', PowerPoint slides. Available online: http://
jumpjet.Info/Emergency-Preparedness/Neighborly-Response/Outside/The_Religious_
Communitie_Response_to_Katrina.pdf.

Chamlee-Wright, E. 2010, *The Cultural and Political Economy of Recovery: Social Learning
in a Post-Disaster Environment*. Routledge, New York.

Chamlee-Wright, E. and Storr, V.H. 2009, 'There's No Place Like New Orleans': Sense
of Place and Community Recovery in the Ninth Ward after Hurricane Katrina',
Journal of Urban Affairs, vol. 30, pp. 615–634.

Chang, K. 2010, 'Community Cohesion after a Natural Disaster: Insights from a Carlisle
Flood', *Disasters*, vol. 34, no. 2, pp. 289–302.

Davidson, R.J. and McEwen, B.S. 2012, 'Social Influences on Neuroplasticity: Stress and
Interventions to Promote Well-Being', *Nature Neuroscience*, vol. 15, no. 5, pp. 689–695.

Drabek, T.E. 2001, 'Understanding Employee Responses to Disaster', *Australian Journal of
Emergency Management*, vol. 15, no. 4, pp. 15–21. ISSN: 1324–1540.

Drabek, T.E. and Key, W.M. 1984, *Conquering Disaster: Family Recovery and Long-Term
Consequences*. Irvington Publishers, New York.

Faciane, V. 2007, 'Vietnamese Community Thriving in Eastern N.O'. *Times Picayune*, 23
April.

FitzGerald, G., Du, W., Jamal, A., Clark, M. and Hou, X.Y. 2010, 'Flood Fatalities in
Contemporary Australia (1997–2008): Disaster Medicine', *Emergency Medicine Australasia*,
vol. 22, no. 2, pp. 180–186.

Graham, H., Mason, R. and Newman, A. 2009, 'Literature Review: Historic Environment, Sense of Place, and Social Capital'. English Heritage, UK, p. 44.

Hay, R. 1998, 'Sense of Place in Developmental Context', *Journal of Environmental Psychology*, vol. 18, pp. 5–29.

Hegney, D.G., Buikstra, E., Baker, P., Rogers-Clark, C., Pearce. S., Ross, H., King, C. and Watson-Luke, A. 2007, 'Individual Resilience in rural People: A Queensland Study, Australia', *Rural Remote Health*, vol. 7, no. 4, p. 620. Available online: www.rrh.org.au.

Howard-Jones, P. 2014, 'Neuroscience and Education: A Review of Educational Interventions and Approaches Informed by Neuroscience'. Full report and executive summary for the Education Endowment Foundation.

Hutchins, G. and Norris, F.H. 1989, 'Life Change in the Disaster Recovery Period', *Environment and Behavior*, vol. 21, pp. 33–56.

Jaycox, L.H., Cohen, J.A., Mannarino, A.P., Walker, D.W., Langley, A.K., Gegenheimer, K.L., Scott, M. and Schonlau, M., 2010, 'Children's Mental Health Care Following Hurricane Katrina: A Field Trial of Trauma – Focused Psychotherapies', *Journal of Traumatic Stress*, vol. 23, no. 2, pp. 223–231.

Jaycox, L.H., Morse, L.K., Tanielian, T. and Stein, B.D. 2006, 'How Schools can Help Students Recover from Traumatic Experiences: A Tool Kit for Supporting Long-Term Recovery'. Rand Corporation Gulf States Policy Institute, TR-413-RC. Retrieved from www.rand.org/content/dam/rand/pubs/technical_reports/2006/RAND_TR413.pdf.

Jaycox, L.H., Stein, B.D. and Amaya-Jackson, L. 2009, 'School-Based Treatment for Children and Adolescents', in E.B. Foa, T.M. Keane, M.J. Friedman and J.A. Cohen (eds), *Effective Treatments for PTSD: Practice Guidelines from the International Society for Traumatic Stress Studies*, pp. 327–345. Guilford Press, New York, NY.

Kaniasty, K. 2012, 'Predicting Social Psychological Well-Being Following Trauma: The Role of Post-Disaster Social Support', *Psychological Trauma: Theory, Research, Practice, and Policy*, vol. 4, no. 1, pp. 22–33. Available online: http://dx.doi.org/10.1037/a0021412.

Kasapoglu, A., Ecevit, Y. and Ecevit, M. 2004, 'Support Needs of the Survivors of the August 17, 1999 Earthquake in Turkey', *Social Indicators Research*, vol. 66, pp. 229–248.

King, D. and MacGregor, C. 2000, 'Using Social Indicators to Measure Community Vulnerability to Natural Hazards', *Australian Journal of Emergency Management*, vol. 15, no. 3, pp. 52–58.

King, D., Bird, D., Haynes, K., Boon, H., Cottrell, A., Millar, J., Okada, T., Box, P., Keogh, D. and Thomas, M. 2014, 'Voluntary Relocation as an Adaptation Strategy to Extreme Weather Events', *International Journal of Disaster Risk Reduction*, vol. 8, pp. 83–90. ISSN 2212-4209.

LaRose, G. 2006, 'Asian Businesses Drive Eastern New Orleans Recovery'. *New Orleans City Business*, 2 October.

McFarlane, A. 1987a, 'Family Functioning and Overprotection Following a Natural Disaster: The Longitudinal Effects of Post-Traumatic Morbidity', *Australian and New Zealand Journal of Psychiatry*, vol. 21, pp. 210–218.

McFarlane, A.C. 1987b, 'The Relationship Between Patterns of Family Interaction and Psychiatric Disorder in Children', *Australian and New Zealand Journal of Psychiatry*, vol. 21, pp. 383–390. PubMed: 3435378.

Monnier, J. and Hobfoll, S.E. 2000, Conservation of Resources in Individual and Community Reactions to Traumatic Stress', in A. Shalev, R. Yehuda and A.C. McFarlane (eds), *International Handbook of Human Response to Trauma*, pp. 325–336. Kluwer Academic/Plenum Publishers, New York.

Norris, F.H., Baker, C.K., Murphy, A.D. and Kaniasty, K. 2005, 'Social Support Mobilization and Deterioration after Mexico's 1999 Flood: Effects of Context, Gender, and Time', *American Journal of Community Psychology*, vol. 36, nos 1–2, pp. 15–28.

Noffsinger, M.A., Pfefferbaum, B., Pfefferbaum, R.L., Sherrieb, K. and Norris, F.H. 2012, 'The Burden of Disaster: Part I. Challenges and Opportunities Within a Child's Social Ecology', International Journal of Emergency Mental Health, vol. 14, no. 1, pp. 3–13.

Norris, F.H., Friedman, M.J., Watson, P.J., Byrne, C.M., Diaz, E. and Kaniasty, K. 2002, '60,000 Disaster Victims Speak: Part 1. An Empirical Review of the Empirical Literature, 1981–2001', Psychiatry, vol. 65, no. 3, pp. 207–239. PubMed: 12405079.

Norusis, M.J. 2003, SPSS 12.0 Statistical Procedures Companion. Prentice Hall, New Jersey.

Pant, A.T., Kirsch, T.D., Subbarao, I.R., Hsieh, Y.H. and Vu, A. 2008, 'Faith-Based Organizations and Sustainable Sheltering Operations in Mississippi after Hurricane Katrina: Implications for Informal Network Utilization', Prehospital and Disaster Medicine, vol. 23, pp. 48–54. PubMed: 18491661.

Peek, L. 2008, 'Children and Disasters: Understanding Vulnerability, Developing Capacities, and Promoting Resilience. Children, Youth and Environments', vol. 18, no. 1, pp. 1–29.

Pfefferbaum, R.L., Pfefferbaum, B., Jacobs, A.K., Noffsinger, M.A., Sherrieb, K. and Norris, F.H. 2012, 'The Burden of Disaster: Part II. Applying Interventions Across the Child's Social Ecology', International Journal of Emergency Mental Health, vol. 14, no. 3, pp. 175–187.

Pina, A.A., Villalta, I.K., Ortiz, C.D., Gottschall, A.C., Costa, N.M. and Weems, C.F. 2008, 'Social Support, Discrimination, and Coping as Predictors of Posttraumatic Stress Reactions in Youth Survivors of Hurricane Katrina', Journal of Clinical Child and Adolescent Psychology, vol. 37, no. 3, pp. 564–574. PubMed: 18645747.

Prinstein, M.J., La Greca, A.M., Vernberg, E.M. and Silverman, W.K. 1996, 'Children's Coping Assistance: How Parents, Teachers, and Friends Help Children Cope after a Natural Disaster', Journal of Clinical Child Psychology, vol. 25, no. 4, pp. 463–475.

Pynoos, R.S., Goenjian, A. and Steinberg, A.M. 1995, 'Strategies of Disaster Intervention for Children and Adolescents', in Extreme Stress and Communities: Impact and Intervention, pp. 445–471. Springer, Netherlands.

Queensland Government 2009, 'Emergency Services Minister Visits Flooded North West, Queensland Government'. Available online: http://statements.cabinet.qld.gov.au/MMS/StatementDisplaySingle. Accessed 7 September 2010.

Robbins, S. and Lozano, J.A. 2015, 'Homeowners Clean Up in Texas; Death Toll Climbs to 19'. Associated Press, 27 May. Available online: http://hosted2.ap.org/APDEFAUL T/386c25518f464186bf7a2ac026580ce7/Article_2015-05-27-US-Severe%20Weather/id-f48f040e1e1c4761b4c7e04922cba65f, retrieved on 1 June 2015.

Saniotis, A. and Irvine, R. 2010, 'Climate Change and the Possible Health Effects on Older Australians', Australian Journal of Primary Health, vol. 16, pp. 217–220.

Save the Children 2007, 'Legacy of Disasters: The Impact of Climate Change on Children'. Save the Children, London.

Scheeringa, M.S. and Zeanah, C.H. 2008, 'Reconsideration of Harm's Way: Onsets and Comorbidity Patterns of Disorders in Preschool Children and their Caregivers following Hurricane Katrina', Journal of Clinical Child and Adolescent Psychology, vol. 37, no. 3, pp. 508–518. PubMed: 18645742.

Stuber, J., Fairbrother, G., Galea, S., Pfefferbaum, B., Wilson-Genderson, M. and Vlahov, D. 2002, 'Determinants of Counseling for Children in Manhattan after the September 11 Attacks', Psychiatric Services, 53, pp. 815–822.

Towers, B. 2015, 'Children's Knowledge of Bushfire Emergency Response', International Journal of Wildland Fire, vol. 24, pp. 179–189.

Tyler, K. 2006, 'The Impact of Support Received and Support Provision on Changes in Perceived Social Support among Older Adults', *International Journal of Aging and Human Development*, vol. 62, pp. 21–38.

Tyler, K. and Hoyt, D. 2000, 'The Effects of an Acute Stressor on Depressive Symptoms Among Older Adults: The Moderating Effects of Social Support and Age', *Aging*, vol. 22, no. 22, pp. 143–164.

Vigil, J.M. and Geary, D.C. 2008, 'A Preliminary Investigation of Family Coping Styles and Psychological Well-Being among Adolescent Survivors of Hurricane Katrina', *Journal of Family Psychology*, vol. 22, no. 1, p. 176.

Weems, C.R. and Overstreet, S. 2008, 'Child and Adolescent Mental Health Research in the Context of Hurricane Katrina: An Ecological Needs-Based Perspective and Introduction to the Special Section', *Journal of Clinical Child and Adolescent Psychology*, vol. 37, no. 3, pp. 487–494. PubMed: 18645740.

Woods, C., Usher, K., Buettner, P., West, C., Mills, J., Boon, H., Chamberlain-Salaun, J. and Mason, M. 2012, 'Tropical Cyclone Yasi: Preparedness, Loss and Distress'. Report, James Cook University, Queensland, Australia.

6 The mesosystem in disaster resilience

Alison Cottrell

In Bronfenbrenner's person-person-context-time model, what are referred to as 'proximal processes' – or interrelations among the different systems in which individuals operate – are considered important (Bronfenbrenner 2005; Bronfenbrenner and Evans 2000; Bronfenbrenner and Morris 2006; Tudge *et al.* 2009). These proximal processes or interrelationships equate to some extent with notions of social networks and social capital. Just as Bronfenbrenner argued that individuals are influenced by context and relationships, so did later social theorists. Tierney (2008), for instance, refers to structure, process and agency in the context of disasters. Like Bronfenbrenner, Tierney argues that while individuals do have agency, in that they make choices, these choices are influenced by their relationships (processes, networks, mesosystem) with social structures (microsystem, macrosystem and exosystem), and that these relationships and choices will change over time (chronosystem).

This discussion will focus on the mesosystem structures and processes available to support the development of resilience for communities and individuals, and in so doing extends the notion of proximal processes beyond that of the microsystem into the macrosystem and the exosystem. The reason for doing so is because the smaller social units influence and are influenced by the larger social units, even into the international sphere (see Chapter 7). That is, networks are 'nested' with increasing levels of social complexity (Doreian and Stokman 1997; Hawkins and Maurer 2010).

The mesosystem constitutes proximal processes or social networks that have a direct or an indirect impact upon an individual and family or household and those other groups and places in the community to which neighbours, friends and extended family belong. These may consist of actual memberships of groups and organisations, such as recreational clubs, local community groups, religious groups, cultural societies and so on, as well as those places where family members spend a significant amount of time: the workplace; school; child care centres; etc. The broader support structures of this system underpin the resilience of the wider community, which indirectly provides strength to individuals and families who are not direct members.

The mesosystem also constitutes the interconnectedness and the roles of social networks in supporting communities and individuals through the three phases of disaster: preparation and mitigation; the acute or response phase; and post-disaster recovery. The mesosystem can also be extended to include the processes and linkages of the exosystem that support communities and individuals with the goal of developing resilience (Hawkins and Maurer 2010; see also Chapter 7).

To explore mesosystem processes, the four Australian case studies undertaken by Boon *et al.* (2012) and another case study by Cottrell *et al.* (2013) will be used as illustrations. Boon *et al.* (2012) conducted research in the communities of Ingham (flooding) and Innisfail (cyclones) in Queensland and Beechworth (bushfire) and Bendigo (drought) in Victoria. Cottrell *et al.* (2013) reported on the impact of a small 'tornado' in the city of Townsville, Queensland.

Social networks – structures and processes

Social networks are an important part of social capital (Coleman 1988; Portes 1998; Putnam 1993), which is seen to contribute to disaster resilience (Aldrich 2012; Aldrich and Meyer 2015; Boeck *et al.* 2006; Dynes 2005; Haines *et al.* 1996; Hurlbert *et al.* 2000; Nakagawa and Shaw 2004; Paton 2008; Paton and Gow 2008; Tierney 2008). Social capital is one of several capitals available to communities, including natural, financial, human and manufactured (Morse *et al.* 2009). Social capital is seen as a social structural resource. At the micro level, social capital is seen as the resources embedded in networks, which enable actors to acquire more external social resources and help people to obtain information, knowledge and social support.

Networks can also be considered as consisting of individuals, organisations or technologies (often referred to as actors) that form nodes in a network. The relationships between actors are referred to as ties (relations or proximal processes). These nodes and ties make a network, and these networks contribute to building society (Aldrich 2012; Portes 1998; Kirmayer *et al.* 2009; Paton 2008; Paton and Gow 2008; Putnam 1993; Tierney 2013). The main function of networks is to facilitate information flow, and these networks are maintained for purposes other than disasters. There are three main types of networks: bonding; bridging; and linking. Bonding networks are between immediate family, neighbours, close friends, business associates and so on. Bridging networks link different groups within a community, such as groups with different ethnic, geographical and occupation backgrounds but with similar economic status and political influence. The third type is the linking network: the ties between community and people with influence in formal organisations. All three types of network are important for sustaining communities, especially in times of crisis. It is important to recognise that in some cases individuals from bonding and bridging networks may also be part of linking networks (e.g. government or NGO), not simply linked to them, say through service provision. In the post-crisis context especially, bonding networks may well be the first to come into play, followed by bridging and linking networks. Sometimes these networks are described as horizontal (bonding and bridging) and vertical (linking) (Olsson *et al.* 2004; Ryan *et al.* 2008).

Doreian and Stokman suggest that social network structures are easier to describe than their processes. Their definition of social network structures is one of a 'set of social actors with social relations' (Doreian and Stokman 1997: 1); for example, friends (actors) with a relation through friendship, or organisations with the relation of referring clients. Networks can also be nested within other networks. In terms of processes, Doreian and Stokman argue:

> ...we view a social network process as a series of events involving relationships that generate (specific) network structures. More glibly, *network processes are a series of events that create, sustain and dissolve social structures*.
> (Doreian and Stokman 1997: 3, original emphasis)

Aldrich (2012), though, warns us that social capital can be 'Janus-faced', that it can be positive or negative (see also Coleman 1988; Portes 1988). Likewise, Boeck *et al.* (2006) suggest that bonding capital with little bridging or linking capital reduces the resources available to people, and reduces resilience and adaptive capacity. In some cases, strong bonding capital can prevent a move away from a negative situation into a more broadly sanctioned lifestyle. Similarly, subgroups within communities can be in conflict, resulting in difficulties for adapting to new circumstances. Additionally, sometimes networks are not obvious, that is, they may be latent, and only manifest in times of need. When a disaster occurs, there may be a flurry of short-term 'bonding' activity, with a return to pre-event levels after some time. These 'new' networks may be a consequence of the need for new types of links specific to the disaster response and recovery context (Varda *et al.* 2009). There may also be emergent networks that are either temporary or sustainable over time. Romantic notions about communities need to be set aside, but so should notions that (modern or urban) communities are bereft of social relationships. These relationships change over time (Leadbeater 2013; Schoch-Spana *et al.* 2007; Varda *et al.* 2009).

The disaster context provides 'concrete' examples of the networks that exist in a social setting and the proximal processes, to use Bronfenbrenner's terminology, involved with those networks. Bronfenbrenner's theory starts with the individual as the focus, and so this discussion will begin with individuals. In other contexts, a discussion that flows from the broad scope of the exosystem to that of the microsystem would be an equally valid starting point (Varda *et al.* 2009).

It is important to recognise that, like all heuristic devices, these categorisations are not discrete entities. They are also 'nested' with the potential for some networks to cross more than one category. For example, in some small communities, bonding and bridging networks may have high levels of overlap. In other cases, bonding and bridging networks may have strong ties or connections into linked networks (Bronfenbrenner 2005; Doreian and Stokman 1997). These social networks provide an opportunity to integrate the different levels of social structure into a coherent framework (Hawkins and Maurer 2010) Bronfenbrenner's theory allows this integration to be more clearly illustrated.

Bonding networks: families, close friends and neighbours

In the emergency and disaster management context, it is not uncommon for agencies, under the pressure of limited resources, to 'forget' that members of communities do indeed act to remedy their circumstances and help others. Haines *et al.* (1996, 2002) demonstrated that for the context of Hurricane Andrew, individuals with strong ties to others who are similar provided informal social support, which led to better outcomes in terms of their physical and mental health than individuals without those strong ties.

The relations reflected in the processes of the mesosystem, which include the support of family, neighbours and friends, are not only expressed in the form of physical acts of help but also as emotional support. It is necessary to recognise that in the disasters context affected people can be both service seekers and service providers at the same time (Varda *et al.* 2009).

Bonding networks were important to all the case study communities in Beechworth, Bendigo, Ingham and Innisfail:

> ...we had some friends and (friend's) dad and uncle. They were fighting the fire and I was back at the house with the girls filling their fire trucks and making sure everything was right at the house...
>
> (Boon *et al.* 2012: 158)

The support of family, friends and neighbours was important for individuals during preparation for a disaster and during the disaster itself. In the town of Ingham, which was affected by flooding, approximately two-thirds of those surveyed report feeling emotionally prepared for the event. In the other three locations, closer to half felt prepared. In all locations, people reported families as important: Ingham 67 per cent; Innisfail 79 per cent; Beechworth 51 per cent; and Bendigo 54 per cent. Friends were also important: Ingham 69 per cent; Innisfail 74 per cent; Beechworth 46 per cent; and Bendigo 46 per cent. Neighbours helped in all locations, but to varying degrees: Ingham 64 per cent; Innisfail 76 per cent; Beechworth 45 per cent; and Bendigo 39 per cent.

Cottrell *et al.* (2013), reporting on recovery from the Townsville tornado, also identified family, friends and neighbours as important. Participants in the survey reported that immediately after the event they helped themselves (two-thirds), and/or were helped by family (half), friends (40 per cent), and neighbours (30 per cent). The need for help reduced during the few weeks after the event and by that stage help was mainly coming from themselves and their insurance companies. The ways people were helped clearly depended on their circumstances. Most people reported help with cleaning up, while others mentioned child care, food and just checking up. Help in the few weeks after the event mainly concerned continued cleaning up and repairs. Some of the participants in the survey were able to help others as well, primarily with cleaning up. At 18 months following the event, two-thirds of the respondents reported being 'good' (12/19), 'back on track' or 'slowly getting there'. There is no doubt about people's perceptions that family, along with friends or neighbours (meso-system links) played a key role in their recovery from the event.

Examples of Bonding Networks from the Townsville Tornado Study included:

> We stayed at friends and they took care of our children while my wife and I were cleaning our house.

> My friend helped for four consecutive days to clean up the shop and save what could be saved.

> They helped to clean the yard and begin to repair the house.

> Friends checked on us to make sure everything was all right and we stayed with them for few days until the power was back.

> The owner of the house was very efficient and repaired the fence very quickly. We received money for the loss of power.

> My children and grand-children made sure that I was never alone the whole time I did not have power, they helped clean up and gave me food.

> We stayed at friends for few days, they kept our kids while we were dealing with the house with the help of some neighbours.

> The neighbours cleaned my yard because I was overseas during the tornado. My parents called the neighbours to check if everything was in order. The insurance was really bad and refused to be cooperative first.

> My son came to clean up and repair damages.

> Friend and family helped to clean up and made sure we had food.

> Friends and family came to help cleaning up and moving stock.

> The neighbours helped a lot cleaning up debris.

> Cleaning up and thinking about something else.
>
> (Cottrell *et al.* 2013: 42)

Bridging networks

Emotional and physical support by members of the community (bridging capital) are often seen as vital for the recovery of individuals and small towns. Additionally, as suggested by Doreian and Stokman (1997), these actions sustain the bridging networks.

An example of mesosystem interactions supporting community resilience through bridging networks is provided by Chamlee-Wright and Storr (2009), who found that church provision of resources and goods fostered social cooperation and community redevelopment after Hurricane Katrina. In particular, they found that the community surrounding the Mary Queen of Vietnam (MQVN) Catholic Church provided goods and resources to residents in the New Orleans East Vietnamese-American community. This allowed the community to rebuild its identity, overcome coordination difficulties and successfully take political action to protect itself.

In Ingham, where flooding was an issue, strong cohesive social networks ensured help was distributed across the community:

> Personality wise, friendship wise, even people that you've hardly met and talked together, we're closer because we've got things to talk about and a commonality. I think that's made us stronger.
>
> (Boon *et al*. 2012: 158)

The community was viewed by respondents as being very tightly knit through family and friend networks and through local associations that involved many of the residents. Non-governmental organisations and charity groups provided significant counselling and financial support to the community. Special mention by key informants was given to groups such as Lifeline, Red Cross, the Lions Club, St Vincent De Paul Society and the Hinchinbrook Community Support Centre, the local community organisation.

> ... flood time is a really good time for me, it is a very social time, everyone goes around and looks at the water and chats to the neighbours ... it pretty much defines our identity in this town. Anyway it really does. I have never been somewhere that is so frequently flooded, and is so accepting of flooding.
>
> (Boon *et al*. 2012: 164)

> I think having meetings for the whole town in the recovery phase and knowing that everyone can feed into that it just helps. We learn our shortcomings and we know how to improve on those shortcomings for the future instances ... I did notice even among the businesses they were helping each other with staffing if somebody [a shop assistant] couldn't get through to their shop.
>
> (Boon *et al*. 2012: 164)

Local and national businesses (exosystem facilities managed locally) were seen as aware of the community's needs, remaining open and available to supply the community with what they needed even though employees as individuals were also affected by the disaster.

> I guess I spent a lot of time at the local shop. It was still open. It was quite a good outlet because you could still get to talk to other people. I think people congregated at the pub or the shop. I guess it was a bit of a social outlet. Just sharing what was happening in their life at the time.
>
> (Boon *et al.* 2012: 164)

In Bendigo, which experienced drought (Boon *et al.* 2012: 161–162), interviewees described how people adapted to the drought with support from local community organisations, council and state government (exosystem and macrosystem support). The smaller landowners, particularly those with shared interests such as horses, helped each other source fodder and cover the cost of transport. For farmers, there was support from all levels. A livestock feed co-operative

> ... saw it as our job to source fodder for our members.
>
> (Boon *et al.* 2012: 161)

This was part of the group's ethos, that it would support its members through tough times. The cooperative

> ... supported a lot of our commercial farmer members through the drought financially by way of giving them things that they needed and carrying the debt until they could come good.
>
> (Boon *et al.* 2012: 161)

The experience of the cooperative was that not one of its customers failed to pay outstanding debts.

Those individuals, including the elderly, who remained connected to the community and knew others around them, were deemed to have coped better:

> I think [even if you are from a low-income background] but you're still strongly connected, and feel a part of your community, have good strong community networks or engage with community groups. So hence, you'll see that – so you can be low income and old ... huge generalisations here, but you can be an older person on a low income so the pension only, but if you engage with the CWA and the Senior Citizens Hall and you go and play bridge every Wednesday with neighbours and Doris and all that and you've got family and you know the butcher, the baker, the candle-stick maker, you know, you're well placed, your buffeted, your connected, you're not going to be left alone if you're liked ... so you reach out to help people [and] people [will] reach out to help you.
>
> (Boon *et al.* 2012: 169)

Social networks, especially among some ethnic and Indigenous groups, were seen as a strong positive influence and helpful coping mechanism. The

Indigenous community in Innisfail was seen as fairly resilient because its members were less dependent on businesses and farms, and because of family cohesiveness and people's sense of place within the community.

> The indigenous community is a perfect example [of resiliency]: you can be low income but because you're part of a community and you have a place in community – as long as it's a reasonably functioning community which I think it's fair to say, you know – the communities out the back of Tully.... In the scale of things, uh, you know, are still quite a cohesive community there. You had high needs – you had high needs all over the place but often that sort of setting is an example of resiliency, having resilience through social connectedness, and having a place in the world I guess and a place in your community.
>
> (Boon *et al.* 2012: 169)

Bridging networks, in terms of relationships with local schools, local businesses, churches and voluntary agencies, were evident from the Townsville Tornado study:

> They organised transport to the evacuation centre for the families who did not have their own transport means. Qbuild (state government agency) arrived even before we called them, they assessed the damages and needs, and called many trades to put things in order to welcome the children as soon as possible.
>
> The school next door helped as well, providing sandwiches and drinks.
>
> The members of the congregation helped to replace dislodged tiles and removed debris.
>
> Employees helped with the damage in the store, they cleaned up damaged office and building surrounds.
>
> (Cottrell *et al.* 2013: 42)

One local government-funded primary school only had a couple of students who were directly affected by the tornado, and they were helped through the school with donations of school materials from other families. However, another local government-funded primary school played a crucial role in the recovery of children and their families after the tornado event. The school itself suffered damage from the tornado. Several buildings had structural damage, such as a brick wall being down, water and electricity interruption, a part of the roof lifted and windows broken, resulting in minor damage inside the buildings. This situation limited the possibility of opening the school on the day of the tornado. The isolation and small size of the stricken area had several consequences: in particular, the lack of accuracy concerning those affected in the first hours following the event. This resulted in an early misconception that no schools had been affected.

The loss of power and precarious state of the building could have been a reason for the school to close over several days; however, the principal and staff insisted on coming in to clean and keeping the doors open to welcome children who needed shelter. Opening the school had a variety of advantages: first, the children had shelter while parents could deal with the situation; and second, it limited the trauma experienced by the children because they were able to return to 'normal life' as soon as possible. That is why the school opened the following day: a generator had been provided by the energy company, the State Department of Education offered counselling and the children were gathered in the school's two safe buildings.

The role of the staff went beyond cleaning and welcoming the children. On the first day, staff also visited families that were recognised as the most vulnerable, to check if they were fine, assess their needs and organise transportation to the emergency centre and delivery of first necessities. Help and solidarity in the first days also came from the neighbouring Catholic primary school that had not been affected by the tornado. It provided the Vincent School staff with sandwiches and drinks, which helped to maintain a secure and comforting place for the children. The school supported the affected families as much as possible by providing services over the days following the event, such as lunch boxes, access to washing machines and phone-charging facilities.

Because the school had been affected by the tornado, every family was indirectly affected; in addition, around 50 families had more or less serious damage to their properties, and half a dozen families moved because of anxiety and forced relocation.

An episode during art class showed how the actions of the school were important for the well-being of the children after the tornado: when students were asked to draw the meaning of the four pillars of the school (respect, learning, safety and success), many of the children drew the tornado for the safety pillar. This showed that the school represented a secure and safe place for the children and the community.

Help between families was organised to provide transport for children to get to school, as some families could not use their vehicles and buses could not access the area. Collaborative networks already existed between many of the families, as the school community is mostly comprised of extended families and neighbours. Support was needed on various levels, from transport provision to help filling in forms. The tornado revealed that some families did not know where and how to apply for governmental support. Aware of this issue, the school distributed a flyer gathering phone numbers and basic information on how to to get help. In this way, the linking networks were facilitated through bridging networks.

A positive outcome of the tornado was the strengthening of links between the school and families, as it was an opportunity for the school to have a more supportive and community role for the families than during its general education activity. The tornado helped to build a stronger feeling of community within the school.

The local veterinary practice played an important role in caring for animals. The practice normally prepares for the cyclone season by bringing in a generator when a cyclone warning is given. However, as with most residents, the tornado caught the practice unawares. It had no power for 24 hours, but was able to operate in a rudimentary way because the damage to the building was limited. Four staff went around the streets to check on people and collect disoriented animals, and a couple of staff also helped with cutting up fallen trees in the neighbourhood after they had dealt with those on the practice's own property. Many of the animals were clients of the practice and had identification discs so they could easily be placed with their owners. Other people came into the practice to see if their animals had been placed there. The practice ended up with only one cat that had to be sent to the RSPCA. One staff member lost a house, but was rehoused in the area.

Local churches also played a role. One church provided three of the most needy people with AU$1,000 each to assist their recovery, as well as other support. Several other churches also provided support. The organisation to provide this support developed after a previous cyclone (Yasi), when spontaneous help was very evident. Hence, network ties were created in a previous event, maintained at a low level post event and then intensified after the next event.

Social networks are facilitated when there is a sense of community or community spirit. Many interview participants commented not only on the help that was provided by family, friends and neighbours, but also by strangers from within and outside the community. They emphasised that the community 'banded together' and tried hard to look out for each other's interests. There was a common feeling amongst stakeholders that

> there was a real ... quite beautiful community spirit.
>
> (Boon *et al.* 2012: 169)

People checked on and helped each other. Reasons people gave for why they thought they were being helped were normative and ranged from simply 'it is what you do' to reciprocal relationships, good relationships and it is a 'nice thing to do'.

> It is what you do.

> That is what you do.

> It is the way things are, support is normal behaviour as I stayed one week without power, they gave me food.

> My family cares about me and they take care of me as I took care of them all my life.

My son came as soon as he heard about the tornado on the news. He was worried for me.

I have kids so all the family feels concerned. They have to help. The street looked terrible, it was a real disaster, we needed help.

They are good friends and they have kids too so they know that it can be difficult

She is a good friend.

They knew I needed help, it is common sense to help friends.

They are good friends and we have children so we needed a place with power to stay. The owner is a friend of ours.

We have good relationship, during bad times help is needed.

Because they like us and they wanted to help.

My neighbours are really nice and I helped them before.

When extreme events occur, everybody feels the will to help. This is how people like to live in society.

They were shocked too by the tornado. Helping is a nice thing to do. Congregating in my front yard.

There was no power, the employees felt it was the right thing to do.

The members have ownership as church families, they take pride in the facility that had been established over 127 years.

Concerning the staff, they consider the school, the children and the families as part of their community so they had to be there to help each other. They helped cleaning the school just as they would have cleaned their house.

Concerning Qbuild, it is their job and we have a really good relationship with them.

(Cottrell *et al.* 2013: 43)

People gave similar reasons for why they helped others:

We helped our old neighbour to clean up her yard. She is old and incapable of doing it. It is a nice thing to do in such situations.

I helped the real estate agency and the other businesses around.

Neighbours. We helped to clean up, there was nothing else to do as nothing was really wrong in our house.

Neighbours. I helped to clean up their yards and roads, and cut trees.

We helped the neighbouring business. We helped clean up, it was the right thing to do.

I helped the neighbours for shopping. They needed help.

We helped friends who were impacted as well. We cleaned up their yards, cut trees, make sure they had what they needed.

We helped all the families with lunch boxes and giving access to washing machines and electricity to charge phones for the families who lost power. We are a big family.

We helped the people around the church.

We provided food parcel assistance as we do in normal times. It is a biblical mandate, it is part of our call as followers of Christ to help others.

(Cottrell *et al.* 2013: 43)

Linking networks

People are 'linked' to communities outside their routine sphere of influence by media coverage of events, but also by service provision from government and non-government agencies. At an even more abstract level, people become linked to the macrosystem of government agencies, particularly through changes in policy and legislation that affect them.

Schools, churches and voluntary agencies not only provided the linkages between groups (mesosystem) in the local community but they also contributed to linkages (linking networks) with higher levels of those organisations and beyond, to the local community and into government agencies such as local and state government.

In addition to assistance provided in Innisfail by family and community networks of friends, neighbours and co-workers (mesosystem), small local and regional food businesses, restaurants and non-profit community organisations (bridging networks) were all mentioned as contributing food or water to meet immediate basic community needs. Nearly all stakeholders who were interviewed mentioned the distribution of free food cooked by local cafés and sent in by out-of-town restaurants, as well as donated food distributed by the Salvation Army and water distributed first by a bottling manufacturer and later on by the government. A number of

NGOs and local non-profit organisations were also very active in the post-cyclone period and helped the community during recovery with economic and material assistance, as well as counselling services (linking networks). These included the Red Cross, the Seventh Day Adventist Church, St Vincent de Paul and several small local organisations. Smaller community-based organisations helped people with bills, fuel vouchers and advocacy.

In addition to offering material forms of support, some noted that even for those who did not need or want such assistance their presence provided a useful opportunity simply to talk:

> I do remember people coming around and offering to help, the church and the Red Cross and everything were coming around and offering help but yeah I suppose it was available but like people are they go 'nah we are right' but some people just come and had a chat which was good at times.
>
> (Boon et al. 2012: 169)

The rural financial counsellor in Bendigo pointed out that one of the most important programmes for the farming community was 'interest support': it kept banks from foreclosing on properties. The counsellor also talked about the importance of the AU$20,000 grants that were given to irrigation communities:

> The grants in irrigation communities were relatively easy to get but [were] critical to the economic survival of small businesses in the community.
>
> (Boon et al. 2012: 161)

People sought information on how to manage gardens, which species were drought tolerant, how to feed stock, where to access feed and how to manage paddocks. The Department of Sustainability and Environment (DSE) ran 'Smartwater' workshops for gardeners and weed management workshops for landholders, while the Bendigo Equine Industry Cluster ran workshops on how to feed stock in the drought. Some residents grew drought-tolerant plants with support from gardening clubs. According to a health service key informant, women got a great deal of satisfaction out of learning about native plants.

> The group members were mostly women in their 70s. They saw their native gardens as being part of a network that supported the wider environment, created a refuge for native plants and animals. They created a corridor through Bendigo which isn't really recognised.
>
> (Boon et al. 2012: 363)

In 2000, the Victorian Department of Primary Industries hosted a programme called 'Smart Gardens', which provided urban communities with information on water regulations, rain water reuse, using tanks and grey water. The severity of the restrictions had left people stranded and they wanted all the information they could get. As one respondent indicated,

Three hundred people turned up … the department was shell shocked!

(Boon *et al.* 2012: 161)

Phone calls and messages of goodwill from outside the community (the macrosystem) were also greatly appreciated, giving residents a psychological boost and allowing them to counter some of the negative media affecting the region.

> …there were people ringing and checking that Beechworth was okay and that I was okay, and that was very humbling…. It was also a good opportunity for me because [of] being in the Chamber [of Commerce] and the Chamber is very involved in getting the message out to the community [about] Beechworth – to the tourists in Melbourne – so I'm using these networks to say 'Please spread the news that we're okay'.
>
> (Boon *et al.* 2012: 159)

Government-funded activities such as community barbeques, concerts or trips away bring people together, encouraging them to talk and to share an enjoyable experience.

> I went on one of those weekends down to Lorne and it was lovely … it was three hundred women and I enjoyed it very much, and it was very sobering for me because everybody I spoke to had lost their home…
>
> (Boon *et al.* 2012: 159)

Service provision at the macrosystem levels following the most recent 2009 fires was seen as having improved considerably compared to the 2003 fire event. The experience of the 2009 fires and the establishment of the Bushfires Royal Commission resulted in many legislated changes to planning and operations, from CFA to local, state and federal government levels. One example is that the Country Fire Authority realigned its management boundaries to coincide with local government boundaries for smoother operations. The creation of Emergency Management teams, including police and emergency services, local council and state agencies such as the Department of Human Services, meant that responses were now coordinated across agencies, with responsibilities clearly defined. The Bushfire Royal Commission is an example of how the microsystem and macrosystem can interact for change via the process of hearings.

One particular tool that highlighted the influence of macrosystems and exosystems on individual and community resilience was the Vulnerable Persons Register. It provides support for vulnerable people, their carers and families to plan and prepare for fire, and enables a rapid response when emergency action such as evacuation is necessary.

> It's a strategic thing, also if there's a bad weather week they will be contacted by an appropriate person for the council or whatever and say 'Have you enacted your plan?' And if they haven't got a plan I think the program

was to contact the carer or contact the relatives and say 'We haven't got a plan. This is your mum and dad, or whatever, do you think we need something?'

(Boon *et al.* 2012: 159)

Linking networks and relations were fostered by strong, effective leadership within the council and hospital in Ingham, resulting in appropriate help being made available to community members.

The hospital, mayor, council and essential services such as electricity and water were reported as exemplary in their leadership and dedication to supporting the community. Their efforts resulted in there being no reports of undue hardship experienced by community members. These exosystem functions, amenable to intervention and future policy amendments, were essential for the well-being of the individuals in the community.

A lot of the nursing staff stayed here [in the hospital] for ten days ... it was very humbling really because they had families at home under water quite often but they were here with us. It was really strong community commitment.

(Boon *et al.* 2012: 163)

The council here done a mighty job to give a hand in the clean up, to get rid of all the stuff, they did that as hard as they could to repair the roads.

(Boon *et al.* 2012: 164)

Examples of linking networks from the Townsville tornado study included:

The insurance was very helpful and gave money quickly.

The insurance came right away to assess damage.

The insurance company was quite prompt.

The army cleaned up two days.

The department of communities gave cheques of $xxx.

Emergency services helped as well. They closed the area and assessed damage.

(Cottrell *et al.* 2012: 42)

The Combined Churches of Townsville and Service Community Organisations in conjunction with the City Council built on the social capital that had emerged during a previous cyclone, making it longer term. The Combined Churches and Community Organisations registered volunteers (356 volunteers in 2012) to provide longer-term support based on that that which emerged after

Cyclone Yasi. This community support comes in the form of 'N2N' – neighbour to neighbour – where church community members are encouraged to look out for all their neighbours, not only those in their church. The local churches view N2N as having showed effective results after the tornado in March 2012, because the supportive network was already in place.

Near the area most affected by the tornado is the office of Volunteering North Queensland (VNQ), which has a section that deals with convergent volunteering in emergency or disaster situations. VNQ has links with the local Lions Club to register volunteers for emergency situations so they are covered for insurance and can be organised. Through VNQ and Lions, a coffee cart was established near the most affected area to provide food and drinks and to serve as an information centre. VNQ also contributed wherever possible to damage assessments and identifying and providing assistance needed. In addition, as volunteers arrived at the area, including State Emergency Services (SES) and Rural Fire Service (RFS), VNQ was able to identify those tasks to be completed, roster someone to those tasks and then check they were completed.

In Innisfail, the immediate response by the local disaster management group, the army, State Emergency Services and local council was widely viewed by residents as efficient and well coordinated:

> I think [the response] was really well coordinated between the disaster management response group locally, the SES, and the army. I think they worked really well to get everything done.... That side of it I think was handled particularly well, even though there were people complaining, but they would complain no matter what.
>
> (Boon *et al.* 2012: 170)

In general the role of government at all levels in assisting recovery efforts was also viewed positively, including assistance provided to businesses (reportedly AU$10,000) and the injection of cash into the community

> Collectively it was fantastic. Within two months, everything is down and flat, it was tidy and clean. It was amazing the speed they've got the town back to normal. I think it was because the incentives they gave us were spot-on.... But they [the incentives] didn't come until a little bit later and at first people would jump in anyway without incentives. That was a week later when the government gave everyone $1,000. There was no cash around. But ATM didn't work so you couldn't get fuel out because there was no electricity and generators ran out.
>
> (Boon *et al.* 2012: 170)

Besides financial support, psychological services and support were also provided by the state government through the Queensland mental health programme, which was described as helping farmers deal with depression:

We had a lot of growers meetings after the cyclone … and we had people from Centrelink (national government agency) from Queensland Health (state government agency) and they did talks on mental health issues and that side of it … there was people everywhere here and in Tully, Babinda, if you needed help you could go and talk to someone privately and it was a very good response just a month after the cyclone, the first couple of weeks there was probably a gap, after that once people got on the ground here, if you needed somebody they were here.

(Boon *et al.* 2012: 171)

The state government's response phase, which lasted six months, assisted people with accommodation and daily living requirements. Two community recovery mental health teams were then set up to provide extra assistance, in conjunction with various agencies, for another 12 months. A large increase in mental health cases was expected but did not occur; there was a large call for assistance immediately after the cyclone but it soon tapered off.

Immediately after the Townsville tornado event, the police, Ergon Energy and Townsville City Council initiated action. The police acted to close streets and check on people. Ergon Energy acted quickly to restore power where possible, so that most people had power within 24 hours, some within three days and only a few lost power for longer because of more complex situations. Because Townsville is a major centre for Ergon, and its residents were prepared for bad weather conditions, the company was able to act reasonably quickly. Townsville City Council activated its Disaster Management Group, which had been on standby because of warnings provided by the Bureau of Meteorology. The event occurred early on a working day, so by the time the Department of Housing and Public Works opened for work they were aware of the issue and the need to check on their clients. Consequently they were able to act swiftly.

Through the Local Disaster Management Group a recovery centre was established at the local Police and Citizen's Youth Club. Red Cross, Lifeline, St Vincent de Paul and Queensland Health all had a presence at the recovery centre, which remained open for three days. Outreach teams were operating to check on people, and did so for up to 10 days. A hotline operated for 10 days as well, offering counselling services and other support. After that, needs were met through normal services provided by agencies. Several grants were available, including emergency assistance, contents and structural assistance. The Department of Communities, Child Safety and Disability Services identified the key issues as reconnection of essential services (particularly electricity), safety and support for immigrant families, many of whom are refugees. Concerns remain around people moving to remoter suburbs, and the impact on immigrant communities, especially refugees.

Most people reported insurance companies arriving very promptly and dealing with claims promptly and amicably, although there was one business in particular that had ongoing issues. A member of the military also had issues because he was overseas at the time and unable to report the damage quickly.

The Townsville City Council activated a Disaster Recovery Plan, which operated for one year after the tornado and included five community 'fun day' events. These events were held in local parks, the best attended being those held in the park nearest the Vincent State School. Apart from providing positive activities for the community, the events also allowed agencies to advertise their services. Agencies included: Good Beginnings; Save the Children – Deadly Blokes and Kids; Recovery and Resilience Team Queensland Health; Kirwan Fire Station; Defence Force; EMQ; Smith Family; Volunteering North Queensland; and Medicare Locals. In addition, a number of Townsville City Council sections were represented. The council reported a diversity of attendants, including Aboriginal, Torres Strait Islander and immigrant families.

At one of these events three months after the tornado, the Townsville City Council conducted a survey and identified problems, including communication about rubbish collection, charity and financial support, mental health support and the reopening of an occasional child care centre – a council-owned facility that had been damaged. Positive outcomes identified by that survey included community response, community spirit and strength, neighbourhood spirit, police presence and State Emergency Services' door knocking to check on residents.

At the last community event one year after the tornado, a final survey was conducted that found very positive response to the community fun days, with people identifying them as opportunities to link to others in the community and support services that were available.

The case studies show how bonding, bridging and linking networks enmesh to provide a system of support for individuals and communities. Sometimes, though, networks are not available, or 'fail' under the stress of an event.

Fragmentation of networks

Coleman (1988) identified obligations, expectations and trustworthiness of structures as critical to the maintenance of social capital. In the disasters context, these three factors are tested.

In Townsville, the city council identified that there was confusion over the council's role. It appeared that people thought the council should provide all the services they needed. This is not an uncommon issue. In many surveys, people are unclear about agencies' roles.

In the Boon et al. study (2012), two groups identified as failing to cope well after the event were itinerants or 'transients' and 'newcomers'. Transients were seen as less prepared financially or in terms of awareness of cyclone threat, while newcomers were portrayed as lacking the knowledge and experience to know how to prepare for the event, as well as the deep roots in the community that would have enabled them to connect to sources of advice, support and assistance.

The linking networks were found particularly wanting, indicating expectations on the part of the community and a consequent perception of lack of trustworthiness. There were perceptions of mismanagement of relief efforts. The organisation of the response phase was deemed too centralised, and as a result the lack of local knowledge meant that the relief was inefficient; an example of macrosystem functions that should have been devolved to other organisations.

> They [EMQ] had some real challenges. Our eldest daughter was moved over to the SES coordination because she works for the council. It was challenging, logistically. You had non-locals coordinating the distribution of food to areas they didn't understand. What we saw in this flood was [an] every man to himself mentality. I mean we were flying choppers here, when the rain stopped we were taking food out, my husband was flying, and he said he was frustrated in that he did a trip from town to Longpocket carrying dog food and then he would come back to town and he would be given an emergency parcel of medicine to go to a farmer on the same path he had just gone on. For a couple of boxes of milk an EMQ chopper, which costs probably 8 or 9,000 an hour, to drop a little item.
>
> (Boon *et al*. 2012: 164–165)

The distribution of the state relief funds was also deemed to be poorly coordinated, by those in need and by the employees of the government agency.

> …well the way it worked I feel wasn't the best way, because we had so many people sitting in rows of chairs all very traumatised, and the Department of Housing people, the Department of Communities people, and the other people sitting at the tables there at the other end of the high tower and these people they had to gradually, one seat by one seat, move up until they got to the front and they would shepherd them up to see these people to talk about their trauma. It was awful … there was elderly people who couldn't walk and you had to help them move it was just traumatic for them and for myself, and it was hot and it was steamy.
>
> (Boon *et al*. 2012: 164–165)

The financial relief offered by the state and federal governments by way of grants was greatly appreciated. However, in settling claims, insurance companies were regarded as failing to support local businesses. This made financial recovery in the wake of the global financial crisis more difficult for the community. By contrast, non-governmental organisations and charity groups provided significant financial support to local businesses as they bought charity goods from them; this assisted the financial recovery of the community, which enhanced community sustainability.

> It all [post-flood insurance claims and business] went down south … so that the loss of those 20 days … nothing made that up so there was no bounce back no recovery. You don't only lose that … there's the replacement of stuff that gets replaced by insurance companies that goes for about a period of six months … we are not getting that business, that business was going

out of town ... for me and my business when we replaced the fridge we know that fridge was in the house for 16 years so we can't make that again so that's taken a whole slab of business from my business for the next 12 to 18 to 24 months because all this stuff that people get new here it was never supplied through our business it was supplied through Sydney outlets and Brisbane outlets. That will now affect my business for the next 10 years until we get on that rotation again.

(Boon *et al.* 2012: 164–165)

At an individual level (microsystem) networks can fragment because of workload issues. Although the drought in Bendigo had been a focus for collective action in all sorts of ways – gardening groups and neighbours supporting each other – not everyone felt they had become more connected as a result of the drought. There was government and private sector support at the exosystem and macrosystem levels, but less evidence of collective, community resilience. Respondents explained that it was difficult to maintain community groups and networks due to the constant workload at home.

It was difficult to run meetings because people wouldn't come on watering night, or they would have to leave early to get home to water, which was affecting people's lives and careers. How those watering restrictions ran our lives!

(Boon *et al.* 2012: 363)

The nature of the drought, grinding on from year to year made it difficult to maintain community support networks and consistent services from government. For example, during the drought years after 2000, the number of rural counsellors in the region increased from three to eight. Because the drought went on for so long, government funding had a stop-start effect on employment, resulting in a high level of turnover as contracts ran out and counsellors moved on. The necessity of building trust within the community was continually being compromised. Smaller landholders in particular appeared to fall through the government support net, being ineligible for financial assistance and rarely seeking counselling. The council officer responsible for drought relief said,

I didn't come across these people at work, probably because they're not networked in as much. I don't think they came in to counselling and we didn't go out to them.

(Boon *et al.* 2012: 162)

Coleman (1988) indicated that the operation of some networks can interfere with the operation of others. The kinds (e.g. economic, material, medical or health), extent and timing of assistance provided by local and regional non-government and private bodies and state and federal government agencies were critical to both individual and community for post-cyclone resilience, but also created a dependency that inhibited the development of resiliency.

A concern about government assistance was raised by a couple of the interview participants, who felt that a major downside was that assistance was provided to the Innisfail community by all levels of government and a range of non-government organisations with the result that the community's resilience was eroded. They argued that people now expected financial assistance following a major disaster, and were unwilling to help themselves. Some said that many people displayed a lack of integrity and self-sufficiency in the aftermath of the event.

> I think the concern at the moment is mostly that there was considerable assistance afterwards and there's a bit of an expectation now that, assistance will be there for any event and we found that in the floods because we have annual flooding every year and with the following floods that occurred people were starting to take white goods down into the water instead of putting them up because they think they might get a new washing machine or whatever and they were starting to ring up before that was even announced 'what's the number to get the money?' So it's set a precedent now that we have to reverse.
>
> (Boon et al. 2012: 171)

This dilemma of conflict with government provision of services and 'self-sufficiency' has led to notions of resilience being institutionalised into government policy (Council of Australian Governments 2011).

The fragmentation of networks around unrealistic expectations arises from poor communication, especially from the exosystem and macrosystem to the microsystem.

Integration of networks

Communications are essential to networks, particularly in the disaster context (Varda et al. 2009). The Boon et al. study (2012: 205) indicates clearly just how the different forms of networks can contribute differently to information sources in communities, especially in the disasters context. Analyses showed that communications at the different sites were significantly different.

For example, in Ingham the sources of information ranked from friends or family (80 per cent), radio or television (80 per cent), neighbours (78 per cent), websites (71 per cent) local council (55 per cent), mobile phone (44 per cent), State Emergency Services (43 per cent) to state government agencies (36 per cent).

In Innisfail, in rank order, it was radio and television (79 per cent), friends or family (70 per cent), State Emergency Services (54 per cent) neighbours (51 per cent), local council (50 per cent), state government agencies (48 per cent), websites (37 per cent) and mobile phone (30 per cent).

In Beechworth, the order was radio and television (86 per cent), neighbours (64 per cent), family and friends (62 per cent), CFA (60 per cent), websites (34 per cent), local council (26 per cent), state government agencies 23 per cent and mobile phone (21 per cent).

In Bendigo, radio and television were most important (71 per cent), then friends and family (58 per cent), neighbours (55 per cent), local council (45 per cent), websites (42 per cent), state government agencies (41 per cent), the Country Fire Authority (27 per cent) and mobile phone (9 per cent).

These figures indicate the variety of information sources that people use. These sources of information span all levels of the system from microsystem to exosystem. The dominant forms in each community suit the availability to the community as well as the type of event. Bendigo's event was a 'slow onset' one and showed a lower level of engagement with information seeking generally.

Conclusion

Social networks contribute to disaster recovery in a variety of ways. First, family, friends and neighbours (bonding networks) are important for basic support in terms of having somewhere to stay should the need arise, emotional support, cleaning up and food. In the immediate recovery phase, local organisations – in the form of support agencies, churches, schools and businesses (bridging networks) – are also important for providing people with support, including cleaning up, food, finances and counselling. Larger organisations, such as large NGOs and government agencies (linking networks), are also critical in terms of providing mechanisms for accessing financial and counselling support in particular.

These networks reflect the level of social capital embedded in the community through values entrenched in the community agencies and government. It is clear that helping behaviour is a broader cultural value that is acted upon during disasters without prompting by others. Additionally, the existence of government and agency policies that not only espouse support for communities but also provide the mechanisms for that support to eventuate are indicative of social capital. The disaster management arrangements that relate to response and recovery are clearly part of that social capital. Bronfenbrenner's theory provides a clear illustration of how the different levels of social scale interact through the mesosystem (proximal processes/networks) to support individuals.

References

Aldrich, D.P. 2012 *Building Resilience: Social Capital in Post-Disaster Recovery.* The University of Chicago Press, Chicago.

Aldrich, D.P. and Meyer, M.A. 2015 'Social Capital and Community Resilience', *American Behavioral Scientist*, vol. 59, no. 2, pp. 254–269.

Boeck, T., Fleming, J. and Kemshall, H. 2006 'The Context of Risk Decisions: Does Social Capital Make a Difference?' *Forum Qualitative Sozialforschung/Forum: Qualitative Social Research*, vol. 7, no. 1, art. 17, January. Available online: http://nbn-resolving.de/urn:nbn:de:0114-fqs0601170 last accessed 28/8/12.

Boon, H.J., Millar, J., Lake, D., Cottrell, A. and King D. 2012 *Recovery from Disaster: Resilience, Adaptability and Perceptions of Climate Change*. National Climate Change Adaptation Facility, Queensland (Publication Number 26/12, ISBN: 978-1-921609-63-3).

Brofenbrenner, U. 2005 *Making Human Beings Human: Bioecological Perspectives on Human Development*. Harvard University Press, Cambridge, MA.

Bronfenbrenner, U. and Evans, G.W. 2000, 'Developmental Science in the 21st Century: Emerging Theoretical Models, Research Designs, and Empirical Findings', *Social Development*, vol. 9, pp. 115–125.

Bronfenbrenner, U. and Morris, P.A. 1998, The Ecology of Developmental Processes', in Lerner, R.M. (ed.), *Handbook of Child Psychology, Volume 1* (5th edn), pp. 993–1028. Wiley, New York.

Chamlee-Wright, E. and Storr, V.H. 2009, ' "There's No Place Like New Orleans": Sense of Place and Community Recovery in the Ninth Ward after Hurricane Katrina', *Journal of Urban Affairs*, vol. 30, pp. 615–634.

Coleman, J.S. 1988 'Social Capital in the Creation of Human Capital.' *American Journal of Sociology*, vol. 94, supplement, pp. S95–S120.

Cottrell, A., Vachette, A. and King, D. 2013 'Community Preparedness, Recovery and Resilience: The Townsville Tornado of March 2012'. Report Prepared for Department of Community Safety, Centre for Disaster Studies, James Cook University, Townsville, p. 88.

Council of Australian Governments 2011 'National Strategy for Disaster Resilience'. Australian Government, Canberra.

Doreian, P. and Stokman, F.N. 1997 'The Dynamics and Evolution of Social Networks', Chapter 1 in P. Doreian and F.N. Stokman (eds) *Evolution of Social Networks*, pp. 1–17. Gordon and Breach, New York.

Dynes, R.R. 2005 'Community Social Capital as the Primary Basis for Resilience'. Preliminary Paper no. 344, University of Delaware, Disaster Research Center, Newark, NJ.

Haines, V., Hurlbert, J. and Beggs, J. 1996, 'Exploring the Determinants of Support Provision: Provider Characteristics, Personal Networks, Community Contexts, and Support Following Life Events', *Journal of Health and Social Behavior*, vol. 37, no. 3, pp. 252–264.

Haines, V.A., Beggs, J.J. and Hurlbert, J. 2002, 'Exploring the Structural Contexts of the Support Process: Social Networks, Social Statuses, Social Support, and Psychological Distress', *Advances in Medical Sociology*, vol. 8, no. 2, pp. 269–292.

Hawkins, R.L. and Maurer, K. 2010, 'Bonding, Bridging and Linking: How Social Capital Operated in New Orleans following Hurricane Katrina', *British Journal of Social Work*, vol. 40, pp. 1777–1793.

Hurlbert, J., Haines, V. and Beggs, J. 2000, 'Core Networks and Tie Activation: What Kinds of Routine Networks Allocate Resources in Nonroutine Situations?' *American Sociological Review*, vol. 65, no. 4, pp. 598–618.

Kirmayer, K.L., Whitley, R., Dandeneau, S.F. and Isaac, C. 2009 'Community Resilience: Models, Metaphors and Measures', *Journal of Aboriginal Health*, November, pp. 62–117.

Leadbeater, A. 2013 'Community Leadership in Disaster Recovery: A Case Study', *Australian Journal of Emergency Management*, vol. 28, no. 3, pp. 41–47.

Morse, S., McNamara, N. and Acholo, M. 2009 'Sustainable Livelihood Approach: A critical analysis of theory and practice'. Geographical Paper no. 189, University of Reading, Reading.

Nakagawa, Y. and Shaw, R. 2004 'Social Capital a Missing Link to Disaster Recovery', *International Journal of Mass Emergencies and Disasters*, vol. 22, no. 1, pp. 5–34.

Olsson, P., Folke, C. and Berkes, F. 2004, 'Adaptive Comanagement for Building Resilience in Social-Ecological Systems', *Environmental Management*, vol. 34, no. 1, pp. 75–90.

Paton, D. 2008, 'Community Resilience: Integrating Individual, Community and Society Perspectives', in K. Gow and D. Paton (eds) *Phoenix of Natural Disasters: Community Resilience*, pp. 13–31. Nova, New York.

Paton, D. and Gow, K. 2008, 'Rising from the Ashes: Empowering the Phoenix' in K. Gow and D. Paton (eds) *Phoenix of Natural Disasters: Community Resilience*, pp. 1–9. Nova, New York.

Portes, A. 1998, 'Social Capital: Its Origins and Applications in Modern Sociology', *Annual Review of Sociology*, vol. 24, pp. 1–24.

Putnam, R. 1993, *Making Democracy Work: Civic Traditions in Modern Italy*. Princeton University Press, Princeton.

Ryan, L., Sales, R., Tiliki, M. and Siara, B. 2008, 'Social Networks, Social Support and Social Capital: The Experiences of Recent Polich Migrants in London', *Sociology*, vol. 42, no. 4, pp. 672–690.

Schoch-Spana, M., Franco, C., Nuzzo, J.B. and Usenza, C. 2007, 'Community Engagement: Leadership Tool for Catastrophic Health Events', *Biosecurity and Bioterrorism: Biodefense Strategy, Practice and Science*, vol. 5, no. 1, pp. 8–25.

Tierney, K. 2013, '"Only connect!" Social Capital, Resilience and Recovery', *Risk, Hazards and Crisis in Public Policy*, vol. 4, no. 1, pp. 1–5.

Tierney, K. 2008, 'Structure and Process in the Study of Resilience'. Fourteenth World Conference on Earthquake Engineering, 12–17 October, Beijing, China, pp. 8.

Tudge, J.R.H., Mokrva, I., Hatfield, B.E. and Karnik, R.B. 2009, 'Uses and Misuses of Bronfenbrenner's Bioecological Theory of Human Development', *Journal of Family Theory and Review*, vol. 1, pp. 198–210.

Varda, D.M., Forgette, R., Banks, D. and Contractor, N. 2009, 'Social Network Methodology in the Study of Disasters: Issues and Insights Prompted by Post-Katrina Research', *Population Research Policy Review*, vol. 28, pp. 11–29.

7 The exosystem and the community in disaster resilience

David King

Bronfenbrenner's model defined the exosystem as one or more settings in the community that do not directly involve the developing person (Bronfenbrenner 1993) – specifically the model defined, for the individual child, the parents' workplace, social networks of the family and the neighbourhood or community. These are, therefore, things that take place outside the individual's personality, family or household. In examining community resilience and adaptive capacity the focus is on the individual and the household and the immediate community. Some elements of the community itself are theoretically part of the exosystem, but the idea of linkages between two or more settings places the exosystem in an external relationship to person, household or community.

The exosystem consists of those community entities and organisations that support the individual, the family and whole communities. These comprise organisations as well as infrastructure: the facilities and operations provided by institutions and NGOs such as hospitals, defence forces, emergency responders, churches and community groups, councils, educational institutions, transport infrastructure and so on. This chapter will examine different types of organisations, the ways in which they interact with individuals and communities, the sorts of services, support and infrastructure they provide and the part they play in enhancing resilience, response in times of crisis and recovery following a disaster.

This chapter draws on illustrations through the four Australian case studies of Bendigo, Beechworth, Ingham and Innisfail, where resilience was enhanced by adaptability, which is an individual-level variable, and predicted by a sense of place, a microsystem-level variable, which in turn was supported by microsystem support from family and friends. All these links showed the importance of mesosystem networks in these feedback loops, as well as positive exosystem experiences, including communications from media and microsystem connections (Boon *et al.* 2012).

The exosystem includes: other people and places; other communities, such as the workplace; extended family and the broader community; and formal and informal organisations. An individual, family, household or community that is not resilient, or is dysfunctional, will be less able to utilise the services of organisations and institutions. Adaptation and resilience are enhanced through diversification, especially in the realm of economic opportunities. Thus, larger communities and settlements inherently possess a greater range of resources and diversity of organisations and institutions.

The exosystem thus consists of entities and organisations that may be accessed by individuals, the family and community. This viewpoint may suggest that exosystem organisations are static, present and functioning, waiting to be called upon by the individual or the community. There is also the issue of the resilience of the organisations themselves. Bronfenbrenner's theory assumes that the exosystem comprises organisations that contribute to community resilience, but organisations may themselves be dysfunctional and lacking in resilience. This may be a consequence of lack of governance or of disconnection between levels of government, institutions and the community. The community may be inherently more resilient than that some of the organisations that service and support it. In relation to development studies, this is the basis of Migdal's 'weak state, strong society' concept, a situation common in the developing world (Migdal 1988).

The case studies of resilience carried out in Bendigo, Beechworth, Ingham and Innisfail drew exosystem informants from business, community groups, local government, emergency management organisations, local medical organisations, real estate companies, NGOs and churches. Research questions relating to the exosystem covered teams of local community groups, emergency management, gas supply, soil erosion, water supply and quality, weed problems, internet, mobile phone access, livestock and crop loss, insurance and neighbourhood and local government counsel preparation (Boon *et al.* 2012).

Organisations and all of their roles, linkages and memberships are clearly a core part of what constitutes the exosystem and its effectiveness. This chapter explores roles and issues around the diversity of exosystem organisations, but first examines the exosystem's relationship to resilience, structures and infrastructure, communication and information and social capital.

The exosystem's relationship to resilience

The exosystem comprises external variables: physical, psychological, social and economic resources that exist within or are available to a community (Berkes 2007; Klein *et al.* 2003; Mowbray *et al.* 2007; Norris *et al.* 2008; Paton 2006). Examples of such support include health providers, emergency management services or local government management of resources and recovery processes. 'At the level of community, strong social networks, accurate and timely communications, economic, social and infrastructure resources as well as effective governance would appear to be implicated in promoting resilience' (Boon *et al.* 2012: 35).

Smith (2010) similarly reported a case study in New Zealand, showing that community resilience is affected by proactive planning and rapid execution of a city council community recovery plan. This report noted that the case study highlighted a common reality that planning for disaster recovery occurs after a disaster strikes, and further emphasised the need to explain more effectively the value of pre-event planning for post-disaster recovery to local officials (including land use planners), state and national agencies, professional associations, non-profits and the private sector (including the insurance industry) (Smith 2010; Boon et al. 2012: 39).

Cutter et al. (2008) used a theoretical model (DROP: disaster resilience of place) to select indicators to measure community resilience. These indicators were based on different types of resilience that contributed to overall community resilience and required different forms of measurement. The types of resilience that Cutter et al. (2008) proposed would act together to produce a resilient community of place were: ecological (e.g. biodiversity, governance and management plans); social (e.g. communications, risk awareness and preparedness, disaster plans, the purchase of insurance – some of these depend on the demographics of the community); economic (e.g. measures of property loss and the effects of business disruption post event); organisational, including institutions and organisations (e.g. assessments of the physical properties of the organisations such as number of members, communications technology, number of emergency assets (e.g. vehicles, hospital beds) and measures of organisational response to disasters such as leadership); infrastructure (e.g. physical systems themselves such as the number of pipelines, exit and delivery road miles); and community competence (e.g. local understanding of risk, counselling services, mental health, quality of life and emotional health) (Boon et al. 2012).

Community economic resilience and resources can help support individuals' resilience (mental health, quality of life perceptions and collective self-efficacy), but individual resilience alone is not sufficient to promote community resilience if the infrastructures, governance and economic underpinning of communities are not present.

There is some overlap between mesosystem and exosystem, where community networks interlink and are part of one system while drawing from the other. For each of the resilience-building indicators listed above, there is agreement across places. Each place had experienced a quite different disaster:

Table 7.1 The four case studies from Victoria and Queensland defined variables that support resilience

Exosystem/mesosystem variable	Beechworth	Bendigo	Ingham	Innisfail
Social networks	✓	✗	✓	✓
Leadership	✓	✗	✓	✓
Communications	✓	✗	✓	✓
Financial assistance	✓	✓	✓	✓
Future preparedness	✓	✓	✓	✓
Community spirit	✓	✗	✓	✓
Volunteers	✓	✗	✓	✓
Council coordination	✗	✓	✓	✗

Source: Boon et al. 2013: 172.

bushfire/wildfire in Beechworth; long-term drought in Bendigo; recurrent as well as specific flood events in Ingham; while Innisfail had experienced two severe tropical cyclones five years apart. These variations in experience are important in terms of defining the needs and support that different communities require from supporting organisations.

Infrastructure and protective structures

Structures – buildings and related spaces – contain the activities of organisations that comprise the exosystem and provide services, community spaces, activities and social interaction. Structures are built or funded by the organisations that occupy them or by government, developers and the private enterprise construction industry. Infrastructure is also constructed and funded by a range of organisations to provide linkages, communications, access, essential services and protection. Some structures and infrastructure are built specifically to protect people and communities against natural hazards. These include shelters, refuges and emergency housing, as well as structures such as tsunami barriers, seawalls, river levees, drainage channels, flood storage and dams. Most infrastructure is provided for routine needs but becomes a critical facility during a disaster, when its functioning capacity may be put under stress, and even a lifeline (e.g. hospitals, sewerage systems, transportation evacuation routes, power).

Transportation access for facilities in the case of an emergency or disaster powerfully influences the capacity for response and recovery. Issues of access and remoteness are a constraint on service provision and economic development during normal times, but place severe constraints on community resilience during and after a disaster. Roads are cut or blocked and power lines collapse, and without power water and sewage cannot be moved.

Protection measures such as levees and dams provide people with a physical security and give politicians a solid measure to suggest that something tangible has been done to mitigate natural hazards. Unless funds continue to be spent on the maintenance of protective measures they decay over time. Lack of maintenance of flood control infrastructure puts communities at risk of catastrophe while providing people with a false sense of security. The failure of levees during the 1993 Mississippi floods severely damaged communities, such that there followed a period of reduced population growth on the floodplain, but growth accelerated a decade later. Like many other natural hazard experiences, flood event experience decays over time (Collenteur *et al.* 2015). Surveys of planners in Queensland at the time of catastrophic flood events in 2011 found a lack of consensus in relation to the usefulness or desirability of protective measures, especially levees (King *et al.* 2013). Just as natural levees are impermanent features in the landscape, engineered constructions only have a limited life span. The problem remains of passive communities developing a dependence on organisations, especially government, to construct protective measures.

There have been many instances of community response to hazard threats in raising houses and building local dykes. Equally, though there is often a lack of coordination between communities and organisations (Marfai *et al.* 2015). Mitigation measures that involve and strengthen the resilience of households include flood proofing of non-residential buildings, elevation of residential buildings, education programmes and the relocation of buildings and infrastructure. Respondents in Queensland case studies following flood and cyclone reported carrying out preparation of business equipment and plans (e.g. generators, back-up options) and expressed a dependence on infrastructure following cyclone Larry.

> [It is hard to get people to realise] community members as well as agencies to come to terms with that stuff can't be … yeah, you can't snap your fingers and have it appear, particularly your transport connections are strained. It took 48 hrs or whatever to get the road open. There's a tiny little runway there that came down – has limited capacity in terms of the planes and set-down there … I guess there was a large number of people who were very dependent on relief very early in the piece.
>
> (Boon *et al.* 2012, IKI2, 168)

At state or provincial government and local council levels many countries have developed floodplain management plans. These involve local government natural resource managers and land use planners in a variety of roles to tackle disaster risk reduction, communication, relocation and climate change adaptation. 'The challenge is to develop a cooperative hazards governance approach that is founded on coordinated policies, laws and institutions, cooperative professional practice and collaborative communities' (Glavovic *et al.* 2010: 679). Glavovic *et al.* (2010) also stress the planning legacy issue and prevention measures in poorly sited settlements, and identify an extensive range of organisations impacting on land use planning and its capacity to reduce risk.

Exosystem: essential services and insurance payments

Essential services are a combination of the lifelines provided by critical infrastructure and the goods and services that constitute day-to-day living, as well as additional services that are part of response and recovery. Heavy machinery and equipment are essential in the initial response period, but as additional equipment must come in from outside the disaster-impacted region there is also reliance on access provided by roads, airports and wharves.

A study in Cairns used cost benefit analysis of willingness to pay to assess the prioritisation of essential goods and service availability following a natural disaster. For Cairns residents, the most likely disaster is a tropical cyclone, for which there are good warnings and a period of time during which people can prepare for the impact. There is also a beginning-of-season campaign to raise preparation awareness among residents, businesses, government, NGOs and suppliers of essential services. The cost benefit analysis approach showed the overwhelming importance of reconnection of electricity and sewerage, well ahead of all other things including fresh food resupply (Dobes *et al.* 2015).

Our case study research in Bendigo, Beechworth, Ingham and Innisfail also assessed the relative importance of the exosystem macro-scale variables in the recovery process at each site. Residents were asked if essential services were disrupted and if insurance payments were delayed. The question about gas supply was substituted by soil erosion for Bendigo residents, where this was a local drought issue. Bendigo residents reported a high level of soil erosion, which caused unavoidable economic stress. However, following the cyclone in Innisfail, respondents experienced the most significant impact upon essential services (water supply problems, electricity supply, mobile phone problems and delays of insurance claim payments). These results are consistent with reports showing that Cyclone Larry resulted in more extensive negative impacts overall than the other disaster events (Boon *et al.* 2012).

Other variables impacting the communities, such as transport, food shortages and alternative accommodation availability, showed the importance of infrastructure to support the response and recovery phases of a disaster. Infrastructure damage, evident in flooding of essential transport systems, resulted in blocking Ingham's access to other towns. This led to the residents suffering lengthy food shortages and mail disruptions, though overall Innisfail residents experienced the greatest food shortages and the greatest dearth of alternative accommodation availability during the recovery stage (Boon *et al.* 2012).

Respondents also described a skew in relief and insurance that constrained recovery in removing immediate benefits from the community.

> It all [post-flood insurance claims and business] went down south … so that the loss of those 20 days … nothing made that up so there was no bounce back no recovery. You don't only lose that … there's the replacement of stuff that gets replaced by insurance companies that goes for about a period of six months … we are not getting that business, that business was going out of town … for me and my business when we replaced the fridge we know that fridge was in the house for 16 years so we can't make that again so that's taken a whole slab of business from my business for the next 12 to 18 to 24 months because all this stuff that people get new here it was never supplied through our business it was supplied through Sydney outlets and Brisbane outlets. That will now affect my business for the next ten years until we get on that rotation again.
>
> (Boon *et al.* 2012: IFG7, 165)

Communication and information

Good communication, especially of warnings for hazard preparation along with hazard information and education, enhance the resilience of individuals, families and communities. A significant amount of education and preparedness takes place within the family and community through interpersonal relationships and networks. People have the greatest trust for information that comes from people they know. This network of personal relationships is enormously expanded by social media, thereby increasing the range and quantity of information available. However, social media and all of its associated information technology is a part of the infrastructure of communication and information technology, primarily a tool for the exchange and passage of messages that emanate from outside the household and community and are thus part of the exosystem.

A study carried out by Campbell *et al.* (2006) to examine post-event community resilience ranked and compared the risks posed by hurricanes to the coastal towns of Rhode Island, USA, from an evacuation and engineering perspective. The study concluded that resilience was linked to the material and conceptual resources available within reach of the community (Boon *et al.* 2012: 42). Communications and early warning systems have land use planning implications. Nirupama and colleagues have shown how rapid urbanisation and a tourism boom contributed to impacts of floods and landslides (Nirupama *et al.* 2015). Hazard risk evolves with new developments, where government and especially planners will have initial knowledge of increased risk and thereby the responsibility to communicate that risk, as well as practise mitigation of the hazard impact.

Kapucu (2008) conducted a multi-method study that included a survey sent to emergency managers to assess how the experience of four hurricanes in Florida affected community preparedness. They did this by examining how effectiveness in coordinating community disaster response efforts affects future public preparedness. Their findings suggest that pre-season planning by local emergency managers, open and effective communication between emergency managers and elected officials, and the use of appropriate technology to provide communication during the response phase all had a significant impact on community responses. Thus individuals' exosystem organisation and coordination perceptions had an effect on preparedness, which in turn translated into a higher likelihood of community resilience (Boon *et al.* 2012: 43).

Risk communication builds on social capital as a means to achieve community resilience. Hoppner *et al.* (2012) argue that social capacity is multi-faceted and 'we suggest subdividing the concept further into four key elements: knowledge capacities, attitudinal/motivational capacities, social/organisational capacities and emotional/psychological capacities' (Hoppner *et al.* 2012: 1756). 'Knowledge capacities' involves

> Knowledge about the hazard and the risk, Knowledge about how to prepare for, cope with and recover from hazardous events, Knowledge about other actors involved in the handling of hazards, Knowledge of formal institutions such as legal frameworks and laws, and Knowledge about values, norms and beliefs of different actors.
>
> (Hoppner *et al.* 2012: 1756)

'Social/organisational capacities' includes 'Communication skills and ability to establish and maintain trustful relationships, organisation skills, and networking and cooperation abilities' (Hoppner *et al.* 2012: 1756).

Social capital

Aldrich and Meyer argue that there is overemphasis on physical infrastruc-ture, whereas it is social infrastructure that builds community resilience. 'Informal ties, particularly neighbours, regularly serve as actual first respond-ers' (Aldrich and Meyer 2015: 256). Social capital is core to community resilience, but contains networks and community organisations that build trust. Social capital depends upon involvement in community organisations, i.e. 'bridging social capital'. This enables access to resources and knowledge. The report states that people who were members of organisations received more support after disasters. 'Number of non-governmental organizations, clubs, and social groups have also been shown to positively correlate with post-disaster population recovery' (Aldrich and Meyer 2015: 260). Three mechanisms to develop social capital all work through organisations: time banking, which rewards volunteerism; social events, which bring people together; and settlement planning and design, which create places and spaces of interaction (this is a priority in urban design anyway) (Aldrich and Meyer 2015).

Pyles and Cross (2008) surveyed the perceptions of residents in a primarily lower socio-economic-status African American neighbourhood of New Orleans post Katrina, to explore the role of social capital, particularly civic engagement and social trust, in community resilience and revitalisation efforts ($n = 153$). Findings revealed high levels of participation in neighbourhood cultural, recovery and political activities were linked to ratings of happiness, older age and higher incomes (Pyles and Cross 2008: 43).

People respond according to social norms. Communities with social problems and low trust perform more poorly during disaster, i.e. there are more deaths. Political influence by the ruling party means better infrastructure for supportive areas, i.e. seawalls, levees and tsunami infrastructure. Additionally, social capital can be created through policy intervention, such as access to services, and NGO roles in building social cohesion (Aldrich 2015).

A simulated earthquake study in New Zealand found that 'almost half (46%) of the population lacked the recommended basic food, water and medical resources to survive for 3 days and that this increased to almost all (90%) of the population after 7 days' (Thomas and Mora 2014: 486). This scenario prompts relief interventions from authorities to balance shortfall, but interestingly the scenario study showed that communal sharing and support emerged as resources diminished. The researchers consequently urged organisations to encourage collaborative approaches (Thomas and Mora 2014).

Social capital is collaborative in nature. After floods wrought havoc in Ingham, North Queensland, respondents reported the need for social interaction and mutual comfort.

> I guess I spent a lot of time at the local shop. It was still open. It was quite a good outlet because you could still get to talk to other people. I think

people congregated at the pub (at Lucinda) or the shop. I guess it was a bit of a social outlet. Just sharing what was happening in their life at the time.

(Boon et al. 2013: IFG2, 164)

Connection to networks and organisations in the community supported people in dealing with the disaster and beginning the process of recovery.

I think [even if you are from a low income background] but you're still strongly connected, and feel a part of your community, have good strong community networks or engage with community groups. So hence, you'll see that – so you can be low income and old … huge generalisations here, but you can be an older person on a low income so the pension only, but if you engage with the CWA and the Senior Citizens Hall and you go and play bridge every Wednesday with neighbours and Doris and all that and you've got family and you know the butcher, the baker, the candle-stick maker, you know, you're well placed, your buffeted, your connected, you're not going to be left alone if you're liked … so you reach out to help people [and] people [will] reach out to help you.

(Boon et al. 2012 : ISK11, 169)

However, social capital cannot be assumed as a given community strength onto which to build resilience. The Vietnamese government has taken the threat from both natural disasters and climate change to develop policies to enhance adaptation and resilience building. However, the experience of Vietnam illustrates a broad global problem: the limitations of cultural transferability. Governments and management make generic statements out of the context of local and cultural realities. Furthermore, organisational and institutional theory argues that 'organisations have to respond to the demands and expectations of different stakeholder groups in order to maintain legitimacy and assure their own survival' (Garschagen 2013: 40);

organisations incorporate resilience elements and terminology in a fairly shallow way which is nevertheless sufficient to satisfy the expectations of the resilience oriented institutional environment. However, the actual structures and procedures of these organisations are barely changed – even though resilience theory would ultimately require significant changes – in order to ensure legitimacy from the Vietnamese bureaucratic institutional environment.

(Garschagen 2013: 41)

Loss of social capital

While social capital supports community structures and features that enhance resilience, the loss of social capital diminishes resilience and increases vulnerability. Community resilience is overlain upon pre-existing vulnerabilities, with hazard risk being especially significant. A community also has powerful socio-economic and demographic vulnerability characteristics that affect its members' capacity to draw benefits from exosystem organisations. Social capital is unequally distributed, among social classes, for example (Murphy 2007: 298). Socio-economic vulnerability reduces social capital. For example, the four towns studied in Queensland and Victoria were all rural settlements, with small populations, experiencing degrees of remoteness as well as issues of rural decline and economic pressures. These community problems were exacerbated by natural disasters.

Demographic indicators that were derived from the 2011 Australian census showed significant losses of younger people from the communities, as well as mean household incomes and educational levels that were below the national average. Characteristics such as these influence other variables, with internet access below 50 per cent in Ingham and Innisfail, although over 60 per cent in Bendigo and Beechworth. The corollary of this is inevitable lower interaction with social media and information technology. The number of businesses in these case study towns were either static or declining in North Queensland, and increasing moderately in the Victorian towns. The standard of living was decreasing in all of the case study places, in terms of the growth in net income relative to increase in rent and mortgage payments. Small and rural towns are in greater danger of loss of social capital, as populations age or decline and services that are part of the exosystem are reduced.

Exosystem: connectedness and sense of place

Sense of place, community and the connected nature of networks are important elements of resilience. The Queensland and Victorian resilience case studies examined these aspects. We asked respondents to rate their sense of connectedness and sense of place, both important variables in supporting community resilience. While Innisfail respondents were the least happy with their community (five years after the event), Bendigo respondents were the least likely to recognise their neighbours, which may be a function of the community's greater size. Bendigo respondents perceived that they had to look after themselves at all times as the event unfolded, implying that they felt little support from council or other governance bodies. Conversely, Ingham respondents were the most likely to know the names of their close neighbours and had closer relationships with their neighbours. Ingham respondents were the most able to work with community members after the event. Queensland respondents reported being more connected to neighbours – more neighbourly – than Victorians during the event.

Hazard preparedness and consideration of leaving the community, individual-level behaviour that is known to have an impact upon community resilience, were also influenced by variables found in the exosystem, mesosystem and microsystem of the individual (Boon *et al.* 2012: 242).

Roles and types of organisations

This chapter has so far examined the services and support mechanisms that constitute contributions made by the exosystem to individuals, households and communities. These have been discussed under broad categories of infrastructure and protective structures, essential services and insurance payments, communication and information, social capital and connectedness and sense of place. It has been shown that these things are provided by agencies or organisations external to the immediate community, although some elements, such as networks, become inextricably intertwined with the functioning of the household and community. For the most part, though, external organisations constitute the exosystem. This chapter goes on to examine the range and diversity of types of organisations and their roles.

Hutter *et al.* (2013) stress the role of organisations in building resilience. Murray *et al.* (2015) discuss the legal and institutional framework of risk governance. The long process of recovery involves time and timing. Over time, strategies change and evolve away from their original plans involving alternative approaches of formal and informal governance. Murray *et al.* suggest that polycentric governance contains flexibility, innovation, scale and time: 'Governance regimes are polycentric and multi-scale, giving rise to many centres of decision-making that are formally independent of each other' (Murray *et al.* 2015: 446). 'The governance of volcanic risk in Auckland is a polycentric system. There is not a hierarchical concentration of management, but responsibility for outcomes resides with numerous groups of people and organisations that become operational or govern in distinct phases' (Murray *et al.* 2015: 461). Embeddedness is slow, changing culture, norms and traditions which influence the way people perceive and interact. The institutional environment is a composite of political, legal and economic processes that determine rights and obligations – i.e. land use planning constraints – where institutional arrangements are formal and bureaucratic. Resource allocation is more flexible and immediate. Thus, there exists a large number of agencies, categorised under governmental agencies, civil society, private or market agents and hybrid organisations. Civil society consists of formal agencies and informal plus emergent community groups. There is also the highly significant role of the private sector in recovery, especially the insurance industry but also retailers of supplies, skilled trades and infrastructure providers. On top of this there are hybrid organisations, which provide services in communication, education, research, warnings, etc. (Murray *et al.* 2015)

Table 7.2 below displays some basic examples of types of organisations that may be involved at different phases of a disaster. There are agencies that have a specific responsibility to respond to a disaster and consequent community recovery. Those that have a direct, primary role usually have an additional responsibility to help people prepare for likely events, through education, preparedness campaigns and warnings. Organisations with an indirect role exist for a non-disaster primary purpose, but in times of crisis they shift their resources to

Table 7.2 Organisations involved in emergency and disaster management

Direct (primary role)	Indirect (other primary role)	Residual and emergent
International agencies	Businesses	Cultural norms
Levels of government	Economic organisations	Community networks
Emergency services	Recreational organisations	Internet and social media
Defence forces	Religious organisations	Residual/traditional leadership
Essential services and lifelines	Cultural groups	Volunteers
Non-government organisations	Interest groups	Fixers and tradespeople
Privatised specialists	Political groups	Illegal/circumscribed groups
Grass roots organisations	Media	Neighbours
Community organisations	Government departments	Migrants and visitors

Source: adapted from King 2007.

the immediate needs of response and recovery. The same is true of those groups that are defined here as residual and emergent, but these are generally non-organised elements. An example of illegal and circumscribed groups was the role of the Taliban in providing leadership in remote parts of Pakistan following catastrophic floods and a slow government response. Cultural norms may be crucial in prompting volunteerism, while social media has recently mobilised groups of people, but also builds upon pre-existing social norms.

The scale of disaster response and recovery influences the capacity and types of agencies involved, i.e. provincial rather than district and community. For example, a lack of decentralisation hampered earthquake recovery in Baluchistan (Ainuddin *et al.* 2013). In Brazil, an Amazonian case study showed state responsibility for disaster risk reduction and emergency management at the expense of local engagement. An extensive range of government agencies was involved, but generally it was a low priority for most of them, with considerable funding complexity and lack of resources (Szlafsztein 2015).

Two levels of organisations are government and community led, where community organisations and social capital have tended to be neglected. These comprise a 'plethora of communities, including neighbourhoods, families, churches, service and hobby clubs and other civil society organisations' (Murphy 2007: 298). Emergency management should not be separated from the community in which it functions. It tends to command and control, but works in the community as well. Communities need capacity and interdependency between communities and agencies. Strong social capital can generate inward-looking communities. Policy and politics can create or destroy social capital. 'Organisations are: Established (Type I); Expanding (Type II); Extending (Type III); and finally, Emergent (Type IV)' (Murphy 2007: 298). Established organisations continue to perform the same tasks that they would undertake in a non-disaster context (e.g. the coroner's office). Expanding organisations increase in size and undertake new activities during disasters. These first two types of organisations are groups whose goals, internal structure and social capital networks are geared towards emergency management in the more formal sense of a municipal response. The next two are more likely to involve civil society organisations that evolve to meet the needs of the stricken communities. Extending organisations take on tasks that are novel, but their authority structure remains unchanged (e.g. a service group mobilises to help disaster victims). 'Emergent organisations are groups that develop to meet disaster needs perceived to be unmet by other responders' (Murphy 2007: 304). Emergent organisations developed from within the community, out of social, infrastructural responses and politics. Thus, there are very great differences in response to crisis between community fluidity and formal agency structure.

Community experiences of organisations

Following the disasters in the communities we studied (Beechworth bushfire, Bendigo drought, Ingham floods and Innisfail tropical cyclone), the exosystem organisations that were directly responsive to each of the disasters showed an improvement in their operations in the period following each of these disasters. For example, following the 2009 catastrophic bushfires, a vulnerable persons register was compiled by the emergency response agencies in order to assist vulnerable families. However, a problem connected with drought was a tendency for exosystem organisations to be oriented mostly towards the needs of farmers. There was more limited government support (exosystem level) for the rest of the community. Respondents in Ingham, following severe floods, identified strong leadership from the local government council. NGOs, especially charities, were strongly involved in recovery while local businesses exhibited a strong sense of community. NGOs supported and used local businesses.

However, problems were identified with the government's relief handouts: people felt that such handouts were demeaning. People identified a feeling of disempowerment during the response period, where responders took over and failed to consult local communities. This phenomenon has also recently occurred in Vanuatu following Cyclone Pam, where international agencies moved in and took over. On the other hand, the presence of relief providers and agencies was reassuring, even for those households that did not need them.

The cyclone impact in North Queensland placed the greatest responsibility on the exosystem. Respondents in Innisfail recorded the highest rating of local government council activities. The local exosystem was cited as especially important. Following Cyclone Larry in 2006, respondents stated that recovery came from an extensive range of government and NGO organisations. It should be noted that Larry was a stand-alone event, a disaster declared before its impact, so that agencies were prepared and waiting to intervene; it was a kind of 'boutique' disaster. Cyclone Yasi in 2011 was around the seventh disaster declaration in Queensland during a season of major disasters that stretched all of the organisations that were involved in response and recovery.

Communications and information were reported in all four case studies as being available to most of the population. The most common source of communication and information was through radio, TV and the internet. There was a perception in the case study communities that local government councils performed effectively and reasonably well; positive perceptions were higher in North Queensland following cyclone and flood than in Victoria following fire and drought. Respondents felt that neighbourhoods themselves were better prepared than local councils.

A summary of exosystem problems in the four case studies lists the following: soil erosion in Bendigo; information; water; electricity; mobile phones; delays in insurance payouts; transport and loss of access; food shortages; and alternative accommodation.

On the other hand there were many positives: restoration of power and sewerage (the restoration of power was critical to recovery, especially for small businesses); debris removal; road access; financial assistance; counselling; council support; statewide support; defence force contribution; connectedness and a sense of place (i.e. social capital); local business support and leadership; Red Cross and State Emergency Services or the Country Fire Authority. There was a perception that organisations had been more effective in dealing with flood and cyclone than with bushfire and drought. Specific leadership experiences were highlighted.

Economic impacts on organisations and communities

A global problem is the lack of investment by the private sector in disaster risk reduction and a lack of integration with formal emergency management disaster plans. While a tourist destination is home to all types of organisation as well as residential communities and tourists, the tourist industry is predominantly a private enterprise. Issues identified by Becken *et al.* were

> deficient planning and coastal development, and lack of implementation of legislation – damage to buildings, infrastructure and environmental assets, financial costs to businesses and/or insurance companies, public sector liability and costs. Lack of private sector resources to effectively implement DRR – High costs to businesses in case of a disaster; implications for business viability and reputation, unsustainable burden on the public sector and civic society.
>
> (Becken *et al.* 2014: 964)

Tourist developments increase hazard risk. Planning and government policies frequently run counter to disaster risk reduction, even if large tourist organisations and resorts practise a duty of care.

Small and medium-sized enterprises are especially vulnerable to disasters. In the case of the Chinese earthquakes, for example, damage from the disaster was compounded by loss of production and business. The recovery emphasis is on livelihoods within the community and neglects businesses (Liu *et al.* 2013). Economic development is also linked to lower disaster losses: poorly developed regions had higher death rates and greater losses (Zhou *et al.* 2014). Public finance is important at all stages of the emergency management cycle, but especially in recovery and in ensuring efficient use (Zhang *et al.* 2015).

In the Australian case studies, the respondents' views about their councils' role in the disaster response and their views about the community's recovery and preparedness for future hazards were important issues as they comprised the exosystem of residents' experience. The questions about the council's response to the disaster and preparedness for future events elicited significantly different answers from participants in the four sites. Beechworth respondents were the most confident that their community had recovered from the bushfires, while those in Bendigo were least confident about community recovery. Ingham and Innisfail respondents were more confident than the Victorian respondents that their council could identify those in greatest need, deal with the emotional responses of their constituents after a disaster, recognise the need for outside support and identify individuals to lead future recovery efforts. Similarly, the Queensland respondents were more confident than the Victorian respondents that their councils' responses to the emergency had been effective and that their council was appropriately prepared for a future disaster event. The above results were associated with a much larger proportion of Victorian respondents, indicating that the latter found it difficult to answer these questions. Such a result could reflect less community connectedness. since at least one of the sites, Beechworth, was a small community like the Queensland sites (Boon *et al.* 2012: 223–224).

Informal and community organisations

Bronfrenbrenner's theory cites the church as a significant organisation in the microsystem, although its role also straddles mesosystem and exosystem. It is the change in role from daily community support to disaster responder that places it in the exosystem. Similarly, the mosque is a community institution and focus for organisations in response and recovery. Religious centres and leaders provide communication and information. Cheema *et al.* (2014) identified local leadership as important but noted a difference in the perceived role of the imam as a spiritual leader rather than as someone who would engage directly in relief. Spiritual support was paramount. 'Overall, this study corroborates the finding that community-based religious institutions play a number of interacting and vital roles in developing community cohesion enabling individual, family and community recovery and rehabilitation in the wake of disasters' (Cheema *et al.* 2014: 2221). The roles of the religious centre are cultural, economic, psychological, social and political: 'the social conduct of the mosque is strongly influenced by the organisation of the people (the mosque committee and communities) and influential individuals (the Imam), and there is not one static or homogenous role' (Cheema *et al.* 2014: 2224) However, the writers also note limitations, and especially

Western perceptions of mosques and potential extremist links and controversial gender issues.

Vallance (2015) refers to Arnstein's ladder in relation to the participation of communities in decision making. Emergent community groups following Christchurch earthquakes were informal, experimental and outside formal recovery processes; these included such emergent organisations as Greening the Rubble, and Gap Filler. 'Recovery literature does not often make a distinction between public participation in recovery activities (substantial issues) and public participation in decision-making for recovery (procedural issues)' (Vallance 2015: 1297). Failure to engage the community leads to inefficient use of recovery resources. Autonomous community disaster risk reduction organisations emerge in the context of specific crises, and may be loosely organised or facilitated by government. Consequently, there is a rapid and significant increase in the number of households participating. Such spontaneous organisations may be linked to the traditional local community system. Bajek *et al.* (2008) noted that these often tend to be organised and involve the elderly, although they may be used by government to mobilise population for disaster risk reduction.

Formal organisations, and even emergency management agencies, evolve and change during the process of disaster response and recovery. What has been planned in anticipation of an event does not necessarily survive the chaos of a disaster. This is not necessarily a weakness, as new approaches and models of leadership may emerge. However, organisations may end up supplying services and support that were not formally planned. A broad range of variables that structure the capacity of an organisation emerge post event as constraints or opportunities. A case study from Canada of organisations similar to Australia's State Emergency Services showed variable integration between community response teams that was influenced by funding, leadership, formality of structure and acceptance within the emergency management system (Carr and Jensen 2015). In much of the world, emergency management, disaster risk reduction and especially climate change adaptation are not very high priorities. Day-to-day services and necessities, the economy and immediate needs dominate government and organisational thinking and allocation of resources. Focused personnel are extremely limited and it is usually their role to harness and coordinate all the potential of supporting organisations once disaster happens. The exosystem of hazard response and assistance works as an opaque but visible support system.

Organisations in the exosystem

In order to pull together all of the foregoing organisational complexity of what constitutes the exosystem, Table 7.3 below reclassifies organisations in terms of type, role or specific support to resilience through the exosystem and constraints or issues that emerge for categories at different times, scales and roles.

Table 7.3 lists a range of types of organisations that are involved in disasters, and thus in mitigation, resilience and climate change adaptation. These organisations are extremely diverse. Some are highly structured and well resourced,

Table 7.3 Resilience support, typology and issues of exosystem organisations: what the exosystem does for community resilience

Roles and functions of organisations	Exosystem resilience support	Constraints
Table 7.2 above; types of organisations involved in mitigation, response and recovery	Direct Indirect Residual Emergent Social capital	Overlap Lack of connectivity Poor linkages Conflicting agendas and priorities Primary organisation purpose Leadership change Governance
Timing	Phases of the emergency management system – i.e. PPRR Plans Slow-onset disasters Climate change Sudden-onset disasters Secondary and cascading disasters	Lack of continuity across time Processes – knowledge Events – prediction Personnel – change Managerialism Funding levels and priorities
Scale	Community Local Regional National International	Hierarchical issues Connectivity across time and space Lack of coordination across scales Variable phases and scales within disasters – change in scale at different time phases

Roles	Preparation and prevention Education Response and rescue Recovery Rebuilding – structures and infrastructure Resilience building Vulnerability reduction Communication and warnings	Governance Leadership Lack of engagement of professionals with community Inappropriate warnings and messages Building codes
Infrastructure	Buildings – schools, hospitals, shelters and refuges, government and council buildings, depots, roads, airports, seaports Networks – virtual, electronic, formal, informal, community Government services Essential services and lifelines – power, water, sewerage Protective structures – levees, barriers, etc. Planning – land use, economic, social Livelihoods	Damage Destruction Costs and funding Rebuilding – insurance, relief Diversion of rebuilding materials out of community Building back better – constraints Primary role of infrastructure – unsuitability in disaster

such as departments in the different levels of government, or large business enterprises. Others are less well resourced, much less structured or even lack any kind of formal structure, such as social media networks. Together they may provide a considerable capacity to tackle mitigation, response and recovery. They exist in the exosystem, with some crossover in relation to their engagement or ownership in the local community in the mesosystem, or their primary role in policy or legislation at national or international levels in the macrosystem. The contribution of these organisations and agencies to the exosystem may be categorised as direct, indirect, residual, emergent or contributing to social capital. Direct organisations have as their primary purpose the support of disaster management, such as emergency services, local or provincial government disaster planning and NGOs such as the Red Cross and Red Crescent. Indirect organisations have as a primary purpose the provision of services and goods that are not hazard related, but in a time of crisis their resources and purpose may be redirected. Building companies in the tourist areas of Phuket in Thailand put their staff and machinery in the service of response and recovery following the 2004 Indian Ocean tsunami. The media provides education and warnings prior to hazard impacts and informs the wider community of needs and problems during recovery. Residual organisations such as churches, mosques and temples refocus their buildings and resources in a time of disaster, but they also underscore and encourage values that translate into volunteerism and community rebuilding, not only from their own adherents but as a much broader part of their contribution to society's values. Emergent organisations are unstructured networks, as well as new social-political entities and charities that develop in relation to a specific disaster and may disappear as recovery is completed, or they may remain as part of the new social capital that came out of the event. All of these organisations and entities through their services, memberships and community interaction build or add to social capital.

This diversity and range of organisations also generates constraints and problems, such as overlap, lack of connectivity, poor linkages, conflicting agendas and priorities, primary purpose of the organisation itself and leadership change and governance, which all have a capacity to reduce or skew resilience. Most of these constraints are closely interrelated and are a direct reflection of the differences inherent in all these often well-meaning and well-intentioned but frequently contradictory agencies. The primary purpose of the organisation creates skills and agendas that may not translate effectively. Leadership change may be positive or negative, but may also involve many underlying complex community issues of legitimacy, contested authority and appropriateness. Good governance builds and supports resilience, but, like leadership, it may be too conservative or too radical for the community to encompass. In summary, the diversity and range of organisations contributes services but may also cancel out some of the benefits.

The next functional structure of organisations in the exosystem concerns issues of timing. Different types of organisations will contribute skills, resources and services at different times during a disaster. Emergency management is structured through phases: prevention, preparedness, response and recovery

(PPRR) in Australia, and variants of this in most countries. The system antici-
pates different needs and priorities at stages within the disaster cycle. Preparedness and prevention or readiness and reduction are part of the broader concepts
of disaster risk reduction and hazard mitigation that anticipate the probability of
a natural hazard impacting a community. These pre-event stages are concerned
with the physical protective measures and infrastructure (elements of the exosystem in themselves) and especially with education and preparedness strategies
that culminate in knowledge of warnings and the warnings themselves.
Response is a specialised, primarily emergency management activity, although
extensive post-disaster research indicates that the 'victims' of any disaster are
active, often first, responders. The phase of recovery involves the greatest range
of players, often a whole-society involvement, which begins as a massive intervention and tails off over months or years, leaving smaller numbers of community members and organisations active over the long term. While the
emergency management system is structured in about four phases, these are
neither discreet not equal in time. They run parallel, overlap, neglect or concentrate on sectors of the community and are influenced significantly by the
next group of issues concerned with scale. Slow-onset or sudden-onset disasters
require different approaches to timing and the balance of activities within the
emergency management phases. Other timing issues involve climate change and
secondary and cascading disasters. These organisations and processes in the exosystem also bring constraints and problems, most of all a lack of continuity
across time. There are also knowledge problems associated with prediction of
events and the timing of processes. Both of these are highly susceptible to the
accuracy and reliability of warnings. The table uses the term 'managerialism' to
cover a range of issues such as liability, hierarchical management systems and
process, where things that were important at points in the planning phases
become a hindrance during and after a disaster. Attitudes have to be realigned
and reprioritised.

Like timing, scale configures the types and approaches of organisations in the
exosystem as they confront events of very different sizes. The scale is most
immediately spatial, but it also applies to the size of the impacted population –
the difference between a rural area containing a population of a few thousands
and a major city or urban region accommodating many millions of people. As
disasters may occur over extensive areas, the scale of organisations that contribute to resilience may take place simultaneously at community, local,
regional, national and international levels, or at subsets of these scales. Disaster
events may often be at scales that are specific to the type of hazard. As with
timing, there are similar issues that constrain the effectiveness of organisations
in the exosystem. These include hierarchical issues, connectivity across time
and space, lack of coordination across scales and variable phases and scales
within disasters – there is a change in scale at different time phases. Emergency
managers are careful to address coordination across scales or administrative
zones, but they have no influence on significantly different territories that are
administered by other agencies.

Table 7.3 identifies the roles of organisations as a specific area of resilience. A specific responsibility of many agencies is resilience building itself. Other roles are structured by the emergency management phases, timing, scale and, quite independently of hazard risk, contributions to social capital. Thus, roles of organisations may include preparation and prevention (DRR), education, communication and warnings, response and rescue, recovery and rebuilding of both structures and infrastructure. Vulnerability reduction may be hazard specific, including protective structures, but hazard vulnerability is primarily driven by structural demographic and socio-economic characteristics of households and communities, and it is not in the power of emergency management agencies to reduce these. There are, however, many social, welfare and education providers among government and non-government entities that provide services to reduce structural social vulnerability and thereby contribute to social capital and resilience. As with the other areas of responsibilities of exosystem organisations, there are constraints that reduce the effectiveness of their roles. These include practical considerations of inappropriate warnings and messages, as well as lack of engagement of professionals with the community and consequent issues of governance and leadership.

Infrastructure is provided by the exosystem. The vast majority of it is provided for all of the needs of the community: residential housing and buildings, schools, hospitals, government and council buildings and depots, roads, airports, seaports, government services and essential services and lifelines including power, water, sewerage. Then there are all the other networks: virtual, electronic, formal, informal and community. During the impact of a natural disaster some of these structures will be turned into shelters and refuges. In recovery, essential services are lifelines critical for bringing a community back to a level of functioning normality. Protective structures, such as levees, drainage channels and barriers, are built to deal with specific and local hazards. They give many people a sense of security and safety, as well as false security, in that any structure can only be built to a certain hazard level. Extreme events and change over time reduce the usefulness of protective structures. There are less tangible services provided by the exosystem that enhance resilience. For example, planning of land use, building codes, economic development and social infrastructure is increasingly expected to address hazard reduction through risk avoidance. These intangibles include livelihood approaches that effectively support resilience. The limitations of infrastructure are expressed through physical damage – even total destruction – and the costs and funding allocations of initial construction and rebuilding. Rebuilding depends on insurance, savings and relief funds, with people's willingness to 'build back better' thwarted by replacement policies of both the insurance industry and local governments. There occurs a diversion of rebuilding materials out of the community as outside organisations flood in, take over and supply programmes from existing places and suppliers. Infrastructure, built to serve a specific population under normal conditions, is often found to be unsuitable in disaster.

Conclusion

The exosystem is that 'top-down' component of societies where governments and large agencies decide on the provision of services and deliver them on the basis of perceived needs and funding available. Although individuals may not be explicitly aware of the provision of these services, the services nonetheless can, and often do, contribute substantially to community resilience. However, this is not to suggest that individuals and communities rely solely on these services for resilience to disasters.

References

Ainuddin, S., Aldrich, D., Routray, J., Ainuddin, S. and Achkazai, A. 2013, 'The Need for Local Involvement: Decentralization of Disaster Management Institutions in Baluchistan, Pakistan', *International Journal of Disaster Risk Reduction*, vol. 6, pp. 50–58.

Aldrich, D. 2015, 'The Need for Social Capital: More Trust Meant Fewer Deaths in Fukushima', *Oriental Economist*, vol. 83, no. 5, pp. 9–10.

Aldrich, D.P. and Meyer, M.A. 2015, 'Social Capital and Community Resilience', *American Behavioral Scientist*, vol. 59, no. 2, pp. 254–269.

Bajek, R., Matsuda, Y. and Okada, N. 2008, 'Japan's Jishu-Bosai-Soshiki Community Activities: Analysis of its Role in participatory Community Disaster Risk Management', *Natural Hazards*, vol. 44, pp. 281–292.

Becken, S., Mahon, R., Rennie, H. and Shakeela, A. 2014, The Tourism Disaster Vulnerability Framework: An Application to Tourism in Small Island Destinations', *Natural Hazards*, vol. 71, pp. 955–972.

Berkes, F. 2007, 'Understanding Uncertainty and Reducing Vulnerability: Lessons from Resilience Thinking', *Natural Hazards*, no. 41, pp. 283–295.

Boon, H.J., Millar, J., Lake, D., Cottrell, A. and King, D. 2012, *Recovery from Disaster: Resilience, Adaptability and Perceptions of Climate Change*. National Climate Change Adaptation Research Facility, Queensland.

Bronfenbrenner, U. 1993, 'The Ecology of Cognitive Development: Research Models and Fugitive Findings', in R.H. Wozniak and K. Fischer (eds), *Scientific Environments*, pp. 3–44. Erlbaum, Hillsdale, NJ.

Campbell, A., Thomas, N., Hunter, C. and Levesque, C. 2006, 'Social Risk Index to Hurricanes in the Coastal Regions of Rhode Island', *Journal of the Transportation Research Board*, 1, pp. 121–129.

Carr, J. and Jensen, J. 2015, Explaining the Pre-Disaster Integration of Community Emergency Response Teams (CERTs)', *Natural Hazards*, 77, pp. 1551–1571.

Cheema, A., Scheyvens, R., Glavovic, B. and Imran, M. 2014, 'Unnoticed but Important: Revealing the Hidden Contribution of Community-Based Religious Institution of the Mosque in Disasters', *Natural Hazards*, 71, pp. 2207–2229.

Collenteur, R.A., de Moel, H., Jongman, B. and Di Baldassarre, G. 2015, 'The Failed-Levee Effect: Do Societies Learn from Flood Disasters?', *Natural Hazards*, 76, pp. 373–388.

Cutter, S.L., Barnes, L., Berry, M., Burton, C., Evans, E., Tate, E. and Webb, J. 2008, 'A Place-Based Model for Understanding Community Resilience to Natural Disasters', *Global Environmental Change*, vol. 18, pp. 598–606.

Dobes, L., Scheufele, G. and Bennett, J. 2015, 'Post-cyclone Emergency Services: A Cost–Benefit Analysis for Cairns, Australia', *Natural Hazards*, 75, pp. 869–886.

Garschagen, M. 2013, 'Resilience and Organisational Institutionalism from a Cross-Cultural Perspective: An Exploration Based on Urban Climate Change Adaptation in Vietnam', *Natural Hazards*, 67, pp. 25–46.

Glavovic, B.C., Saunders, W.S.A. and Becker, J.S. 2010, 'Land-Use Planning for Natural Hazards in New Zealand: The Setting, Barriers, 'Burning Issues' and Priority Actions', *Natural Hazards*, 54, pp. 679–706.

Hoppner, C., Whittle, R., Brundl, M. and Buchecker, M. 2012, 'Linking Social Capacities and Risk Communication in Europe: A Gap Between Theory and Practice?', *Natural Hazards*, 64, pp. 1753–1778.

Hutter, G., Kuhlicke, C., Glade, T. and Felgentreff, C. 2013, 'Natural Hazards and Resilience: Exploring Institutional and Organizational Dimensions of Social Resilience', *Natural Hazards*, 67, pp. 1–6.

Kapucu, N. 2008, 'Collaborative Emergency Management: Better Community Organising, Better Public Preparedness and Response', *Disasters*, vol. 32, no. 2, pp. 239–262.

King, D. 2007, 'Organisations in Disasters', *Natural Hazards*, vol. 40, no. 3, pp. 657–665.

King, D., Ginger, J., Williams, S., Cottrell, A., Gurtner, Y., Leitch, C., Henderson, D., Jayasinghe, N., Kim, P., Booth, K., Ewin, C., Innes, K., Jacobs, K., Jago-Bassingthwaighte, M. and Jackson, L. 2013, 'Planning, Building and Insuring: Adaptation of Built Environment to Climate Change Induced Increased Intensity of Natural Hazards'. National Climate Change Adaptation Research Facility, Queensland, p. 361. ISBN: 978-1-921609-75-6.

Klein, R.J.T., Nicholls, R.J. and Thomalla, F. 2003, 'Resilience to natural Hazards: How Useful is this Concept?', *Environmental Hazards*, vol. 5, pp. 35–45.

Liu, Z., Xu, J. and Han, B. 2013, 'Small- and medium-Sized Enterprise Post-Disaster Reconstruction Management Patterns and Application', *Natural Hazards*, 68, pp. 809–835.

Marfai, M., Sekaranom, A. and Ward, P. 2015, 'Community Responses and Adaptation Strategies Toward Flood Hazard in Jakarta, Indonesia', *Natural Hazards*, 75, pp. 1127–1144.

Mowbray, C.T., Woolley, M.E., Grogan-Kaylor, A., Gant, L.M., Gilster, M.E. and Shanks, T.R.W. 2007, 'Neighborhood Research from a Spatially Oriented Strengths Perspective', *Journal of Community Psychology*, vol. 35, pp. 667–680.

Murphy, B.L. 2007, 'Locating Social Capital in Resilient Community-Level Emergency Management', *Natural Hazards*, 41, pp. 297–315.

Murray, C., McDonald, G. and Cronin, S. 2015, 'Interpreting Auckland's Volcanic Governance through an Institutional Lens', *Natural Hazards*, 75, pp. 441–464.

Nirupama, N., Sharma, R., Verma, K. and Panigrahi, S. 2015, 'A Multi-Tier Hazard-Part I: Description of the Event', *Natural Hazards*, 76, pp. 259–269.

Norris, F.H., Stevens, S.P., Pfefferbaum, B., Wyche, K.F. and Pfefferbaum, R.L. 2008, 'Community Resilience as a Metaphor, Theory, Set of Capacities, and Strategy for Disaster Readiness', *American Journal of Community Psychology*, vol. 41, pp. 127–150.

Paton, D. 2006, 'Disaster Resilience: Building Capacity to Coexist with Natural Hazards and their Consequences', in D. Paton and D. Johnston (eds), *Disaster Resilience: An Integrated Approach*. Charles C. Thomas, Springfield, IL, pp. 3–10.

Pyles, L. and Cross, T. 2008, 'Community Revitalization In Post-Katrina New Orleans: A Critical Analysis of Social Capital in an African American Neighborhood', *Journal of Community Practice*, vol.16, no.4, pp. 383–401.

Smith, G. 2010, 'Lessons from the United States: Planning for Post-Disaster Recovery and Deconstruction', *Australasian Journal of Disaster and Trauma Studies*, vol. 2010/1.

Szlafsztein, C.F. 2015, 'Management of Natural Disasters in the Brazilian Amazon Region', *Natural Hazards*, 76, pp. 1745–1757.

Thomas, J.A, and Mora, K. 2014, 'Community Resilience, Latent Resources and Resource Scarcity after an Earthquake: Is Society Really Three Meals Away from Anarchy?' *Natural Hazards*, 74, pp. 477–490.

Vallance, S. 2015, 'Disaster Recovery as Participation: Lessons from the Shaky Isles', *Natural Hazards*, 75, pp. 1287–1301.

Zhang, Y., Ma, Y., Chen, A. and Lin, Y. 2015, 'Research on Chinese Public Finance in Response to Domestic Natural Disasters', *Natural Hazards*, 77, pp. 1799–1810.

Zhou, Y., Li, N., Wu, W., Liu, H., Wang, L., Liu, G. and Wu, J. 2014. 'Socioeconomic Development and the Impact of Natural Disasters: Some Empirical Evidences from China', *Natural Hazards*, 74, pp. 541–554.

8 The macrosystem in disaster resilience

David King

The macrosystem is defined by Bronfenbrenner as an overarching pattern of the microsystem, mesosystem and exosystem characteristics of a culture or subculture and consists of its belief systems, body of knowledge, resources, customs, lifestyle, opportunities and their structures, hazards and life options (Bronfenbrenner 1994). In this chapter, we will emphasise those components of society that directly contribute to the safety, resilience and adaptive capacity of people and communities in the face of natural disasters and hazards that will be exacerbated by climate change.

The policy landscape operates at multiple levels, such that the lack of or presence of particular national and international policies has impacts upon community and individual disaster resilience and vulnerability. The impact of governance and socio-economic and demographic trends and influences upon policy development is a component of the policy analysis.

At the international level, the chapter will primarily examine the work and strategies of the ISDR, which is supplemented by the WMO, IPCC and major international NGOs. Policy approaches such as the Hyogo Declaration are examined in order to trace their impact from the global scale to the local community and individual. National-level policies illustrate the means by which international strategies are translated through national policies to provincial and local levels of government. The chapter identifies a range of national initiatives, and in relation to the Australian case studies particular importance derives from such strategies as the Council of Australian Governments review, productivity commission, climate change policies and community resilience policy. Core policy and strategic developments that extend from the international to the community, through all levels of government and NGOs, are vulnerability and resilience, with extension from resilience towards the future for climate change mitigation and adaptation in both developed and developing countries. Community development policy in its broader perspective considers vulnerability, resilience and climate change adaptation. At local government levels, specific policies in areas of land use planning, settlement design for hazard resilience, governance and infrastructure provide a focus for analysis. A local government climate change policy of protect, accommodate or retreat is an emerging framework that deals with the impact of increasing hazard impact. The chapter focuses on:

- The policy landscape.
- The impact of a lack or presence of particular national and international policies upon community and individual disaster resilience and vulnerability.
- Influence of macrosystem policies at household and community levels – case studies.

The policy landscape

The hazards policy landscape influences and contributes to resilience, but it only works if it is relevant and socially acceptable. It may seem to be a framework of safety across government, society and community, but it only contributes to the resilience of individuals and households if it has been translated into their lives and is accepted by people.

Policy is driven by social values and governance. Values are extremely diverse; for example, materialistic, spiritual, religious, social control, independence vs individualism, self-sufficiency, dependency, social hierarchy and acceptance or rejection of science and technology. Internationally there is a pervasive influence of liberal, Western, technologically driven values, which emphasise and place responsibility on the individual as well as encouraging acceptance of technology and its solutions. This Western influence has driven the values of the United Nations and other international agencies.

Governance is equally variable in terms of political and social systems, resources and finance, the capacity of states to govern and to provide services and leadership and their social acceptance and authority in times of crisis. Equally variable is social capital, which is not a standard set of societal characteristics. Social capital may exist with or without strong governance: Migdal's (1988) weak state and strong society. Social capital is constructed by values, culture and resources.

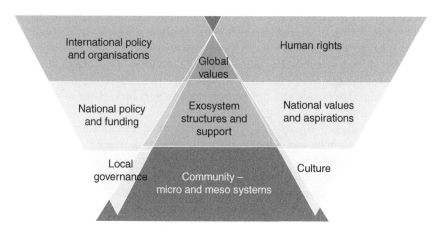

Figure 8.1 The focus of policies, strategies and needs between macrosystem and microsystem.

The exosystem supports the individual, household and community through organisations, infrastructure, services and NGOs that are tangible and close, both geographically and socially. The macrosystem exists outside this direct relationship as a much less tangible set of influences that primarily impact upon the individual through the exosystem and mesosystem. The macrosystem is top down but draws on deeply rooted values and societal processes.

At the top of the hierarchy of the disaster risk reduction macrosystem sit the international policies and strategies of the United Nations International Strategy for Disaster Reduction (UNISDR). United Nations strategies for disaster reduction are complemented by other UN agency policies, such as the Millennium Goals and the United Nations Convention on Climate Change. The IPCC (2012), along with the World Meteorological Organisation's models of climate change (WMO 2010), predicts an increase in economic losses and exposure of people and assets to natural disaster. Trends in urbanisation have contributed extensively to increased disaster risk, such that city growth will cumulatively contribute to much greater risk exposure alongside the effects of climate change. Furthermore, the IPCC predicts greater migration from hazard-prone locations.

The UNISDR developed plans and strategies through world conferences at Yokohama in 1995, Kobe in 2005 and Sendai in 2015, and through the concentrated efforts of the International Decade for Natural Disaster Reduction (IDNDR) through the 1990s. The Kobe conference in 2005 produced the Hyogo Framework for Action (HFA), which reinforced the goals of the IDNDR that called upon government intervention at multiple levels for disaster risk reduction. Before 1990, disaster risk reduction was dominated by response agencies, especially emergency management, alongside hazard knowledge research that was primarily scientific in nature. Both of these continue to play important and expanded roles. However, the IDNDR shifted responsibility to governments, mainly to engage communities and increase awareness and preparedness.

Through the 1980s and 1990s extensive research and policy emphases identified community vulnerability to natural hazards (Wisner 1993; Cannon 1994; Blakie et al. 1994). The problem with vulnerability assessment is that vulnerability is largely structural in nature. Many characteristics of vulnerability, such as poverty or lack of education, and factors not conducive to mitigation in the short term such as demographic characteristics like the very young and the very old, are things that people and communities can do very little about in the short to medium term.

Building resilience emerged as a better policy than vulnerability reduction, because it gave agencies and communities achievable goals that could be targeted (Anderson-Berry and King 2005). Vulnerability tends to stress the negatives in society or individuals, those things that people can do little about. Resilience stresses the positives: aspects of people and communities may be enhanced and developed to reduce disaster risk. Initially, definitions of vulnerability and resilience had linked the two concepts, suggesting that they were at opposite ends of the same continuum. In fact, they are parallel sets of conditions, where some aspects of vulnerability or resilience are on opposite ends of the scale, such as household income, but where many others are entirely different measures. For example, social networks contribute to resilience, while a stratified socio-economic system may be seen to increase vulnerability, yet these are not necessarily mutually exclusive. People may be both vulnerable and resilient at the same time. Thus, policy has shifted strongly towards emphasising the building of resilience.

Internationally, however, vulnerability reduction still has an important role. In one sense, vulnerability is defined by proximity to a natural hazard zone. Resilient communities may be located on a coastline subject to storm surge, or on a river floodplain: they are thus both vulnerable and resilient. Consequently, policies specifically address hazard zones and the vulnerability of risk through land use planning, protective measures such as levees and flood control and hazard reduction through activities such as controlled burns of bush and forest.

At another level, international agencies, especially the United Nations, strive to reduce vulnerability caused by underdevelopment: poverty, poor health and social disadvantage. The United Nations Millennium Goals set targets of vulnerability reduction for social justice, which also reduce the vulnerability of communities to natural disasters.

Following the IDNDR of the 1990s, the world disaster conference in Kobe in 2005 stressed the importance of building the resilience of nations and communities, rather than targeting vulnerability. The international strategy for 2005 to 2015, the Hyogo framework, established outcomes and goals to mainstream disaster risk reduction into sustainable development and planning. It was also designed to develop and strengthen institutional mechanisms to build hazard resilience alongside greater incorporation of disaster risk reduction approaches into emergency management preparedness, response and recovery phases (UNISDR 2007). Unfortunately the mid-term review of the HFA found many of the goals of 2005 to have been only partially achieved, so that the world conference in Sendai in 2015 built on the existing framework rather than establishing an entirely new direction in disaster risk reduction.

The Sendai framework sets an overall goal to

> Prevent new and reduce existing disaster risk through the implementation of integrated and inclusive economic, structural, legal, social, health, cultural, educational, environmental, technological, political and institutional measures that prevent and reduce hazard exposure and vulnerability to disaster, increase preparedness for response and recovery, and thus strengthen resilience.
>
> (UNISDR 2015: 37)

It then sets seven targets, unlike the more general statements made by the HFA:

1   Substantially reduce global disaster mortality by 2030, aiming to lower average per 100,000 global mortality.

2   Substantially reduce the number of affected people globally by 2030, aiming to lower the average global figure per 100,000.
3   Reduce direct disaster economic loss in relation to global gross domestic product (GDP) by 2030.
4   Substantially reduce disaster damage to critical infrastructure and disruption of basic services, among them health and educational facilities, including through developing their resilience by 2030.
5   Substantially increase the number of countries with national and local disaster risk reduction strategies by 2020.
6   Substantially enhance international cooperation to developing countries through adequate and sustainable support to complement their national actions.
7   Substantially increase the availability of and access to multi-hazard early warning systems and disaster risk information and assessments to people by 2030.

(UNISDR 2015: 37)

The Sendai framework then identifies priorities for action over the 15-year plan period. These are summarised as follows.

1   Understanding disaster risk – comprising an understanding of disaster risk, vulnerability, capacity, exposure of persons and assets, hazard characteristics and the environment.
2   Strengthening disaster risk governance to manage disaster risk – at national, regional and global levels, the management of disaster risk reduction in all sectors and ensuring the coherence of national and local frameworks of laws, regulations and public policies, roles and responsibilities, the public and private sector.
3   Investing in disaster risk reduction for resilience – involving public and private investment, DRR through structural and non-structural measures, and issues of the economic, social, health and cultural resilience of persons, communities, countries and their assets, and environments. This priority refers to innovation, growth and job creation as secondary outcomes.
4   Enhancing disaster preparedness for effective response, and to «Build Back Better» in recovery, rehabilitation and reconstruction – recovery, rehabilitation and reconstruction phase is an opportunity to «Build Back Better» through integrating disaster risk reduction measures, preparedness needs to be strengthened for more effective response and ensure capacities are in place for effective recovery. The priority also identifies women and the disabled as leaders in DRR equity.

(UNISDR 2015: 37)

These priorities are followed by guiding principles that place shared responsibility on states, all levels of government and stakeholders, engagement of all of society, coherence of disaster risk reduction and sustainable development, addressing underlying risks, legislation, local government empowerment, multi-hazard approaches and global partnerships. There is no direct reference in the targets, priorities and guiding principles to climate change, but it is referred to throughout the framework document. Climate change is identified as exacerbating hazards, as well as contributing to new risks and increased vulnerability alongside a range of factors that include urbanisation and poor governance. Disaster risk reduction, sustainable development and climate change are referred to as linked elements. The mandate of the United Nations Framework Convention on Climate Change supports the UNISDR framework, but exists separately, with its own goals and targets. The Sendai framework identifies poverty reduction, sustainable development, natural resource management, the environment, urban development and adaptation to climate change (UNISDR 2015).

Translation from the global to the local

Developed countries had an easier task of mobilising international strategies through multiple levels of government to the local and community levels. Developing countries understood the necessity for disaster risk reduction but were much more constrained by lack of resources as well as the besetting problems of governance constraints. Yet at the mid-term review of the HFA (ISDR 2011), most countries in the world had achieved less than had been expected, regardless of their level of development. At the Kobe conference in 2005 when the Hyogo framework was agreed there was enthusiastic support for positive action in reducing disaster risk. The conference took place just one month after the Indian Ocean tsunami, with many delegates and international representatives having come directly from the disaster zone. Both Kobe in 2005 and Sendai in 2015 were chosen as venues because of their experience of recent catastrophic disasters. Unfortunately, an enthusiasm to bring about change on the global stage faced complex governance issues.

Australia's three levels of government illustrate some of these complexities. Agreement to implement the HFA was signed off through the Department of Foreign Affairs and Trade and communicated to responsible departments at the Federal (Commonwealth) level and passed down to state-level governments and departments through the Council of Australian Governments (COAG). The COAG had already begun the process of mainstreaming disaster risk reduction some years before the Kobe conference, having initially established the National Strategy for Disaster Resilience in 2011. Within state governments, responsibility for disaster risk reduction lies primarily within the appropriate emergency management department, but the national strategy had placed responsibilities across state governments. Each responsible state government department then communicated disaster risk reduction activities to various sections of local governments. Depending upon the size and the level of resources of local government, progress was extremely variable. A significant section of most local governments is its planning department, and it was from the planners that spe-cific action was required. Therefore, land use planning is presented as an example of the difficulties that slowed the process of disaster risk reduction.

Mainstreaming land use planning into disaster risk reduction

The intent of the HFA strategy for land use planning was followed in a piece-meal manner, demonstrating some successes, but also a significant proportion of failures and constraints. Initiatives developed and agreed at the international level were endorsed by national governments, but the agreement had then to be actioned through legislation to multiple levels of government over a period of time.

The most fundamental constraint is that land use planning is oriented towards the promotion and facilitation of new developments, whereas con-siderations of disaster risk reduction and climate change adaptation are still rel-atively minor issues. Bottlenecks to attitudinal change among planners are political and economic realities that continue to be influenced by climate change scepticism. Additionally, there are tight development costs that begrudge expenditure by developers on disaster risk reduction or restrictions on land use. Attitudinal change is slow and requires education and open minded-ness, not only among planners (who are generally open to ideas of disaster risk reduction and climate change) but the private enterprise entrepreneurs and pol-iticians who drive the process.

Land use planning is structured through legislation, requiring new laws and their implementation in order to practise disaster risk reduction and climate change adaptation in new developments. Again, it is the politicians and private sector that drive legislative change with planners acting primarily as respond-ents and facilitators. Once the legislation is activated, further bottlenecks occur. First, land use planners can only specify disaster risk reduction actions on land that is proven to be hazard prone. Comprehensive, highly detailed hazard mapping has to take place (one-metre differences in height are critical for surge and flood). Detailed mapping is slow, expensive and further constrained by boundary and jurisdictional issues.

Responsibility for mapping, information, communication and community education, awareness and resilience building falls primarily on local govern-ments, whose resources and capacity are the lowest in the political system. Fur-thermore, there are enormous inequalities between the resources and capacity of city councils in contrast to rural local governments, especially remote and indi-genous communities.

Local government areas inherit the legacy of past planning decisions, where most hazard risk resides. Planners' capacity to reduce risk in communities that are already well established in hazard zones is extremely limited. A priority is disaster risk reduction retrofitting of infrastructure and lifelines in hazard-prone areas, although this is also constrained by limited resources balanced against more immediate community and economic needs. Hazard proofing infrastructure requires long time periods to implement (a decade to realign and floodproof a highway is not unusual). Alongside these bottlenecks to land use change, rapid urban growth and urbanisation continue alongside strong population growth, adding to the constant need for new infrastructure and housing. Climate change exacerbates the need for stronger disaster risk reduction through adaptation and community resilience.

In Australia, there have been successes in the area of land use planning for disaster risk reduction. The enormous task of detailed hazard mapping has advanced, although it is only after mapping has been completed that strategic plans may be modified effectively (hazard zones are more easily applicable at the strategic plan level as they require less detail than a residential development plan). This whole process of mapping and strategic plan production has taken 15 years in Queensland, with land use planners only now in a position to place conditions on hazard vulnerability in new urban subdivisions. Meanwhile, development applications continue to be made and approved without the benefit of accurate hazard maps. Consequently, many approved hazard-prone developments remain in the pipeline. As mapping has moved ahead, alongside advances in IT, information has been made available to communities. However, information is not the same as education, and many local governments are still wary of releasing too much information and mapping.

Building codes, although not the direct responsibility of planners, have been extremely successful in reducing the risk of cyclonic destruction of residential dwellings. The use of building codes, within urban design, extends to such features as raised slabs and high-set living areas, enabling planners to specify a range of conditions for building in areas of minor to moderate flood risk.

Integration of disaster risk reduction into a broad range of legislation and government departmental jurisdictions has enhanced the role of land use planners in furthering awareness. Where disaster risk reduction has become a priority for institutions and is incorporated into specific legislation, such as the construction of critical infrastructure, planners are able to incorporate additional risk reduction strategies into planning decisions.

Planning case studies

Two category-4–5 tropical cyclones devastated coastal communities south of Cairns, Queensland in 2006 and 2011. Storm surge was especially destructive during Cyclone Yasi in 2011. Beachfront communities were established when land was cheap and disaster risk reduction was not part of land use planning practice. Beachside communities are the clearest example of the risk legacy and all are ultimately threatened with sea level rise and a long-term likelihood of 'retreat' as beachfront land is eroded and inundated. However, many residents of these communities are retirees who do not expect the climate change threat to eventuate in their lifetimes, despite having recently experienced a five-metre storm surge. Residents who have rebuilt expressed a stoic attitude of endurance and resilience. On the other hand, many housing blocks remain empty following complete destruction of dwellings, while many more that have been rebuilt are for sale. An out migration of disaster-impacted residents has already taken place.

The communities of Tully Heads and Hull Heads (150 km south of Cairns) were severely damaged by storm surge, especially dwellings that had been built along the beach ridge. People evacuated well in advance of the cyclone warning so there was no loss of life. Storm surge obliterated some dwellings constructed of light materials such as timber, but even where substantial block-built houses withstood the impact of the sea, saltwater ingress ruined their interiors. Almost all had to be rebuilt.

After the 2011 floods had occurred throughout Queensland and Cyclone Yasi in the North, the Queensland government established a disaster response planning agency, the Queensland Reconstruction Authority (QRA). QRA planners consulted impacted communities and provided advice and guidance for rebuilding. In Tully Heads and Hull Heads, the QRA worked with the Cyclone Testing Station (CTS) of James Cook University to design stronger dwellings built to cyclone standards and able to withstand a severe storm surge. The sketch design is illustrated in Figure 8.3, along with a sturdy example of the built dwelling that reflects the QRA/CTS design (Figure 8.4).

Figure 8.2 Storm surge destruction from Cyclone Yasi at Tully Heads/Hull Heads, 2011 (David King).

Figure 8.3 Sketch design of a storm surge-resistant house (source: QRA 2011).

Figure 8.4 Reconstructed dwelling at Tully Heads/Hull Heads, 2014 (David King).

The rebuilding of Tully Heads and Hull Heads is a best-practice example of a land use planning response agency engaging in extensive community consultation to meet the desires of residents to rebuild to a higher safety standard. However, residents are still living on the same fragile beach ridge that remains as susceptible to sea level rise and storm surge as before. In most cases, this was the only land that the residents owned; insurance coverage paid for rebuilding the house, usually for replacement rather than building back better, which incidentally is a priority of the Sendai framework. The hazard risk has not been mitigated. The solution is a short-term adaptation, but, as noted by residents, probably long enough to cover their lifetimes, and meanwhile the location is paradise. Relocation was not an option for people who had invested all they owned into living on the beach. The planners were impeccable in their community consultation, but there has been minimal hazard reduction.

Future trends in land use planning

Four groups of climate change and hazard planning strategies have been recognised and are in various stages of incorporation into planning policies (Thomas *et al.* 2012). These are: *do nothing* (an approach favoured by climate change sceptics but virtually no one in government); *retreat*; *defend* or *protect*; and *adapt* or *accommodate*. The retreat policy places responsibility for action on planners at local and state government levels, as well as on individuals and households. Individuals and households retreat by migrating away from the hazard zone, sometimes as refugees driven out by loss of housing and livelihood but more often balancing risk against opportunities and reduced risk elsewhere. Planning drives retreat by re-zoning hazard-prone land or areas that have been devastated by a disaster, such as at Grantham in Queensland's Lockyer Valley following catastrophic flash floods in 2011, or re-zoning land that has been eroded or lost through erosion. Defend or protect strategies are put in place through the exosystem where physical infrastructure is built, such as levees, drainage channels, walls and land reclamation. The decision either to protect or to abandon protection, is generated at the macrosystem level and passed down to local government and other exosystem agencies, including both planners and engineers. The adapt or accommodate strategy puts responsibility, action and costs on individuals or communities. The macrosystem strategy that leads to adaptation is building resilient communities, which then funds programmes, agencies and groups to raise awareness and preparedness. This may also filter down to the policies of insurance companies, such as enhancing capacity to build back better.

UNISDR (2015) recommends extension of land use planning as an agency of DRR. Guiding principles identify areas such as public planning, prevention of accumulation of new risk, open information and knowledge generation. Reference is made to the need to incorporate risk reduction into governance frameworks for local government, civil society and the private sector. Consequently, land use planning for disaster risk reduction requires development and resourcing in specific priority areas in order to translate macrosystem concepts into microsystem and exosystem realities (King *et al.* 2013).

1　Governments need to target local communities and the constraints of local government.
2　Community resilience through land use planning requires information, consultation and education and awareness in order to empower communities and households so that they are able to use the information that becomes available, in order to enhance their own risk reduction and climate change adaptation.
3　Comprehensive plans for disaster reduction need detailed mapping that requires significant government resources and policy initiatives. Mapping processes that are under way in many countries still have some way to go, especially in non-metropolitan regions.
4　There needs to be integration of legislation across government sectors with disaster risk reduction and climate change adaptation fully incorporated into planning legislation as well as in related legislation and jurisdictions that impinge upon land use planning.
5　A priority for reduction of existing risk (the legacy of past planning decisions) is critical infrastructure: hazard proofing lifelines that will be critical to evacuation and recovery in the event of disaster, and relocating infrastructure that is threatened by climate change (residential properties are much more difficult to relocate in the short to medium term).
6　Future disaster risk reduction and climate change adaptation must be built into strategic plans that indicate future settlement growth. Hazard zones must be clearly mapped, identified and strict conditions applied to the sort of land use that will be permitted in these areas. Hazard mitigation, climate change adaptation and disaster risk reduction need to be conditions of development at the local government level.
7　Urban design is evolving to incorporate disaster risk reduction and climate change adaptation. Design principles play an important role in recovery and reconstruction where there is enormous potential to build back better and to hazard proof future communities. Urban design (for example the new urbanism movement) has been effective in establishing principles of sustainability, but so far that sustainability has neglected hazard reduction and climate change.

Land use planners were not recalcitrant or obstructive. The experience of incorporating disaster risk reduction into local area plans was simply a long and costly process. Decisions to restrict residential development in hazard-prone areas required accurate mapping and incorporation into strategic plans or planning schemes. In Australia, several states have been pushed along in this process by catastrophic disasters involving significant loss of life that generated commissions of inquiry. The Bushfire Inquiry and the Queensland Flood Inquiry each generated further sets of recommendations that reinforced existing policies at the macrosystem level. However, despite political, economic and social pressures to prevent such future disasters, responsibility usually falls upon local government, the local community and individual households, where resource limitations act as a brake upon rapid change.

The impact of national and international policies on community and individual disaster resilience and vulnerability

The next section looks at the ways in which the macrosystem reached down and influenced communities, households and individuals who had recently experienced a major natural disaster. The macrosystem includes things such as the relative freedoms permitted by the national government, cultural values, the economy and external events. These things can also affect resilience, either positively or negatively. Macrosystem variables such as type of government, media, cultural systems and religions have a functional presence in the expectations, values, hopes, training and knowledge that individuals and local families in communities carry with them all the time, particularly in their memories and common sense, which can facilitate the process of resilience (Masten and Obradovic 2008; Boon et al. 2012: 24).

For a response to a disaster to be adequate for community recovery and resilience, urgent decision-making needs to bring public and private sectors together to collaborate at the local, state and federal levels. As such, this invokes the role played by politics (a macrosystem issue) as well as the roles played by exosystem and mesosystem organisations to promote the resilience process.

Recent large disasters (Hurricane Katrina, Hurricane Nargis) have demonstrated the role played by politics in supporting community recovery and resilience (Pelling and Dill 2010). Political procrastination and lack of timely government response for reconstruction following disasters such as Hurricane Katrina illustrate the importance and power of macrosystem variables for exacerbating or mitigating disaster impacts upon a community. In relation to climate change adaptation, the broader context within which natural disasters such as droughts, floods and cyclones are embedded and likely to be exacerbated becomes critical, as does the power of national and international politics (Adger 2010; IPCC 2007). Politics strongly impact upon, and sometimes determine, the level of community preparedness, a factor known to support community resilience (e.g. Cutter et al. 2008; Glavovic 2010; Gunderson 2010; Mora 2006; Prosser and Peters 2010).

Marchand (2008) also points out that resilience is enmeshed with the fabric of social life itself, with politics, power, history and environment. Manyena (2006) further highlights issues arising from the failure of politics to support community resilience to disasters, in this case food insecurity and malaria. These arise from a study looking at the role of rural district councils (RDCs) in Zimbabwe in facilitating disaster risk reduction. Local authorities are critical in building disaster-resilient communities, because their proximity to community pressures allows them to design properly tailored long-term solutions to disasters and development problems. Manyena (2006) argues that RDCs grappling with community resilience in Zimbabwe not only have inadequate financial and human resources at their disposal but also poor governance, which exacerbates and increases the difficulties they face.

Influence of macrosystem policies at household and community levels: case studies

The case studies of Bendigo, Beechworth, Ingham and Innisfail indicated that macrosystem factors, such as the financial support available to individuals from state and federal agencies and charity groups, were not directly linked to individual resilience but rather to the idea of potentially leaving the community. These factors supported both individual and community resilience, since without them individuals would have left the community, leaving it depleted in numbers and therefore less resilient.

Macrosystem representatives in the case study communities were identified in Beechworth as government support, representing Indigo Shire Council, Regional Development Victoria, Emergency Management within the Department of Human Services Victoria, and Ovens and King Community Health Service (Boon *et al.* 2012: 54). In Bendigo, macrosystem representatives were the Department of Sustainability and Environment, the climate change adaptation officer, the Department of Human Services, the manager of Strategic Support, the Department of Planning and Community Development, the community capacity building officer and the co-ordinator of the Rural Women's Network Response to Drought and Climate Change. In Ingham, macrosystem representatives were Queensland Health, the director of nursing/ facility manager, the Queensland police service, the emergency response police, Emergency Management Queensland, governmental welfare providers and Community Health (incl. Indigenous Health). In Innisfail the macrosystem representatives were identified as Queensland Department of Communities, Queensland Department of Primary Industries, Queensland Rural Adjustment Authority, Queensland Fire and Rescue Service, Queensland Department of Communities, Queensland Police Service and the local government member.

Macrosystem issues were listed by respondents in the case study communities. These included shortages of food, the disruption of postal delivery, transport disruption and consequent economic losses. Specific comments are recorded in Table 8.1.

Macrosystem positive influences at Innisfail recorded receipt of assistance from the council, charity or welfare groups and state or federal government. Federal and state government grants were much easier to endorse than others, although the Queensland sites received a measurably greater level of assistance than the Victorian sites. On the other hand, councils in Bendigo and Beechworth were considered more helpful than those in Queensland. Charities were not reported as helping except in Beechworth; possibly they

Table 8.1 Macrosystem variables by case study site

Macrosystem		Ingham	Innisfail	Beechworth	Bendigo
		N %	N %	N %	N %
As a result of the event I had difficulty in finding alternative accommodation	N/a	70	63	77	63
	Strongly disagree	6	8	6	8
	Disagree	20	11	15	18
	Agree	2	10	2	9
	Strongly agree	2	8	1	2
As a result of the event I experienced prolonged shortage of food	N/a	21	14	62	35
	Strongly disagree	15	16	13	16
	Disagree	36	42	23	32
	Agree	23	19	1	13
	Strongly agree	6	10	1	4
As a result of the event I experienced lengthy disruption of transport	N/a	17.3	20.9	57	35
	Strongly disagree	5.8	16.8	10	10
	Disagree	20	36	25	17
	Agree	39	20	8	21
	Strongly agree	18	6	0	16

Macrosystem negative influences	As a result of the event I experienced prolonged shortage of food As a result of the event I experienced lengthy disruption of transport/economic loss As a result of the event I experienced lengthy disruption of postal deliveries As a result of the event members of my family experienced health problems
Macrosystem positive influences	I received assistance from the council I received assistance from charity groups/welfare groups I received financial assistance from state or federal government
Preparedness (individual and microsystem levels)	My household is well prepared for future events
Exosystem preparedness	Our neighbourhood is well prepared for future events Our council is well prepared for future events
Macrosystem preparedness	State government: emergency services, etc. are well prepared for future events affecting our community Commonwealth government: emergency management, health, social security, etc. are well prepared for future events affecting our community

Source: Boon et al. 2012: 195.

were overwhelmed. Local-level support was more prominent for Beechworth than Bendigo. Macrosystem negative influences identified prolonged short-ages of food, lengthy disruption of transport and associated economic loss at Bendigo only, and the experience of lengthy disruption of postal deliveries and associated mental health problems also at Bendigo only (Boon *et al.* 2012: 209).

Macrosystem support for community recovery

Many participants had attended some form of state government-funded fire recovery activity, such as community barbeques, concerts or trips away (exosys-tem and macrosystem influences). Although the subsequent spending of the Bushfire Recovery funding was severely criticised, most people expressed their appreciation of the activities that brought people together, encouraging them to talk and to share an enjoyable experience.

> I went on one of those weekends down to Lorne and it was lovely ... it was three hundred women and I enjoyed it very much, and it was very sobering for me because everybody I spoke to had lost their home...
>
> (Boon *et al.* 2012: 159)

Service provision at the macrosystem and exosystem levels following the 2009 fires was seen as having improved considerably compared to the 2003 fire event. The experience of the 2009 fires and establishment of the Bushfires Royal Com-mission resulted in many changes to planning and operations, from CFA to local, state and federal government levels. One example given was that the Country Fire Authority had realigned its management boundaries to coincide with local government boundaries for smoother operations. The creation of Emergency Management Teams, including police and emergency services, local council and state agencies such as the Department of Human Services, meant that responses were coordinated across agencies, with responsibilities clearly defined.

A valuable tool that highlighted the influence of macrosystems and exosys-tems on individual and community resilience was the Vulnerable Persons Register. It provided support for vulnerable people, their carers and families to plan and prepare for fire, and enabled a rapid response when emergency action such as evacuation is necessary.

> ...it's a strategic thing, also if there's a bad weather week they will be con-tacted by an appropriate person for the council or whatever and say 'Have you enacted your plan?' And if they haven't got a plan I think the program was to contact the carer or contact the relatives and say 'We haven't got a plan. This is your mum and dad, or whatever, do you think we need something?'.
>
> (Boon *et al.* 2012: 159)

The 2009 Black Saturday fires and the consequent Bushfires Royal Commission (a macrosystem-level process) resulted in significant improvements to community infrastructure, such as fire refuges and neighbourhood safer places, as well as improved communications capacity and the equipment, operation and management of the CFA. Community members had lobbied successfully for improvements to telecommunications infrastructure.

> We're better prepared, like to spend more money on the infrastructure of the CFA. And the communications people spent money on phones to improve those … I think we're better prepared because the ABC and the communication people are working on the shortcomings…
>
> (Boon *et al.* 2012: 160)

Local government and state government agencies had shifted their focus to fire awareness campaigns, more timely responses, maintaining community mental health and creating a more coordinated, 'big picture' approach. These approaches are rational local responses that are reinforced by national and international strategies.

At Bendigo, drought tested individual resilience but did not build community resilience. Interviews revealed some individual resilience but strong overall community resilience to drought. The resilience pre-existed the specific hazard experience. Particular themes identified included: prolonged stress for individuals and families; exosystem and macrosystem support for farmers in particular; lack of social connections, and variation in preparedness. Exosystem and macrosystem support was good but geared mainly to farmers. Interviewees talked about how people adapted to the drought with support from local community organisations, council and state government (exosystem and macrosystem support). The smaller landowners, particularly those with shared interests, helped each other locate fodder and cover the cost of transport. For farmers, there was support at all levels. A livestock feed cooperative 'saw it as our job to source fodder for our members' as part of its ethos to support members through tough times. The cooperative 'supported a lot of our commercial farmer members through the drought financially by way of giving them things that they needed and carrying the debt until they could come good'. The experience of the cooperative was that none of their customers failed to pay their debt (Boon *et al.* 2012).

The rural financial counsellor interviewed pointed out that one of the most important programmes for the farming community was 'interest support', which kept banks from foreclosing on properties. The counsellor also talked about the importance of the AU$20,000 grants that were given to irrigation communities: 'The grants in irrigation communities were relatively easy to get but was critical to the economic survival of small businesses in the community' (Boon *et al.* 2012: 161).

Marked site variations were observed between the four case study sites. Ingham experienced the least food shortages and highest postal delivery disruption.

Bendigo had the greatest economic loss but lowest mental health problems. Bendigo residents reported the greatest level of economic loss, probably because of the long-term nature of the drought. Evaluations of macrosystem preparedness for future events suggest that state and commonwealth governments, especially emergency services, health and social security, are well prepared for future events.

People who reported dependency on exosystem and macrosystem support expressed a greater intention to leave the community, implying that these people were those more vulnerable to disaster event impacts. In all, it was indicated that a disaster-resilient person is adaptable, has connections to the community and can work with others in the community, as well as having a sense of place and possibly some prior experience of disaster. A resilient person was unlikely to have received support from institutions at the macrosystem level, although the macrosystem indirectly and intangibly supports the exosystem and its capacity to support people and communities. Most importantly, a resilient person is highly unlikely to want to leave the community. In Innisfail, those who thought of leaving were influenced by their families' health and a weak sense of place; unlike Ingham residents, those who received assistance from macrosystem institutions were also more inclined to want to leave. The 2006 and 2011 censuses indicate that significant numbers of people had left the Innisfail region, resulting in an absolute population decline. By contrast to Ingham residents, they were influenced also by infrastructure problems, climate change concerns and lower financial capacity, showing that Innisfail residents were more dependent on external support systems than Ingham residents, as confirmed by the rates of macrosystem assistance received, which were more extensively and uniformly applied than in Ingham. Their strong evaluation of council functions, five years after the occurrence of the cyclone, was based solely on their ratings of the support they received from the exosystem: local community groups, the council and formal rescue services. These data confirmed that, with the passage of time, the council was considered to be well placed to respond to any future disaster events.

At Beechworth those who received macrosystem assistance experienced infrastructure macrosystem problems, had prior disaster experience and more than likely received exosystem support during the fires. However, unlike those in Innisfail and Bendigo, this did not predict their desire to leave the community, echoing Ingham residents' reports.

There were clearly differences between the communities with regard to individuals' resilience and whether they considered leaving the community. However, there were also strong common themes across the groups. Financial capacity was critical to preparedness. Moreover, the severity of the impact of the disaster as manifested in macrosystem infrastructure negatives was another important factor influencing residents' consideration of leaving, and possibly leading to a decrease in community resilience. Interestingly, assistance received from macrosystem institutions, such as various levels of government, was also linked to a desire to leave, possibly because those who received macrosystem support were likely to be the most vulnerable community members. Residents were asked if: (1) they seriously considered leaving; (2) whether ideally they would like to leave the community; and (3) if they had difficulties in finding alternative accommodation. This means that those people who received assistance from the macrosystem (government, etc.) may consequently have been made more resilient by default; the resilience of the community might have also been increased as a result, since these residents remained in the community.

Perhaps counter to expectations, macrosystem variables, such as the financial support available to individuals from state and federal agencies and charity groups, were not directly linked to individual resilience but rather linked to consideration of potentially leaving the community. From this perspective, it is reasonable to surmise that these variables were in fact both individual and community resilience supports; without them, it is likely that individuals would have left the community, leaving it depleted and therefore less resilient. Expenditure patterns, which are dependent on micro and macro-level policies, can strengthen development and recovery as well as help put in place disaster risk reduction measures (UNISDR 2004). Thus, overall macrosystem support boosts community resilience and also decreases individual vulnerability, indirectly boosting individual resilience (Boon *et al.* 2012).

Conclusion

The macrosystem is an overarching influence upon people and their communities, but in existing at an intangible level it seldom exerts a direct impact upon either disaster risk reduction or climate change adaptation. It works at other levels, such as through the exosystem, to bring support to resilience and adaptation at the level of the individual, the household and the community. Inevitably there are many barriers, constraints and limitations that filter the impacts of macrosystem policies and strategies as they percolate downwards through an organisational hierarchy. Only where legislation is enacted does the macrosystem provide a direct incentive to the community. Mostly disaster risk reduction relies on information, education, awareness, preparedness and community actions to enhance resilience and safety. Some players, such as land use planners, have legislative structures to guide decisions, but disaster risk reduction is still in its infancy in most planning jurisdictions. The process of building resilience and adaptation for disaster risk reduction takes time. Initiatives from the IDNDR of the 1990s are only now beginning to show up in actions and behaviour.

References

Adger, W.N. 2010, 'Climate Change, Human Wellbeing and Insecurity', *New Political Economy*, vol. 15, no. 2, pp. 275–292.

Anderson-Berry, L. and King, D. 2005, 'Mitigation of the Impact of Tropical Cyclones in Northern Australia through Community Capacity Enhancement', *Mitigation and Adaptation Strategies for Global Change* (special issue), 10, pp. 367–392.

Blakie, P., Cannon, T., Davis, I. and Wisner, B. 1994, *At Risk – Natural Hazards, People's Vulnerability, and Disasters*. Routledge, London.

Boon, H.J., Millar, J., Lake, D., Cottrell, A. and King, D. 2012, *Recovery from Disaster: Resilience, Adaptability and Perceptions of Climate Change*. National Climate Change Adaptation Research Facility, Queensland.

Bronfenbrenner, U. 1994, 'Ecological Models of Human Development', in *International Encyclopedia of Education*, Vol. 3, second edn. Elsevier, Oxford.

Cannon, T. 1994, 'Vulnerability Analysis and the Explanation of "Natural Disasters"', in A. Varley (ed.) *Disasters, Development and the Environment*. Wiley, Chichester.

Cutter, S.L., Barnes, L., Berry, M., Burton, C., Evans, E., Tate, E. and Webb, J. 2008, 'A Place-Based Model for Understanding Community Resilience to Natural Disasters', *Global Environmental Change*, vol. 18, pp. 598–606.

Glavovic, B.C. 2010, 'The Role of Land-Use Planning in disaster Risk Reduction: An Introduction to Perspectives from Australasia', *Australasian Journal of Disaster and Trauma Studies*, vol. 2010–2011.

Gunderson, L. 2010, 'Ecological and Human Community Resilience in Response to Natural Disasters', *Ecology and Society*, vol. 15, no. 2, pp. 1–11.

IPCC 2007, 'Climate Change 2007: Impacts, Adaptation and Vulnerability. Contribution of Working Group II to the Fourth Assessment Report of the Intergovernmental Panel on Climate Change' (M.L. Parry, O.F. Canziani, J.P. Palutikof, P.J. van der Linden and C.E. Hanson). Cambridge University Press, Cambridge.

IPCC 2012, 'Summary for Policymakers', in *Managing the Risks of Extreme Events and Disasters to Advance Climate Change Adaptation* (C.B. Field, V. Barros, T.F. Stocker, D. Qin, D.J. Dokken, K.L. Ebi, M.D. Mastrandrea, K.J. Mach, G.-K. Plattner, S.K. Allen, M. Tignor and P.M. Midgley (eds)). A Special Report of Working Groups I and II of the Intergovernmental Panel on Climate Change. Cambridge University Press, Cambridge and New York, NY, pp. 1–19.

King, D., Harwood, S., Cottrell, A. and Gurtner, Y. 2013, 'Land Use Planning For Disaster Risk Reduction And Climate Change Adaptation: Operationalizing Policy And Legislation At Local Levels, Global Assessment Review'. UNISDR, Geneva.

Manyena, S.B. 2006, 'Rural Local Authorities and Disaster Resilience in Zimbabwe', *Disaster Prevention and Management*, vol. 15, no. 5, pp. 810–820.

Marchand, M. 2008, 'Differential Vulnerability in Coastal Communities: Evidence and Lessons Learned from Two Deltas', *WIT Transactions on Ecology and the Environment*, no. 118, pp. 283–293.

Masten, A.S. and Obradovic, J. 2007, 'Disaster Preparation and Recovery: Lessons from Research on Resilience in Human Development', *Ecology and Society*, vol. 13, no. 1, art. 9. Available online: www.ecologyandsociety.org/vol.13/iss1/art9/.

Migdal, J. 1988, *Strong Societies and Weak States: State-Society Relations and State Capabilities in the Third World*. Princeton University Press, Princeton, NJ.

Mora, S. 2006, 'Disasters are Not Natural: Risk Management, a Tool for Development', *Geological Society Engineering Geology Special Publication*, vol. 22, no. 1, pp. 101–112.

Pelling, M. and Dill, K. 2010, 'Disaster Politics: Tipping Points for Change in the Adaptation of Socio-Political Regimes', *Progress in Human Geography*, vol. 34, no. 1, pp. 21–37.

Prosser, B. and Peters, C. 2010, 'Directions in Disaster Resilience Policy', *Australian Journal of Emergency Management*, vol. 25, no. 3, pp. 8–11.

QRA 2011, 'Planning for a stronger, more resilient North Queensland, Part 1 Rebuilding in storm tide prone areas: Tully Heads and Hull Heads', Queensland Government, Brisbane.

Thomas, M., King, D. and Fidelman, P. 2012, 'Climate Change Adaptation in Coastal Cities: Insights from the Great Barrier Reef, Australia', *The International Journal of Climate Change: Impacts and Responses*, vol. 3, no. 2, pp. 107–127.

UNISDR 2004, 'Living with Risk: A Global View of Disaster Reduction Initiatives'. International Strategy for Disaster Reduction, Geneva.

UNISDR 2007, 'Hyogo Framework for Action 2005–2015: Building the Resilience of Nations and Communities to Disasters: Extract from the Final Report of the World Conference on Disaster Reduction'. International Strategy for Disaster Reduction, Geneva (A/CONF.206/6).

UNISDR 2011, 'Hyogo Framework For Action 2005–2015: Building the Resilience of Nations and Communities to Disasters: Mid-Term Review 2010–2011'. International Strategy for Disaster Reduction, Geneva.

UNISDR 2015, 'Sendai Framework for Disaster Risk Reduction 2015–2030'. UNISDR, Geneva.

Wisner, B. 1993, 'Disaster Vulnerability: Scale Power and Daily Life', *Geo Journal* vol. 30, no. 2, pp. 127–140.

WMO 2010. *Global Perspectives on Tropical Cyclones; from Science to Mitigation* (World Scientific Series on Asia-Pacific Weather and Climate – vol. 4), ed. J. Chan and J. Kepert. World Scientific Publishing, London.

9 The chronosystem in disaster resilience

Alison Cottrell

The concept of time embedded in the chronosystem is fundamental to Bronfen-brenner's (1979, 1986, 2005) theory. The notions of change and development, be they at the microsystem, exosystem or macrosystem level, are dependent on the passing of time and are evident in the changing nature of the proximal processes associated with the mesosystem (networks).

Time can be perceived as linear and progressive: the conventional view of time as moving forwards, without the possibility of return. Time can also be considered as cyclical, relative and unequal, and as a spiral. Cascading failures can drive communities downwards into decline and further loss, or the spiral can build on successes and enhance adaptation. Time, then, is socially constructed (Franck 2005; Harvey 1990) and defines events in a real or imagined past. Imaginary myth and the creation of myth around historical events link with oral history. People and communities define past events as significant, and populate past times with the power of these events and stories. Myth and oral history are intertwined and non-chronological. Chronology matters less to people than the significance of an event, which may be embellished for greater meaning. Socially or culturally significant events are often understood in terms of the time before and the time after.

Particularly in the disasters context, it is common for cyclical periods to come into play. For example, annual seasons bring with them weather events that lead to natural hazards, and longer-term cyclical weather systems such as El Niño and La Niña influence the potential for drought and storms. Disasters are also influenced by political and budgetary cycles, as well as social trends. In the disasters context, time can be seen to occur in phases. We refer to rapid or slow-onset hazards, as well as the speed of passage and temporal location of a hazard. Time can be stretched or shortened within phases, before, during and after hazardous events. Depending on the location and the people involved, the phases of a disaster can take place in parallel as well as sequentially. There is a lag in response that is driven by remoteness, access and distance. Different people and communities recover at different rates. Time loops take people and communities back to an earlier or pre-disaster state. Resilience can include the term 'bounce back', implying a return in time, but it is not to the same time, or perhaps not to the same 'place'. The loop returns people to a surrogate of the pre-disaster state.

Time decay diminishes the significance of lessons learned and also heals trauma. There is a gradual but irregular loss of the memory of a disaster. Details and awareness are lost over time, along with a loss of fear and of the immediacy of the events. Time can also heal.

Essentially, the chronosystem is about change over time, and whether individuals and communities remain resilient, decline or develop resilience. The following discussion will focus on the different systems identified by Bronfenbrenner, phases of a disaster, the impacts on system changes and, finally, implications for research strategies.

Mesosystem – time, place and networks

Doreian and Stokman (1997) suggest we are compelled to view networks – the mesosytem – over time. Bronfenbrenner embeds the system in time, and disasters provide the context to allow analysis of changes to pre-existing networks, how networks are adapted for the circumstances and how new networks arise. Varda *et al.* identify four ways in which social networks change because of disasters: pre-disaster networks may be sustained, nurtured or broken; ad hoc social networks form and dissipate quickly as needs arise and ebb; emergent networks replace 'broken' or 'lost' ties with 'new' ones; and stationary ties remain unaffected by the disaster (Varda *et al.* 2009: 23, 22). Similarly, Masten and Obradovic (2006) identified that pre-existing networks help sustain those affected by disasters and, where they remain available, enhance the prospects of resilience.

Implicit in Bronfenbrenner's theory is that an individual is located in a place. That place can be a physical one, or a metaphorical, socially defined place. In both cases, the notion of place may or may not change over time. The mesosytem (networks) in which an individual participates may be strongly centred on a given location, which links the individual to a physical place of residence and the networks embedded in the geography of that location. These networks may not remain stable over time, particularly given inward and outward migration of people. There is also the notion of a social sense of place where people's place in social relationships are defined on the basis of the groups to which they belong, as well as their status within those groups. Increasingly, the mesosytem is becoming embedded in virtual place through the development and/or maintenance of relationships through the internet at all levels of social scale, allowing the development of support networks in ways not previously possible.

The phases of a disaster

It is essential to consider all phases of a disaster, to understand the impact of time on vulnerability resilience and sustainability. As an event unfolds, it is possible that aspects of the system that appear to have attributes contributing to vulnerability, resilience or sustainability may change.

In the disasters context, considering the different phases of a disaster help us to refine the understanding of the influence of time on the whole system identified in Bronfenbrenner's theory.

The different phases of the disaster management cycle are labelled slightly differently, depending on the country or organisation in focus. For example:

Planning, preparedness, response and recovery.

(Australia)

Mitigation, preparedness response and recovery.

(United States of America)

Prevention and mitigation, preparedness, response and recovery.

(Canada)

Pre-response, disaster, recovery.

(UNISDR recovery planning)

Prevention, mitigation, response/immediate relief, reconstruction/ rehabilitation.

(South Asian Disaster Knowledge Network)

Nearly all of these phases are represented as a cycle: a closed loop, with feedback mechanisms implied. For the sake of this discussion, the terms before, during and after are used to describe a disaster event. As will become apparent later in the discussion, this allows for variation in the timing of the disaster event regarding those affected.

The Jesuit Conference Asia Pacific provides an effective illustration of the components of the disaster management cycle that relate to the chronosystem of Bronfenbrenner's theory, albeit in another way (JCAP n.d.). This representation has five phases: ordinary time (mitigate and prepare); alert (disaster event warn and identify); ASAP (disaster response and relief); weeks and months (recover and rehabilitate); and months and years after (restructure and redesign – build back better and safer, with social inclusion). Across all these phases, the JCAP identifies disaster area engagement and resilience, organisational networking and communicating in support of community and broader information and accountability for international involvement as occurring. Here, then, the evolution of time phases are posed around a given event, which indicates the notion of the mesosystem (community engagement) and resilience, as well as the exosystem and its organisations' relationship to the mesosystem through communication, as well as the macrosystem, again through the mesosystem. This is a much more socially inclusive model, which incorporates time more effectively, and is more nuanced in terms of activities that occur. Similarly, Gurtner et al. (2008: 15) demonstrate the complexity of activities across the disaster time spectrum (see Figure 9.1).

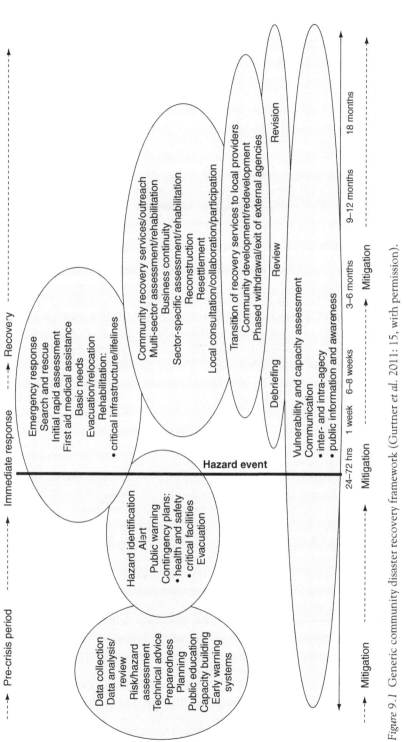

Figure 9.1 Generic community disaster recovery framework (Gurtner *et al.* 2011: 15, with permission).

All systems identified in Bronfenbrenner's theory are engaged at each of the different phases around the context of a disaster, but different types of organisations will contribute skills, resources and services at different times. While the emergency management system is structured in about four phases, these are neither discreet nor equal in time; they run parallel, and they overlap. Neglect or concentration on sectors of the community are influenced significantly by issues as they arise and dominate, and are affected by scale. Slow-onset or sudden-onset disasters require different approaches to timing and the balance of activities within the emergency management phases. Other timing issues involve climate change and secondary and cascading disasters. The organisations and processes in the macrosystem and exosystem also bring constraints and problems, most of all a lack of continuity across time.

Macrosystem

At the macrosystem level, policy and legislative changes occur over time. For example, the UNISDR has seen three major changes at the policy level since 1989. In 1989 The United Nations General Assembly announced the International Decade for Natural Disaster Reduction (IDNDR), which commenced in January 1990 with the support of a secretariat. Its main objective was to reduce the impact of natural disasters. The year 1994 saw the First World Conference on Disaster held in Yokohama (23–27 May). This conference was a mid-term outcome of the IDNDR and established 10 principles (see Chapter 7). The principles of the Yokohama Strategy for a Safer World focused on a broad range of factors associated with the reduction of the impacts of disasters on individuals and communities. The Second World Conference on Disaster Risk Reduction was in Kobe in 2005 (18–22 January); its main goal was to focus on preparedness for disasters in order to reduce death tolls.

The Hyogo Framework for Action (2005–2015): Building the Resilience of Nations and Communities to Disasters was one outcome of the 2005 conference. At this stage, the focus had been refined to the consideration of aspects of risk and resilience. In 2015, the Third UN World Conference on Disaster Risk Reduction (WCDRR) was held in Sendai (14–18 March). By this time, while the focus remained on risk and resilience, there was a shift to identifying more concrete targets. Additionally, there was a shift towards conscious integration of disaster resilience with sustainable development and climate change adaptation. These policy changes have occurred through meetings of international players from the government, non-government, academic and private sectors. Consequently, the meetings influence government policy as well as the outlook of larger non-government agencies, such as the International Federation of Red Cross and Red Crescent Societies (IFRCRC).

The annual reports by the IFRCRC (various 1993–2014) make important contributions to the conversations about disasters and resilience. This can be shown by comparing the topics for international annual conversation and within the Red Cross, with linkages emerging between the two. The First World

Disasters Report of 1993, in collaboration with the Centre for Research on the Epidemiology of Disasters, focused primarily on the provision of disaster statistics. Later reports moved on to consider the challenges faced by response agencies (1994), AIDS in Africa (1994), the ethics of humanitarian assistance (1995), the involvement of those affected (1996), the role of NGOs (1997), good governance in urban environments (1998), environmental change (1999), public health (2000), recovery (2001), risk reduction (2002), ethics (2003), risk and resilience (2004), information (2005), neglected cities (2006), discrimination (2007), HIV and AIDS (2008), early warnings and early action (2009), urban risk (2010), hunger and malnutrition (2011), migration and displacement (2012), technological innovations (2013) and culture and risk (2014). To some extent, these reports reflect the big events of the time, but there is evidence of a developing understanding of the complexities of the disasters context.

These shifts in policy at the international level influence the funding of programmes at national levels. Governments change policy and services delivered (Government of Canada 2015; Government United Kingdom 2015; Smith 2006; Soomaroo and Murray 2012), and the programmes and projects delivered in countries by the United Nations and other agencies change as policies and attendant resources change. Regional and local governments (macrosystem) are strongly influenced by these broader policy changes, evidenced in a shift of focus from response only to response and recovery.

In addition to the international policy context, governments are influenced in policy development by the enquiries that inevitably occur post disaster. These (almost invariably) lead to recommendations for changes in land use planning, community education programmes about risk and preparedness and improved approaches to community information around a particular event (Goode *et al.* 2011).

Community education programmes are an important component of preparedness for disasters, with a concomitant concern about what strategies may or may not be most effective, and at what point in the disaster event. Community engagement is seen as essential for the delivery of effective services in the disasters context. Community engagement requires a significant investment in the development of the mesosytem, and requires time (Commonwealth of Australia 2010). Community involvement in understanding risk at the local level – and developing land use plans appropriate for that risk – take time. Pearce (2003) reported on a community participation process that took eight years from inception to completion.

Exosystem

As a consequence of socio-historical conditions (the chronosystem) in modern, highly industrialised societies, individuals are often deemed to have become more dependent on services and institutions in both their local community (within their exosystem) and larger society (macrosystem). This economic or psychological dependency can become a problem when interactions with these institutions are ruptured by a major disaster such as an extreme weather event. People's expectations regarding assistance are sometimes described as degrading their preparedness, as many fail to take responsibility or lack the economic resources to become self-sufficient, leave before the event or mitigate the risks. Hence, the macrosystem invests considerably in education programmes to prepare people for disasters and to become more self-reliant. However, this is controversial because of the expectation that modern industrial societies will provide support services. Good governance of communities in the disasters and development context is considered to involve the interconnectedness of individuals and communities with larger non-government organisations and governments through the provision of transparent and effective services (Twigg 2009).

Microsystem

A consistent finding is that individuals, households and groups who have strong social networks (in their microsystem) are able to draw on shared material and social resources to sustain them during and through the aftermath of a disaster event. For example, during the period of chaos following a cyclone in Innisfail, the strengths of (microsystem and mesosystem) interactions within the Indigenous community made its members less dependent on organisations in the larger community (exosystem) than were individuals who lacked such close social or cultural ties or relationships. Indigenous community members were able to rely on extended family and neighbours for support for managing or maintaining basic functions and structures. Similarly, those who had to be more self-sufficient owing to their circumstances (e.g. rural fringe dwellers) were likely to cope better because of their capacity to draw on their own resources and knowledge of more traditional methods of survival (Boon et al. 2012). However, resilience can be constrained by these close relationships if other parts of the system are absent. For example, in some communities where the microsystem is not well linked in with the exosystem, an individual or household may be bereft of resources, and may become endangered as a result of trying to support and protect family members or pets (Aldrich and Meyer 2015).

Research processes and time

Research processes occur at a specific moment, and usually ask participants to reflect on what has happened over time. When people reflect on what has happened over time, despite this being 'one point in time' research, there are three main possible outcomes. First, people may have forgotten the initial experience and instead reflect on their current state of mind. Second, they may remember how they felt at the time of an event, but fail to recognise resulting changes. Finally, they may be reflective and able to recognise how their experiences and feelings have changed over time. These variations can result in distortions in perspectives (Denzin and Lincoln 2005; Hay 2010; Neuman 2011).

Time series research is potentially able to determine more accurately changes over time, in terms of experiences and feelings as well as impacts on vulnerability, resilience and sustainability. However, the ethical issues inherent in social research generally, and disaster research in particular, become exacerbated should researchers try to survey individuals and communities repeatedly about their experiences (Citraningtyas *et al.* 2010; IFRCRCS 2003; O'Mathúna 2010).

Conclusion

Time, the chronosystem, is an essential component to Bronfenbrenner's theory for resilience. The chronosystem is represented as moderating all other systems. As such, the theory provides a comprehensive model of the relationships and components of the social systems in which individuals are embedded and allows a broader understanding of those systems. The resilience of individuals, communities, larger organisations and governments all vary over time – sometimes for the better, and sometimes not. To consider resilience as only occurring at one point in time is to fail to understand the dynamic nature of systems and processes associated with the impacts of disasters, communities more generally, and individual growth and change.

References

Aldrich, D.P. and Meyer, M.A. 2015 'Social Capital and Community Resilience', *American Behavioral Scientist*, vol. 59, no. 2, pp. 254–269.

Boon, H.J., Millar, J., Lake, D., Cottrell, A. and King, D. 2012, *Recovery from Disaster: Resilience, Adaptability and Perceptions of Climate Change*. National Climate Change Adaptation Research Facility, Queensland.

Brofenbrenner, U. 2005 *Making Human Beings Human: Bioecological Perspectives on Human Development*. Harvard University Press, Cambridge, MA.

Bronfenbrenner, U. 1986, 'Ecology of the Family as a Context for Human Development: Research Perspectives', *Developmental Psychology*, vol. 22, pp. 723–742.

Bronfenbrenner, U. 1979, *The Ecology of Human Development: Experiments by Nature and Design*. Harvard University Press, Cambridge, MA.

Citraningtyas, T., MacDonald, E. and Herrman, H. 2010, 'A Second Tsunami? The Ethics of Coming into Communities Following Disaster', *Asian Bioethics Review*, vol. 2, no. 2, pp. 108–123.

Commonwealth of Australia 2010, *Manual 45 – Guidelines for the Development of Community Education, Awareness and Engagement Programs*. Attorney-General's Department, Canberra.

Denzin, N.K. and Lincoln, Y.S. 2005 *The Sage Handbook of Qualitative Research* (third edn). Sage, Thousand Oaks, CA.

Doreian, P. and Stokman, F.N. 1997, 'The Dynamics and Evolution of Social Networks', in P. Doreian and F.N. Stokman (eds) *Evolution of Social Networks*, pp. 1–17. Gordon and Breach, New York.

Emergency Management Australia 2003, 'Community Development in Recovery from Disaster'. Australian Emergency Management Manual Series Part III, vol. 3 – Guidelines: Guide 13. Available online: www.em.gov.au/Documents/Manual29-Community DevelopmentInRecoveryFromDisaster.pdf.

Franck, G. 2005, 'Time: A Social Construction?', in F. Stadler and M. Stöltzner (eds) *Zeit und Geschichte/Time and History* (Contributions of the Austrian Ludwig Wittgenstein Society, Vol. XIII), trans. S. Plaza, pp. 78–80. Österreichische Ludwig Wittgenstein Gesellschaft, Kirchberg am Wechsel .

Goode, N., Spencer, C., Archer, F., McArdle, D., Salmon, P. and McLure, R. 2011, *Review of Recent Australian Disaster Inquiries.* Monash University, Melbourne.

Government of Canada 2015, 'Fifth Annual Roundtable on Disaster Risk Reduction: Rethinking Roles in Disaster Risk Reduction'. Public Safety Canada. www.publicsafety.gc.ca/cnt/rsrcs/pblctns/pltfrm-dsstr-rdctn-2014/index-eng.aspx.

Government United Kingdom 2015, '2010 to 2015 Government Policy: Emergency Response and Planning'. Cabinet Office. Available online: www.gov.uk/government/publications/2010-to-2015-government-policy-emergency-response-planning/2010-to-2015-government-policy-emergency-response-planning.

Gunderson, L. and Holling, C. (eds) 2001, *Panarchy: Understanding Transformations in Human and Natural Ecosystems.* Island Press, Washington.

Gurtner, Y., Cottrell, A. and King, D. 2008, 'PRE and RAPID. Community Hazard Recovery Needs and Capacity Assessment'. Unpublished Report, Department of Communities and James Cook University Research Project.

Harvey, D. 1990, 'Between Space and Time: Reflections on the Geographical Imagination'. *Annals of the Association of American Geographers*, vol. 80, no. 3, pp. 418–434.

Hay, I. 2010, *Qualitative Research methods in Human Geography* (3rd edn). Oxford University Press, Melbourne.

IFRCRCS (International Federation of Red Cross and Red Crescent Societies) 1993–2014, World Disasters Reports. IFRCRC, Geneva. Available online: www.ifrc.org/en/publications-and-reports/world-disasters-report/world-disasters-report/.

IFRCRCS 2011. 'Public Awareness and Public Education for Disaster Risk Reduction: A Guide'. International Federation of Red Cross and Red Crescent Societies, Geneva.

IFRCRCS 2003, 'World Disasters Report. Focus on Ethics in Aid'. International Federation of Red Cross and Red Crescent Societies, Geneva.

Jackman, A.M. and Beruvides, M.G. 2013, 'Hazard Mitigation Planning in the United States: Historical perspectives, Cultural Influences, and Current Challenges', in J. Tiefenbacher (ed.) *Approaches to Disaster Management – Examining the Implications of Hazards, Emergencies and Disasters.* In Tech, Rijeka, Croatia. Available online: http://dx.doi.org/10.5772/54209.

JCAP (Jesuit Conference Asia Pacific) n.d., www.ecojesuit.com/enhancing-collaboration-and-action-in-disaster-risk-reduction-and-management-the-jcap-coordination-protocol/7616/). Accessed 23 November 2015.

Linley, P.A. and Joseph, S. 2004, 'Positive Change Following Trauma and Adversity: A Review', *Journal of Traumatic Stress*, vol. 17, pp. 11–21.

Masten, A.S. and Obradovic, J. 2006, 'Competence and Resilience in Development', *Annals of the New York Academy of Sciences*, vol. 1094, pp. 13–27.

Neuman, W.L. 2011, *Social Research Methods: Qualitative and Quantitative Approaches* (seventh edn). Allyn and Bacon, Boston, MA.

O'Mathúna, D. 2010, 'Conducting Research in the Aftermath of Disasters: Ethical Considerations', *Journal of Evidence-Based Medi cine*, vol. 3, pp. 65–75.

Pearce, L. 2003, 'Disaster Management and Community Planning, and Public Participation: How to Achieve Sustainable Hazard Mitigation', *Natural Hazards*, 28, pp. 211–228.

Smith, E. 2006, 'National Disaster Preparedness in Australia – Before and After 9/11', *Australasian Journal of Paramedicine*, vol. 4, no. 2. Available online: http://ro.ecu.edu.au/jephc/vol.4/iss2/7.

Soomaroo, L. and Murray, V. 2012, 'Disasters at Mass Gatherings: Lessons from History', *PLoS Currents*, 4, RRN1301. Available online: http://doi.org/10.1371/currents.RRN1301.

Twigg, J. 2009, 'Characteristics of a Disaster-Resilient Community: A Guidance Note'. DFID DRR Interagency Coordination Group.

Varda, D.M., Forgette, R., Banks, D. and Contractor, N. 2009, 'Social Network Methodology in the Study of Disasters: Issues and Insights Prompted by Post-Katrina Research', *Population Research Policy Review*, vol. 28, pp. 11–29.

Conclusion

Helen J. Boon, Alison Cottrell, David King

This book has demonstrated the use of a theory for assessing and researching individual and community resilience. Resilience is international and national policy. Australia's National Strategy for Disaster Resilience aims to bring together all levels of government, business, NGOs and communities into a comprehensive approach. Specific roles were identified for individuals, businesses, NGOs and volunteers. The strategy stresses the need for joint commitment and concerted effort by all sectors of society. This requires a shared responsibility – not just from emergency managers but across all sectors of society.

The national definition of resilient communities (COAG 2009) identifies characteristics such as the capacity to function well under stress, successful adaptation, self-reliance and social capacity. It lists a number of elements of social capital and partnerships at multiple levels of government. Policy development under the Council of Australian Governments at the national level is oriented towards the community and grassroots.

Maguire and Hagan (2007) suggest properties of resilience that comprise resistance, recovery and creativity. They identify types of communities and types of disasters, as well as different phases. Societies are resilient to some hazards and vulnerable to others. Rogers (2011) relates resilience and disaster risk reduction (DRR) to the PPRR model: prevention (or planning), preparedness, response and recovery. Coles and Buckle (2004) cite the multi-faceted nature of resilience. Thus there is a need for a more structured framework to examine how resilience functions, how it may be blocked or enhanced and its links to disaster risk reduction.

The issue that has inspired the writing of this book is the need for a framework to measure resilience. The introduction examines the need for such a framework in order to understand disaster risk reduction through resilience. Routes and barriers to resilience are identified and Bronfenbrenner's bioecological systems theory is proposed as a useful framework for such an analysis. Bronfenbrenner's original theory was aimed at understanding the context, setting and influences on child development. It involves the connections, networks and interactions that surround a child. The model gives us five nested spaces or systems: microsystem, mesosystem, exosystem, macrosystem and chronosystem. This book shows how those systems can be used to understand resilience to natural disasters. The systems are spaces in which people participate through a process or mode of interaction. The environments in which they live are those that are perceived or understood: in preparing people to deal with natural disasters and climate change, perceptions are as important as reality. The process is phenomenological, with perceptions of the environment influencing behaviour and learning. Resilience and adaptation require learned behaviour to bring about disaster risk reduction.

Chapter 2 reviewed the literature in order to identify problems with the definition of resilience alongside vulnerability and adaptation or adaptive capacity. Disaster risk reduction clearly works most effectively when all communities, organisations and policies interact together. The interconnectedness of people, communities, society and all of its organisations, policies and legislation presents us with a complex, diverse set of scales and levels, thereby reinforcing the need for a structured framework of analysis.

The authors adopted Bronfenbrenner's theory as a means to analyse resilience and climate change adaptation through a research project of the National Climate Change Adaptation Research Facility (NCCARF). Research was based on small communities that had experienced natural disasters. Simultaneously other NCCARF projects, involving this research group alongside other partnerships, examined a larger group of communities that had just endured a natural disaster, and the agencies, organisations and professions engaged in a range of disaster risk reduction activities directly through emergency management or as contributions from professions outside emergency management. These included professions that enhanced resilience through support activities, such as land use planning and building codes.

Case study communities that were the focus of climate change adaptation and resilience studies had between them experienced drought, fire, flood and cyclone within the previous five years. The case study communities of Bendigo and Beechworth in Victoria and Ingham and Innisfail in Queensland provided extensive qualitative and quantitative research data from individuals, households, key informants and archival sources and databases. Data were analysed through the use of the five systems of Bronfenbrenner's bioecological systems theory. This provided both a structure for analysis and a means to vary research questions and consequent methods according to the scale of the system that is the focus of study.

The microsystem provides a focus on individuals and households. Research indicated individual and community vulnerability as well as resilience and adaptive capacity. Social support factors perceived as well as received by individuals provided a stimulus to resilience. Different types of hazards did not necessarily require different resilience attributes, but it is evident from the literature and other research carried out by researchers at the Centre for Disaster Studies that human-induced disasters, such as war and terrorism, leave longer-term scars and trauma than natural ones. Longitudinal studies of individual resilience are also important but are limited in nature because the experience of individual residents is intertwined with community-level factors, especially family, friends and neighbours. Beyond that immediate level are other microsystem supports, such as workplace, churches and schools, which build and complement resilience. Sense of place additionally reinforces positive feelings and emotions, which contributed strongly to recovery and rebuilding after a disaster.

The mesosystem concerns social networks and social capital. Disaster literature supports Bronfenbrenner's assertion that individuals are strongly influenced by contexts and relationships. The mesosystem complements both the macrosystem and exosystem, which provide organisations and policies that are made operable by mesosystem networks. Social networks reinforce resilience through relationships and physical and emotional support. Networks are crucial to social capital and are underpinned by shared values. Networks make operable the services and facilities provided by governments, NGOs and community organisations. The mesosystem is a linking system that empowers the microsystem, exosystem and macrosystem individuals, agencies and their characteristics of resilience.

The exosystem involves linkages and processes of individuals and households with formal and informal organisations and utilises the mesosystem of social networks, but there is a direct interaction between the microsystem and exosystem at the level of close community organisations such as workplace and school. However, the exosystem is primarily a top-down component of service provision. Services and support facilities are provided in a complex continuum of types, roles and functions. The exosystem primarily consists of support organisations, many of which exist distinct from the disaster situation, providing diverse and routine services to the community. These organisations shift their roles and priorities in a time of crisis, although they may also contribute education and disaster risk reduction prior to a disaster. However, most organisations in the exosystem are not established with a primary role of disaster risk reduction.

The exosystem also incorporates infrastructure, which in a disaster may constitute community lifelines and the support framework for recovery and rebuilding. This aspect of the exosystem is passive, requiring individual and community knowledge at the microsystem level and within the functional networks of the mesosystem. Services require community knowledge to be effective, at which point they support and enhance resilience.

The macrosystem includes the overarching structures that support the microsystem, mesosystem and exosystems. It includes belief systems, values, resources and culture. These aspects are implicit in society at individual and community levels, as well as through national and international policies, laws and trends of all kinds. Much of the macrosystem is intangible, relying on the exosystem and mesosystem to translate the big picture to local and individual needs. Policies, information and education provide consistent approaches from international agencies to national and provincial governments, but legislation can only be enacted within states or nations, within the constraints of resources and political will. Barriers and constraints limit or slow down the uptake of macrosystem policies and strategies; similarly, macrosystem aspects of culture and values, which are powerful supports to resilience, are also slow to change.

Shared values contribute significantly to the building of resilience and community strengths, but there are many cultural attitudes, such as fatalism, which are a barrier to disaster risk reduction. Culture and values change slowly, as traditions have to be challenged and modified over time.

The chronosystem gives focus to the idea of time and change in all of the other systems. All policies, changes, modifications and adaptations require the passage of time. Time is more complex than a linear or equal incremental process. Time is socially constructed – cyclical, stretched or shortened, especially in relation to available resources – and perception of a disaster is influenced by time's passing and distance decay. The chronosystem encompasses all systems. Resilience takes time to build, but equally takes time to decay or to be lost. A disaster is an event in time, but it takes place in the continuum of time that is structured in emergency management by PPRR (or RRRR: reduction, readiness, response and recovery). These phases of the emergency management cycle provide a structure for intervention and programmes, with an assumption of the passage of time for their completion (commonly up to five years for effective recovery). However, these phases are not mutually exclusive, as education and preparedness occur during recovery, and recovery often begins during the response phase.

The chronosystem moves each of the microsystem, mesosystem, exosystem and macrosystem into different spaces and phases of resilience. The bioecological systems are dynamic. The use of Bronfenbrenner's framework is essentially dynamic at each of the system levels. This is especially important for understanding how resilience functions at the various levels of scale that are given structure through the focus of these systems. The essence of the concept of 'building community resilience' is a process that is dynamic. This is further reinforced by the link between resilience and climate change adaptation, which requires behavioural change. Central to Bronfenbrenner's theory is the process of interconnection and change that operates through these systems.

The use of Bronfenbrenner's bioecological systems theory as a framework for understanding resilience and adaptation in people and communities confronting natural disasters has been researched in communities that have had direct experience of natural disaster. The research has provided valuable indicators of characteristics, processes and influences, but there is clearly a need for a great deal more research at each system level. Each system represents a different scale of influences, and only by understanding the connection and lack of connection between these scales or systems can we recommend effective strategies and policies. Additionally there is a clear need for longitudinal studies of individuals, communities and organisations, including research into the effect of time itself and the role of memory and construction of past events. Assessment of hazard and climate change education at the microsystem level needs more participatory research into the roles and effectiveness of workplace, school and community organisations in developing information, awareness and knowledge that enhance and build resilience and adaptation. Research also needs to be conducted within and between organisations that contribute to community resilience. The way in which information, strategies and policies cross between the system levels is only partially understood. Bronfenbrenner's framework stresses the interconnection between these levels. That is the focus of this book: understanding the connections of resilience across different scales.

The following recommendations for policy and emergency management emerged from the analysis of communities through the lens of Bronfrenbrenner's bioecological systems theory (Boon et al. 2012).

1   Encourage local support networks.
2   Identify vulnerable groups that do not have microsystem support and put strategies into place to ensure they are given assistance during a disaster.
3   Ensure adequate local health services so people do not have to move.
4   Run health and well-being education classes in relation to disaster preparedness.
5   Develop appropriate plans for socio-economic groups who are unable to insure their properties. Acknowledge individuals in the community with prior experience and use them as mentors, local educators and leaders.
6   Ensure councils are involved in disaster preparedness, response and recovery processes, and engage the community in such processes.
7   Support community events that build sense of place and support social networks.
8   Undertake further research to examine better approaches to provide financial and service support in times of natural disasters for those who are vulnerable.
9   Focus on younger generations for disaster education as they are more receptive and will be the base for community resilience under future scenarios of climate change.
10   Monitor and evaluate longitudinal changes in attitudes to disaster risk and climate change.
11   Response and recovery services need to be flexible and locally based to cater for different disaster events.
12   Ensure there is a scale of levels of preparedness, for major and minor events.
13   Ensure there are government support services for both rapid-onset and longer-term events.
14   Build and maintain community networks during times of drought for town dwellers, farmers, newcomers and vulnerable residents.
15   Provide ongoing counselling services during and after the events.
16   Provide information that accurately describes potential natural hazard impacts to overcome erroneous beliefs about potential risks.
17   Tailor mitigation strategies for disaster risk reduction to each community at a local level.
18   Increase the role of local government in building a sense of place.
19   State government services should not dominate or overshadow local government or volunteer roles.

A final message to policy makers and emergency managers involves the need for patience, persistence and integration. The chronosystem reminds us that awareness, resilience and adaptation require behavioural changes that take time to be realised. Short-term solutions are likely to be inadequate, requiring patience to achieve outcomes in the long term. As a consequence, awareness, education and community resilience-building policy must be persistent: repeated, relaunched, evaluated and redeveloped. Finally, integration is the core argument of this book. Policies and strategies for resilience and adaptation must be integrated across the systems – microsystem, mesosystem, exosystem, macrosystem and chronosystem – linking and supporting at multiple levels and different scales. The theoretical lens used here has examined the complexity and diversity of those elements that must be integrated across resilience and adaptive capacity-building policies and strategies, to create an integrated disaster risk reduction policy.

References

Boon, H.J., Millar, J., Lake, D., Cottrell, A. and King, D. 2012, *Recovery from Disaster: Resilience, Adaptability and Perceptions of Climate Change*. National Climate Change Adaptation Research Facility, Queensland.

COAG (Council of Australian Governments) 2009, 'National Strategy for Disaster Resilience: Building our Nation's Resilience to Disasters'. Australian Government, Canberra.

Coles, E. and Buckle, P. 2004, 'Developing Community Resilience as a Foundation for Effective Disaster Recovery', *Australian Journal of Emergency Management*, vol. 19, no. 4 (November), pp. 6–15.

Maguire, B. and Hagan, P. 2007, 'Disasters and Communities: Understanding Social Resilience', *Australian Journal of Emergency Management*, vol. 22, no. 2 (May), pp. 16–20.

Rogers, P. 2011, 'Development of Resilient Australia: Enhancing the PPRR Approach with Anticipation, Assessment and Registration of Risks', *Australian Journal of Emergency Management*, vol. 26, no. 1, pp. 54–58.

Index

Page numbers in *italics* denote tables, those in **bold** denote figures.

For Product Safety Concerns and Information please contact our EU
representative GPSR@taylorandfrancis.com Taylor & Francis Verlag GmbH,
Kaufingerstraße 24, 80331 München, Germany

Printed and bound by CPI Group (UK) Ltd, Croydon, CR0 4YY
08/05/2025
01864534-0001